Learn HTML on the Macintosh®

Learn HTML on the Macintosh®

....

**David Lawrence
with
Dave Mark**

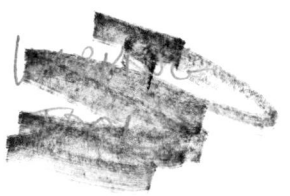

ADDISON-WESLEY DEVELOPERS PRESS

Reading, Massachusetts • Menlo Park, California • New York • Don Mills, Ontario
Harlow, England • Amsterdam • Bonn • Sydney • Singapore • Tokyo
Madrid • San Juan • Paris • Seoul • Milan • Mexico City • Taipei

Many of the designations used by manufacturers and sellers to distinguish their products are claimed as trademarks. Where those designations appear in this book, and Addison-Wesley was aware of a trademark claim, the designations have been printed in initial capital letters or all capital letters.

The authors and publishers have taken care in preparation of this book, but make no expressed or implied warranty of any kind and assume no responsibility for errors or omissions. No liability is assumed for incidental or consequential damages in connection with or arising out of the use of the information or programs contained herein.

Library of Congress Cataloging-in-Publication Data

Lawrence, David, 1949–
    Learn HTML 3.0 on the Macintosh / David Lawrence with Dave Mark.
      p. cm.
    Includes index.
    ISBN 0-201-88793-2 (alk. paper)
    1. HTML (Document markup language)   2. Hypertext systems.
3. World Wide Web (Information retrieval system)   4. Electronic publishing.
5. Macintosh (Computer)   I. Mark, Dave.   II. Title.
QA76.76.H94L39   1996
005.7'2--dc20   96-11105
                                                                                         CIP

Copyright © 1996 by David Lawrence

A-W Developers Press is a division of Addison-Wesley Publishing Company, Inc.

All rights reserved. No part of this publication may be reproduced, stored in a retrieval system, or transmitted, in any form or by any means, electronic, mechanical, photocopying, recording, or otherwise, without the prior written permission of the publisher. Printed in the United States of America. Published simultaneously in Canada.

Sponsoring Editor: Kim Fryer
Production Manager: Sarah Weaver
Production Coordinator: Deborah McKenna
Cover design: © 1996 Andrew M. Newman
Set in 10.5 point Janson by Octal Publishing, Inc.

1 2 3 4 5 6 7 8 9 -MA- 99989796
First printing, June 1996

Addison-Wesley books are available for bulk purchases by corporations, institutions, and other organizations. For more information please contact the Corporate, Government, and Special Sales Department at (800) 238-9682.

Find A-W Developers Press on the World-Wide Web at:
http://www.aw.com/devpress/

`<dedication>`
To all keepers of the Macintosh flame, the red-eyed webmasters who look up and see that the day or night has somehow evaporated, and to Nadine Keyes and the memory of Dan Barker, the best teachers a kid could ever wish for.
`</dedication>`

Contents

Acknowledgments xi
About the Author xv

Chapter 1   Welcome

    Browsing Is Cool; Publishing Is Cooler   2
    Webspeak   3
    The Basics   4
    Instant Gratification   5
    Showtime   5
    We Assume . . .   7
    What You Need   8
    What's in This Package   9
    Lay of the Land   10
    Conventions Used in This Book   11
    Installing Your Web Tools   11
    Time to Explore   14

Chapter 2   Intro to HTML

    Same Language, Different Interpretation   16
    Getting Started   17
    Recognizing Tags   18
    Brief History   18
    Your First HTML Page   19
    Element Tags and Empty Tags   20
    The Paragraph Tags: <p>…</p>   24
    The Heading Tags: <h1>…<h6> and </h1>…</h6>   24
    What's Next   27

Chapter 3   HTML Theory: A Must Read

    Tag Structure   29
    White Space   31

HTML Comments   32
HTML Character Sets   33
HTML Versions   34
What's Next   38

Chapter 4   From the Neck Up: The Head Elements

Instant Replay   40
An Aside: The Short Version   42
Planning the Site   43
Other Head Element Tags   47

Chapter 5   HTML Body Language

The Body Elements   59
Image Is All   72
Block Party   78
List Elements   88
Semantic Format Elements   97
Physical Format Elements   105
What's Next   113

Chapter 6   Hitting the Links

URL Makeup   116
Absolute vs. Relative URLs   122
Creating Links   123
Improving Our Image   129
What's Next   132

Chapter 7   Icons, Buttons, and Image Maps

Some Human Interface Guidelines   134
Graphical Navigation Techniques   136
Creating and Enhancing Graphics Using Photoshop   138
Icon Navigation   144
Button Bar Navigation   147
Text Navigation   148

Image Maps **149**
Server-Side Image Maps **149**
Client-Side Image Maps **156**
What's Next **158**

Chapter 8 **Forms and Tables**

Forms: The Back End **159**
The Front End: The Form Itself **160**
Tables **177**
Building Tables **183**
What's Next **192**

Chapter 9 **Multimedia: Sound and Movies**

Let There Be Sound **193**
Basics of Mac Sound Reproduction **194**
Integration **198**
Listen Up! **199**
Converting Sounds **200**
Movies **209**
What's Next **212**

Chapter 10 **Frames**

Frame Me! **215**
What's Next **223**

Chapter 11 **Population and Maintenance of Your Web Site**

Choosing Your Connection Type **226**
Preparing Your Server **228**
Working Faster **235**
Working with Your Service Provider **235**
Ongoing Maintenance of Your Site **237**

Appendix A   DIGEX Packages

DIGEX Shell Service **239**
Personal-IP—Dynamic PPP Dial-Up Connection **240**
DIGEX Price List and Product Availability
as of April 15, 1996 **243**

Appendix B   HTML Character Equivalencies 245

Appendix C   Calendar 253

Index 273

Acknowledgments

If someone could have realistically conveyed to me a year ago how hard it is to write one's first book, I would have still eagerly taken on the project, but I probably would have taken a deeper breath before plowing on. There are a number of people that I'd like to thank for the part they played in birthing this book.

First, the people closest to the book: my co-author and friend, Dave Mark, with whom a chance meeting a few years ago has blossomed into a friendship/learning experience for which I will always be thankful. To the tireless people at Addison-Wesley who make the publishing side of this process seem effortless, I offer the highest of praise and a toast at the next MacWorld: to Kim Fryer, my editor; Debbie McKenna, my production editor; Janice Borzendowski, my copy editor; Heather Champ, my first tech editor/webmistress/server push addict; The Unknown Other Tech Editor and to Keith Wollman, my managing editor (and the only man in the bunch), who stuck with me when it was clear I needed someone to push me to be 'stuck with'-able.

Next, the people that in some way made it possible for me to get to the point that I could actually tackle a first book: my family and friends from Computing Analysis Corporation: Steven Clough (OH-IO!), Tom Berens, Rick Driscoll, Eileen O'Grady (who's always in girlfriend mode!), Brian Sweeney, Dave Thompson, Doug Ramsey, Greg Eoyang, Sum Dhum Gai, E.B., Rick Jones, Jim Kline, Mark McLendon, Shawn Geddes, Tamara Wiley, and Lara Ledebur; their counterparts at ARPA: Pete Tunanidas, Carla Little-Kopach, Judy Lowe and Phil Harris; the web dudes and dudettes at DIGEX who worked so quickly to get our servers in shape: Doug Humphrey, Doug Mohney, Joe Peck (thanks for the RealAudio help!), Amyn Meruani, and John Todd and his staff of server gods; my friends and family at America Online: Joe Bernui, Scott Stein, Dok Wright and Mark Irwin; Susan Twain, Steve Marinetto, Kathy Ryan, Barry Shuler, Tracy Shuler and the rest of AOL Productions East, South and West (thanks for the Thai food!), Dave Baker and the Cool Team, Tim Barwick, David Gang, Ted Leonsis, Jean Villanueva and Steve Case; Stu Wetstein, Chris Lynch and Jimmy Lynn; the folks at RealAudio; the folks at Now

Software; our friends at Netscape; Matt and Jan and Rita and Peter and Suzanne and Jack and Stu of Online Today; Pat Kenealy and Nancy Jacobs of PC WORLD, Steve Saslow, June Brody, Bob Biernacki and Anita Bonita at SJS and the rest of the crew on the radio show; my millions of listeners without whom each week I'd be talking to nothing but the walls of a lovely radio studio; David and Eileen at Web Developer Magazine; Alan Meckler and Andrew Kantor at Internet World/Mecklermedia; my web design clients, especially Cliff Pia, Todd Cummings, Jonathan Bebisheimer at ACN, Jon Wolfert at Jam Creative Productions, Carolyn Vincent at ATMI, Ken Kohl of KST/Talk 650, Julie Butcher at Adolph Coors Brewing, the fans of Don and Mike, and the Real Bob James (put down that razor blade!).

Special thanks to Tracey Akins at UTK, Jennifer Allen at Waggener Edstrom, Craig Ashwood at Arrow 94.7, Frank Barnako of USA TODAY Online, Barry and Jerry at BJ Pumpernickles, Julie Blumenfeld at Windows Magazine, Bob and Jeff, Bob and Luanne Bole-Becker, Harrell and Betty Bosley, Wendy Bulawa at McGrath Power, Mark Bunting, California Pizza Kitchen, Drew Carey (Go Tribe!), Lee Carnahan, Marie Cloutier-Tuberosa, Holland Cooke, Don Crabb, Kasey Crabtree, Debbie Degutis, Corey Deitz, Bob Dudley, Woody Hume and Julie Visnich at Claris, Ron Duritsch, David Eliot, Adam Engst, Jon Epstein, Dick Ferguson, John and Terry Flint, Ric Ford, Dr. Fred, Joel Furr, Jon Gann, Dan Gillmor at SJMN, MaryAnne Haggerty and Karen Marrero at the Washington Post, Professor Donna Hoffman, Home Office Computing, Scott Horne, Steve Jobs, E. Karl, Roger Kasten, Guy Kawasaki, Brian Kelly for my workspace, Alan Kipust and all of Paper Direct, Leo LaPorte, all of the other David Lawrences who got my e-mail by mistake, Bob Levitus, Jimmy Lynn, Peggy Kilburn, Stu Mark, John McWade of BEFORE&After, Norm Miller, Sue Nail, "Supersplice" Michael Neff, Kathy Newstrom, John Pliesse, David Pogue, Annette Reynolds, Bob Sherwood and the Minidisc Team at Sony, Mike and Alice Simon-Curry, Aaron Singer, Steve Skrovan, the Rockville Starbucks, Mark Steo, Linda Stern, Nancy Tamosaitis, Frank at TDK, John Tesh, Tower Records, Lou Ward and Patty Neiss at Apple, Philip Ward, Esq., Pat Waters, Robin Williams, the other Robin Williams, Bill Wimsatt, Craig Witt and Kyle Simpson, Rich Wood, Steve Wozniak, Rent-A-Nerd and Mike Wyckoff,

Jan Ziff, Alicia Zimmerman of Adelphi Cable, and Howard Zimmerman for their invaluable and selfless contributions.

Finally, I'd like to thank Rarr for her support, encouragement and love, Madison for the endless Pocahontas recitals and the opportunity to play John Smith and Radcliffe, and Eliza Nicole for dzzzzzzzt!

IloveyouallandIpromisetocometobedontimeforachange.

```
<grateful>
  David Lawrence, LearnHTML@aol.com
  Glenwood, MD
</grateful>
```

About the Author

David Lawrence produces online areas for America Online, and hosts a nationally syndicated radio talk show revolving around computers and personal electronics.

His radio background includes Top-40 personality morning shows and general interest talk shows in 8 of the top 20 markets, including New York and Washington DC.

David also does commercial and promotional voice work for national and multinational clients, and specializes in multimedia production and the voicing of prompts for computer telephony applications. You can hear his character voice work on over 600 radio stations across the country and around the world.

He also specializes in audio specific commercial web development, and counts dozens of satisfied clients among his career accomplishments.

David has 20 years in radio as an air talent, 18 years working with computers, 12 years working with Macintosh, 3 years working with HTML and what seems like a lifetime so far as a father.

You can reach him at LearnHTML@aol.com for web or computer questions (especially questions about this book), and VoxTalent@aol.com for everything else.

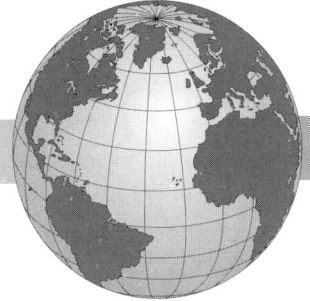

Welcome

Welcome! This is a book you will be glad you bought; the corners of its pages will become dog-eared as you continue to refer to it to expand your knowledge about creating content for one of the most exciting developments in recent computing history: the World Wide Web.

Considering the phenomenon it has become, the World Wide Web began simply enough—as a communications project at the European Particle Physics Laboratory in Switzerland. There, Tim Berners-Lee and his colleagues wanted to find a better way for physicists from around the world to stay up to the minute on research, and to be able to connect with each other quickly and efficiently, no matter what part of the world they were in.

The result, in 1989, was the World Wide Web, a **hypertext** system that uses the global reach of the Internet as its transport mechanism. Users click on links, which display another document that also contains links. The amazing thing is that the documents you link to could be housed on a computer in the cubicle next to yours or one that's halfway around the world. In fact, the unimagined growth experienced by the Internet over the last few years is primarily due to the Web's expansion and acceptance.

From the first time you fired up a Web browser (most likely Netscape Navigator, the most popular, and the one we're using in this book), you probably felt comfortable with it and the Web. Although Web browsers come in two flavors—text-only and graphical—a graphical browser is preferable because it enables you to see in-line images, fonts, and document layouts. Netscape Navigator (which from now on we'll just call Netscape, as it's commonly known) is just such a graphical browser.

Every effort has been made by Web developers to make browsing the Web and the creation of Web documents as simple as possible. As a Web user, you can navigate around the world without ever having to type in any confusing location information or UNIX commands. You simply click on the word or image that highlights where you want to go next. As a Web designer, you create content and arrange it artistically, with very little effort beyond that.

Browsing Is Cool; Publishing Is Cooler

Browsing the Web is certainly a wonderful and exciting adventure, but being one of the creators—publishers—is even more so. The World Wide Web naturally has attracted the attention and involvement of the computing world, but what proves its versatility and ease of use is its appeal to the more universal world of commerce and industry. Its multimedia nature has been embraced by hundreds of thousands of companies, multinational behemoths and sole practitioners alike, as a way to publicize their wares and bring customers to their doors. The Web is a great equalizer; the cost of a Web site is relatively minor, and the results can be spectacular no matter what size your company is.

It's common these days for people to print their e-mail addresses as prominently on their business cards as their phone numbers. And after you learn to create Web content, you'll no doubt want to include the address of your Web site on your business card, too.

Some Internet-wise companies treat their Web sites as an electronic companion to a printed brochure. A brochure, as valuable a promotional tool as it can be, is limited: the reader can't ask it questions or get anything more than what's on the printed page. A Web page, however, can be linked to other brochures from within the company, to other sources—and more.

Some look to Web pages as an eventual replacement for brochures and sales kits. Already a number of companies on the Web are almost paperless. One such is software.net, a company that sells computer software, not from a storefront or through a mail order company, but with a series of Web pages. Its customers search for the software they need and pay for it with a credit card in a secure Web transaction. In some cases, software.net will help customers find the product they want, take the order, then actually download the software, right onto the person's hard drive, ready to install. How's that for one-stop shopping?

It is so easy to create content for the Web that your imagination is your only limit. You can add pictures, sound, movies, and other multimedia effects; there are no complex programming languages to learn, no expensive hardware add-ons to buy. Once you understand the basics of Web page creation, you'll begin to see results immediately.

Webspeak

The basic language of Web design is the **HyperText Markup Language (HTML)**. HTML is the stuff all Web pages are made of, from the most complex commercial site to the simplest collegiate bio. To get a little more technical, HTML is a set of conventions for identifying the sections of a document so that, when accessed by a program called a browser, each section is displayed in a formatted layout.

HTML is composed of a series of **tags** placed in a text file. These tags define the attributes of the text display: whether the affected text will appear in boldface, italics, or all capital letters, for example; how headlines and quotes are distinguished or highlighted; how graphics are displayed; how links are made; and how files are made available for downloading, to name a few. We'll talk more about HTML later in the chapter and as we learn "how to speak it."

Once you learn these tags, you'll have about one-third of the knowledge you need to become proficient at Web site design. You'll gain the second third of this knowledge as you develop the style in which you want your pages to appeal to and capture an audience. The final third of the knowledge is a little more nebulous to define: It's a function of solving the problems that always seem to crop up when Macintosh is used in a world dominated by another platform—in this case, UNIX.

And Speaking of UNIX . . .

One of the reasons we wrote this book is that Macintosh users rarely have had to delve into the arcane world of UNIX. But if you want to become entangled in the wonderful world of the Web (and we assume you do, or you wouldn't be reading this book!), you'll have to learn a little UNIX. Why? Because the vast majority of **Internet service providers (ISPs)** house their customers' Web sites on UNIX computers. And like the majority of people with Web sites, you'll probably use an ISP to host your site.

Don't panic, though; you only have to know enough UNIX to be able to show the world your documents. You already know how to look in a folder on your Mac to find out what files are there and how to share those files with others on a Macintosh network. We'll show you how to do that same thing in the UNIX world so that you can share your creations with all who care to look.

The Basics

If you know how to use a word processor like Microsoft Word or WordPerfect, you already know how to highlight a passage of text and boldface it, italicize it, indent it, and so on. This same process of assigning text attributes will be used in creating Web pages. In fact, the process is even easier to learn than PageMaker, Word, or WordPerfect, so your path to a finished product is more direct.

Familiar Tools

As you create your pages, you'll be working with a simple text editor, namely **BBEdit Lite,** which we'll describe more fully later in this chapter. A full-fledged word processor will certainly work, but it isn't necessary. Fully formed Web pages can also be written in Apple's own SimpleText or its older sister, TeachText. There are a number of tools that help you turn out Web-readable versions of Word, WordPerfect, and PageMaker documents (among other applications), but you'll find yourself coming back to your trusty text editor to adjust the Web page's text to look just right. For your convenience, the CD-ROM bundled with this book gives you BBEdit Lite, which we consider to be the best text editor for creating Web pages.

When you add pictures to your pages, you'll be working with familiar graphics packages as well. Whatever skills you have in drawing, painting, and graphic file manipulation will be directly transferable when you're working to make your Web site visually appealing. As with the text editing applications, many graphics applications that you'll find useful are included on our CD-ROM.

Sound and movies, which are found all over the World Wide Web, are as easy to place in your Web site as they are to work with on Macintosh. Here, too, we've taken the time to select the cream of the crop of Macintosh-based sound and movie-editing applications for our CD-ROM, as well as lots of utilities designed to make the creation of multimedia content in your Web pages a breeze.

Instant Gratification

One of the most rewarding aspects of creating Web pages is that you see your work take shape as you view your efforts with your browser, make adjustments, and finally refine your page. Computer programmers are good role models for this process. They write **source code**, a version of their program that is readable by people (as opposed to machines). They too use a text editor to write their code, as you will to write your pages. Then they compile the code into a version easy for the computer to read, called an **executable program** that is made up of ones and zeroes. If the compiled program doesn't do what they expect, it's back to the source code for tweaking, another compiling process, and another test. You'll be doing the same thing, although the nature of Web page design is such that the results are viewable immediately.

The iterative process of adding or marking up a bit of text, browsing it to see if it's exactly the way you want it, and then going back and further refining the page means you get instant feedback. Your pages show progress quickly, and that leads to a building of confidence in your abilities as a Web designer.

Showtime

Web design brings out the performer in all of us, and in the case of the World Wide Web, your audience is—well—the world! The most powerful moment in creating a Web site comes when you finally make your pages "world-readable." It's a heady experience: one moment you have a fairly private collection of text files, and the next you're getting e-mail from a fan who browsed your home page from a computer in Finland. Or, if you're a numbers cruncher, think of it this way: 30,000,000 human beings can be influenced, entertained, informed, sickened, bored, saddened, or made joyous by what you compose. It's a letter to the editor on a global scale. It's desktop publishing on steroids. The content of your pages will reflect your intellect, experience, dreams, fears, desires, and more (including your HTML coding skills) to the people who drop by to see what you've done.

Window Shop the Web

Although you'll learn virtually everything you need to know in this book to crank out great-looking pages, it's a good idea to browse the Web on a regular basis. You'll see Web pages that make you sit back in your chair and shake your head, wishing you'd thought of that. Well, there's no law against learning from the best, and we'll show you how these creative people accomplished their feats of HTML legerdemain, and further, how to incorporate these innovations into your Web pages.

Working with Text

You'll be looking at styled text from a whole new viewpoint, one with fewer options than the typical Macintosh word processor, but that is simpler to handle and manage. You'll learn how to set off text and highlight passages to draw the viewer's eye to important content. You'll master the various ways headings can be used to attract and/or guide the reader. You'll learn to manage paragraphs and to mix graphics with text. You'll become as proficient with text on the Web as you are on your desktop, and in much less time than it took you to learn your word processor.

Working with Pictures

If you have a thorough grounding in graphic formats like GIF and JPEG, you're well on your way to understanding what you need to know to efficiently display graphics in your Web pages. If you don't understand those concepts, we'll review them. We'll show you how to efficiently prepare your graphics for the Web, which format to choose when creating graphic content, and how to manipulate those graphic files to add pizzazz to your Web site. We'll explore **image maps**—those pictures in Web pages that cause your browser to do different things depending upon where you click. We'll also discuss and examine different styles and techniques that invite the viewer to stay with your site and get the most out of it.

Working with Sound and Movies

Pictures aren't the only elements that you'll add to your Web design palette. Sound is easy to handle on the Macintosh, and is even easier to add to your site. We'll examine the different standard sound file formats, show you the most common ways to provide audio content on your page, and touch on technologies such as RealAudio and StreamWorks.

Movies can be integrated with the same ease as text, graphics, or sound, and you'll learn to work with Apple's QuickTime to make your movies watchable on all platforms.

We Assume . . .

This book is not a beginner's bible on the Macintosh, nor is it a primer for the Internet-impaired, so if you fall into one of those categories, we're sorry to say this may not be the only book you need to buy. If, however, your knowledge and skills fall into the range described in the following, you've made the right choice.

. . . That You Have Basic Mac Skills

We assume that you can open and close a file, save it and save it "as" another format, and that you can point, click, drag, and so on with the mouse. We also assume that you understand how your hard drive is formatted and organized and how Apple's filing system works. Furthermore, you should be familiar with launching and running applications, and using the Clipboard to transfer graphics and text items. Finally, you must understand the basics of the Edit menu: copying, highlighting, cutting/pasting, and the like.

. . . That You Know How to Browse the Web

We also assume that you know how to use the Netscape browser. This includes launching it, navigating the menus, getting to Web sites by typing in **URLs (Universal Resource Locators)**—the strings of characters that identify an Internet resource type and location, clicking on hypertext links and images on Web pages to go places and get things, and creating and managing bookmarks. You also know how to configure your browser to specify all of the **helper applications,** the small utilities that assist Netscape in displaying certain file formats, such as sound and video files. And you know basic Web terminology—you know what a Web site is, as well as a home page. If you aren't familiar with some of these items, you should review Netscape's help documentation, available online right from Navigator's Help menu.

What You Need

You'll need at least a 68040-based Macintosh (a Quadra or better) and 8 MB of RAM to comfortably run Netscape and some of the often-used helper applications. You'll also need System 7.0 or better, preferably System 7.5. You'll need to be able to pass TCP/IP packets back and forth with the Internet, either via a 28.8 modem, or via some other faster connection. There are several ways to do this, and except for one, they all require MacTCP or Apple's newest TCP/IP extension, Open Transport, to be installed and configured in your System folder. You also should have an Internet or HTTP connection to the Web, whether it be through an online service such as CompuServe or America Online or through an Internet service provider (ISP) in your area, that will permit you to browse the Web. If you don't have such a connection, we'll show you how to get one with one of several ISPs we work with . . . each available with a free trial.

Optimal Configuration

Here's what we use to do our Web design:

- Macintosh 7500/110AV
- 64 MB of Newer Technologies' RAM
- 2 gigabyte hard drive from APS
- System 7.5.3 (as of this writing)
- Microtek IISPX scanner (it came with Adobe Photoshop, the full version, free! What a deal!)
- Wacom ArtZ tablet and Paper Power, from the good folks at Piptel
- Iomega Zip Drive for back up
- Sony CD, MiniDisc, and cassette player/recorder for sound
- JVC Stereo Hi-Fi VHS video cassette recorder for video

What's in This Package

Turn to the inside back cover to find the CD-ROM bundled with this book. It is chock full of everything you need to get started right away to create your own Web pages.

We've also made arrangements with the folks at Digital Express Group, one of the top national ISPs, to set aside space on their servers so that you can sign up with them and get started. For four weeks you can play with their system, and they've pledged 5 full megabytes of storage space for your Web site masterpieces. Finally, PSI is represented in our hit parade with a similar deal to try out their popular Pipeline service. You have a lot to choose from, and you can try them all.

But wait! There's more!

How about megabyte upon megabyte of shareware and freeware applications utilities and you can use to design, build, and enhance your Web pages? It's all there, from Web text processors to faceless applications that make converting graphics to universally readable format as simple as cutting and pasting, We've licensed most of these for you, our reader, saving you lots of time and money. Demo or shareware items are there for your convenience to try. If you find yourself using something on a regular basis, please be sure to pay the shareware fee requested by the author.

> Shareware authors rely on an honor code to get paid, and when users of their work don't pay up, we all lose. The shareware author who created the program will get discouraged, stop writing innovative and cheap software, and will most likely take up a career in bill-collecting (where the concept of shareware is virtually unknown). So pay up. It'll make you and the shareware programmer feel great!

Finally, we've provided the actual text files for each of the Web pages we create in the book. If you don't want to type in everything, you don't have to. We've also provided sample HTML pages for some of the neat tricks we'll show you; simply copy and paste any of the HTML files on the CD-ROM, then use them (or their concepts) in your own Web site. One tool we don't give you is Adobe Photoshop. We show lots of examples in our graphics chapters that were created in Photoshop. It's the ideal choice for both originating and manipulating graphics on the Mac, and if you don't have it, you should seriously consider getting it.

Lay of the Land

This book was designed so that you can go from reading the first page to publishing a Web page in two or three hours. To that end, this book is organized to get you up and running with the various tools on the CD-ROM, and then to get you signed on and your Web site started. For those of you who already have Web space available, you can skip this information and get right to the HTML stuff. The rest of the book is devoted to building your Web design toolkit—working with images, sounds, movies, and other multimedia files. In the remainder of this chapter, we'll introduce you to the `Authoring` and `Helpers` folders which contain the text editor BBEdit Lite, the software necessary to sign on to an ISP, and associated utilities for the creation and manipulation of various multimedia file formats. The content of the rest of the chapters is as follows:

- Chapter 2 provides the first glimpse at HTML. We'll describe the structure of HTML text documents and the basic tags you'll need to display text.
- Chapters 3, 4, and 5 dive into the pool of HTML tags, providing an in-depth look at those currently available, a preview of some that will be available soon, and some Netscape-specific extensions to HTML, whose results are usually seen only by you and other Netscape users.
- Chapter 6 explores the mysteries of URLs and hyperlinks: how they work and how to use them to join pages, related items, and other elements in your Web site. We'll also look at how to use URLs and hyperlinks with graphics.
- Chapter 7 works more with graphics and hyperlinks, showing how to construct buttons and image maps.
- Chapter 8 demonstrates how to create forms. You can use them to interact with visitors to your Web site by offering questionnaires, surveys, or guestbooks, among others. You'll also learn how to create tables to format columns of information.
- Chapter 9 gets into the material that can really make your Web site fun: sound and movies.

- Chapter 10 introduces you to frames, one of Netscape's coolest new features. You'll see how you can add a whole new dimension to your Web site by mixing static objects with dynamic content.
- Chapter 11 walks you through the process of finding and working with an ISP to host your Web site.

Conventions Used in This Book

As you go through this book, you'll encounter a few standard conventions intended to make the book more readable. For example, technical terms mentioned for the first time appear in **boldface**.

> Boxes like this one are called **tech blocks**, and are intended to add detail to the subject currently being discussed. These blocks fall into three categories: By the Way, Important, and Warning. By the Way tech blocks are informative or entertaining, but not crucial. Important boxes contain information that you should tuck away in a reasonably responsive part of your brain for easy retrieval. Warnings are, well, warnings. We hope they keep you out of trouble or solve a problem before you know it is a problem.

All of the HTML examples and folder and file names in this book appear in a monospaced typeface called `Letter Gothic`. This includes source code fragments that appear in the middle of running text. Menus and menu items that you click on appear in **Chicago**.

In addition, as we introduce the all-important HTML tags, they will be accompanied by **tag tables** that present, in an easy-to-read format, the parameters of the tag under discussion.

Let's get going!

Installing Your Web Tools

Building a Web site is like building a bookcase (or any other carpentry project, for that matter). Putting together the elements of a good Web site requires proficiency with a number of different tools. And just as a carpenter knows when to pick up a hammer, saw, screwdriver, chisel, and so on, you'll learn how to quickly and easily choose the appropriate application to do the job at hand.

Your HTML Toolkit

There are three main folders on your CD-ROM: `Authoring`, `Goodies`, and `Helpers`. The `Authoring` folder contains the tools that will not only help you build your Web site, but will help you test and maintain it as well. The `Goodies` folder contains some neat applications that we use to make building Web sites easier and more fun, but that we didn't have room to fully explore in the book. The `Helpers` folder contains the latest versions (as of the publication date of this book) of the various helper applications that assist your browser in viewing and playing back multimedia files you'll encounter as you browse the Web.

To install your helper and authoring tools, insert the book's CD-ROM into your CD-ROM drive and drag the `Authoring` and `Helpers` folders from the CD-ROM onto the top level of your hard drive. For the moment, leave the `Goodies` folder on the CD-ROM alone.

The first Web development tool you'll want to become familiar with is your text editor. This is the tool you'll use to create and modify the text files that will become the mainstay of your Web site. As mentioned briefly earlier, the text editor we'll be using throughout the book is called BBEdit Lite. There are other editors that will allow you to create Web files, but we think BBEdit Lite is the best. You can use it for other text-based tasks, too. We've already configured it for use on the Web pages we're going to be building. (Dragging the `Authoring` folder onto your hard drive automatically installs BBEdit Lite.)

Once you've built a Web page or two, you'll view them (browse them) using Netscape. You'll create and edit your Web pages in a cycle: You'll use BBEdit Lite to input your Web page text and HTML tags. Next, you'll save your text as an HTML file, switch to Netscape, and reread the HTML file from your hard drive. If you see something you'd like to change, it's no problem. Just go back to BBEdit Lite, change your text, save it, and switch back to Netscape to test again.

Using the Toolkit

To make sure everything was properly copied from the CD-ROM, let's fire up Netscape and take it for a spin. If Netscape 2.0 is not already installed on your Mac, we recommend that you get a copy. Netscape 2.0 is

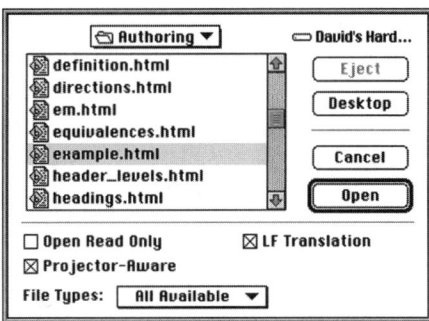

Figure 1.1
The Authoring folder on our hard drive.

the latest version of the browser as of the writing of this book, and all of our HTML examples in this book were written with it in mind. It's the market leader, after all. You can download a copy from the Netscape home page <http://www.netscape.com>. Remember you will need to pay for it, unless you're part of an educational institute, a non-profit group, or a library. Or you can buy a copy in your local software store. That said, you can use other browsers such as Internet Explorer or Mosaic to view our HTML examples, but they may not support all of Netscape's fun features.

> A Web page doesn't necessarily have to be accessed via the Internet. As long as the files that make up the Web site are made up of text files embedded with legal HTML tags, your browser won't care if the Web pages are on your hard drive, on a CD-ROM, or on your cousin's Mac in Bay Village.

Now let's use Netscape to look at an HTML example.

1. Once Netscape has started, select **Open File** from the **File** menu. When prompted for a file to open, navigate into the Authoring folder.
2. Select the file named example.html and click on the **Open** button (Figure 1.1).
3. Once you click the **Open** button, Netscape will use the information in the example.html file to create the Web window shown in Figure 1.2. Your new window should contain the spiderworks banner (that's our company!) followed by a list of options.
4. Now click on the "works" side of the spiderworks logo (it has white text on a black background). Netscape should jump to a new Web page containing a congratulatory message (Figure 1.3).

Figure 1.2
The Web window built from the HTML file example.html.

Cool, huh? If you ran into a problem, quit Netscape and start the process again. If you still can't get the darn thing to work, try recopying the Authoring folder from the CD-ROM onto your hard drive and reinstalling Netscape. To return to the page of the Web site that contains the spiderworks logo, click on the **Back** button.

Time to Explore

Take a look at the entire CD-ROM-based Web site we've built for you to use in conjunction with this book. Take as much time as you want to explore everything there. We know that there are some of you who will want to jump ahead and look at the advanced stuff. That's fine. We'll be back here, waiting for you when you're done. Bear this in mind as you're perusing: Almost everything you see will be used later as an example to illustrate some skill you'll learn, or some behavior of your Web tools you'll want to know about. You might even want to try bookmarking some of the pages that are particularly interesting to you. Have fun!

Figure 1.3
If you see this window, your test was successful!

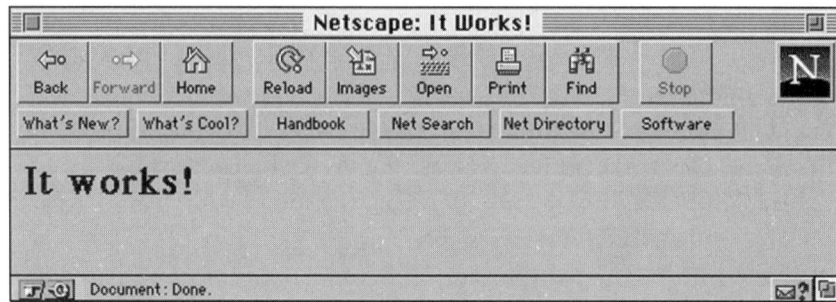

Intro to HTML

Every Web page starts life as an HTML document, and, as we've mentioned, all you really need to create these documents is a text editor. What distinguishes HTML documents from other text files is that they contain the tags we told you about in Chapter 1. Remember, these tags tell the browsers how to display text and graphics, where links go, and so on. Unsurprisingly, HTML text file names end in .html. This file extension is important, because some browsers rely on the extension of the file name to determine what to do with the file.

In your Web travels, you'll no doubt encounter an HTML document with a file name that ends .htm, instead of .html. No, it's not a typo. Files that end in .htm were created on computers that run DOS or Windows 3.1 or lower, which means file names must take the form `filename.ext`, where `filename` is limited to eight characters or fewer, and `ext`, the extension, is limited to three characters or fewer. Hence, .html gets shortened to .htm. This limitation will disappear as Windows 95 and its looooong file-naming convention becomes more dominant in the PC market, but for now, a three-character .htm text file extension is your clue that the author of the document didn't use a Mac.

The beauty of HTML tags is that they allow you to arrange the elements that make up your Web page virtually any way you want, and you don't have to consider whether your audience is using a Macintosh, a PC, a Sun, or Silicon Graphics workstation, or any other type of computer to access your Web pages. The HTML tags "speak" a sort of universal language, understood by all Web browsers.

Same Language, Different Interpretation

That said, it's important to note that while all browsers understand HTML, they may put, shall we say, a different "accent" on it. The Web browser on your machine—Netscape, we assume, if you're working along with us—interprets the HTML file in a way that makes sense for your computer, which means that the same Web page might look slightly different when viewed in the Mac version of Netscape than in the Windows 95 version of the browser. The same Web page might also vary slightly in appearance when viewed in two different Macintosh Web browsers on the same computer, such as Netscape and Intercon's NetShark.

HTML is a standard, and as such is always changing. There have been two versions already—HTML 1.0 and 2.0. Currently, HTML is moving toward version 3.0, known as HTML+ at one time. The HTML 3.0 standard is expected to be finalized in 1996, although it was not at the time this book was written. The fact that HTML 3.0 has not been finalized affects how browsers display HTML documents. Netscape is currently the browser with the most advanced features (some of which are not part of any HTML standard), and it will likely support 3.0 before the others. As we go along, we'll tell you which tags are 2.0, which are 3.0, and which are Netscape-only.

This slight variation in appearance is an important point, and one that will come up again as we learn how to design Web pages for the way Netscape interprets HTML. But we will also take into consideration the other popular browsers in use, and make sure that our pages look good in them as well. The variations in browsers are, for the most part, minor; nevertheless, it's valuable for the success of your documents that you understand the subtleties that set browsers apart. We'll talk about these differences throughout the book, make sure to highlight those that are really important, and warn you about the ones that are merely annoying.

Getting Started

Dumping the information you want to display into an HTML document is easy. Just type away, or copy and paste from another document, or open a text file you've already created. The actual text in an HTML document is often referred to as the **source**, since it is the source from which the browser will create the displayed information for the end user. The source for a Web page will show you the text along with the HTML tags used to mark up the text.

> It's possible to look at the source for any Web page that you encounter. Most Web browsers that we know of will allow you to view the source for a Web page right in your browser and to save a Web page as a source (HTML) file and/or as a text file to your hard drive.
>
> To view the source for a Web page in Netscape, click on the **View** menu and then on **Document Source**. To save the page as a source file or as a text file (giving you only the text you'd see displayed in the browser), click on the **File** menu, then click on **Save As**. You'll have the option of saving the page as either a source or text file in the resulting dialog box.
>
> Viewing the source is a good trick to keep in mind when you encounter Web pages that are well designed or have some cool feature that you want to learn how to do. Save the source to your hard disk to review at your leisure.

The main difference between an HTML document and a document created in a word processor is that most word processors allow you to change the characteristics of text *within* a document. For example, you can use your word processor to modify a paragraph's font, size, style, alignment, spacing, color, and so on. With HTML, we'll be using tags to accomplish all these things. For now, the important thing to remember is that all HTML documents consist of plain text.

When you begin using BBEdit Lite, you might notice the **Font & Tabs** item in the **Text** menu. This item lets you change the font, size, and style of text of your HTML source. Resist the urge to use a fancy-schmancy font! Pick a font that's readable and stick with it. Letter Gothic 9-point is used for all of the HTML source in the book because it's monospaced, which means that you can easily align characters in a line of text. It is also fairly compact, allowing you to pack quite a bit on the screen, without making the text hard to read.

Monaco 9 also works well as a source font because it is monospaced and compact, like Letter Gothic. Monaco is also a system font, and has therefore been available on every Macintosh since the first 128K. Because it's part of the Macintosh operating system, it loads faster. We use it...and recommend it.

Recognizing Tags

A simple convention is employed to distinguish text from tags: the less-than and greater-than signs (< >, also called angle brackets) are reserved in HTML to begin and end tags; that is, text that is enclosed between these brackets comprises HTML tags. (This would seem to mean that you can't use those two characters in your text for anything other than to define HTML tags, but later we'll explain how it is possible for you to do so without confusing the browser.)

Other Tag Uses

As we've briefly mentioned in Chapter 1, in addition to using tags to format text (assign attributes to text), you can use tags to link two documents on the Web, display graphics, or make it possible to download a file. Tags used in these ways create **hotspots** on which the viewer can click to invoke the link, the display, or the download.

In the next few chapters, you'll learn everything you need to know about tags. But now we'll give you some background on the development of HTML and tags, which should help you better understand HTML tags before you begin working with them.

Brief History

HTML is a language that owes its origins to a very simple declaration a few years back by the International Standards Organization (ISO) regarding SGML, or Standard Generalized Markup Language. Think of SGML as the big house in which HTML has a room.

In general, when using a markup language, you are mimicking the process of proofreading or editing, and this is true of computer markup languages as well. You review the text, change it to suit the composer or editor or to correct errors, and then present it to the viewer. With markup language, you can create a structured document that has the major elements, such as the head, title of the document, body, etc., clearly delineated so that it's portable to a variety of programs and platforms.

Initially, HTML was designed to simplify the display and viewing of styled text and graphics in documents on various computing platforms that have access to the World Wide Web, and to allow hypertext linking between these documents. (Remember Tim Berners-Lee and his cast of physicists?) Later, HTML was upgraded for more functionality with version 2.0. HTML 3.0, which is being argued about even as we write, will add even further functionality, and refine and simplify some of the more confusing aspects of HTML 2.0.

You also need to be aware that our friends at Netscape have complicated the standardization process by introducing their own HTML tags. And because Netscape is the most commonly used browser, it would be detrimental to the quality of your Web pages not to implement these HTML additions.

Throughout this book, we'll work in HTML 2.0 and 3.0 but we'll also identify and define those Netscape-specific tags that you'll see and want to know about. We'll do our best to keep you updated on all HTML developments at our Web site, http://www.spiderworks.com.

If you'd like to get more technical information on any of the HTML standards we mentioned, point your browser to http://www.w3.org. There you'll find more information on the subject than you'll ever need. Keep in mind, though, the documents you read there today may be completely different next week, next month, or next quarter since the 3.0 standards have not yet been set. They'll definitely be different next year.

Your First HTML Page

We've got some very exciting Web pages to show you later on in the book, but the sample pages we're about to show you now are intentionally baby-step simple, so that we can more clearly demonstrate the fundamental HTML concepts.

All of the projects in this book are in the Authoring folder you copied from the CD-ROM to your hard drive. Follow along by opening the

Figure 2.1
Opening a sample Web page on the CD-ROM.

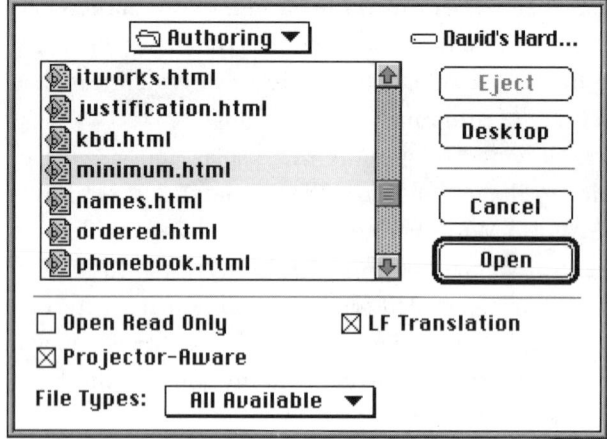

sample HTML files in BBEdit Lite (to see the source) or in Netscape (to see the results). Let's open the project, called `minimum.html`, using BBEdit Lite, as shown in Figure 2.1. As the name implies, this file contains the minimum amount of information needed to create your first Web page.

The following is `minimum.html`'s source code.

```
<html>
<head>
<title>xxxxx</title>
</head>
<body>
yyyyy
</body>
</html>
```

Be aware that some of the tags that you'll learn in this book are not required to make your documents readable, and in fact may disappear in future versions of the HTML standard. Nevertheless, it's a good idea to understand these tags, as they add to your overall knowledge of HTML, and they may become necessary again as the language standards evolve and new functionality is added to the World Wide Web.

Element Tags and Empty Tags

Let's get some HTML terminology under your belt:

- An **element** is composed of a set of tags and the text contained between the tags.

- **Element tags** are used in pairs: an opening or **start tag,** and a closing or **end tag**. The start tag consists of two brackets framing the tag name, such as <tag>. The end tag consists of two brackets framing a slash and the tag name, such as </tag>. The element tags are usually used to apply a process or look to a block of text or graphic.
- **Empty tags** perform tasks that are not dependent upon enclosing text in the HTML document. This includes indicating where a graphic belongs on a Web page, which is done with the <img> tag. Empty tags do not have end tags.

In this book, we will indicate when tags enclose text by using the **<tag>…</tag>** convention, where the three periods indicate text. We will use **<tag>** by itself when there is no text be enclosed.

> When using empty tags, *don't* use an end tag. Although some of the browsers you'll encounter will just ignore an empty end tag, such as </img>, others will abort. One of the first things to look for if your browser doesn't give you what you want is an errant empty end tag…or a missing end tag to an element.

Warning!

In the sections that follow, we will take a look at all of the tags that appear in `minimum.html`'s source.

<html>…</html>

Our very first tag! As you would guess, **<html>** tells your browser that the text in the file it's about to interpret is, in fact, HTML. It is usually the first tag in the document. Actually, <html> is one of those tags that we touched on earlier that isn't really necessary since most browsers assume that the files they browse are HTML; hence, you'll see that some people leave it out. Its companion end tag, </html>, usually the last tag in an HTML text file, also is unnecessary for the proper interpretation of your Web page by most browsers. We recommend, however, that you leave it in. You never know when the standard will change to require the <html>…</html> tags.

> **Important!** Tag names are case-insensitive, which means they can be typed either in upper- or lowercase, or a combination if you have the stamina, and the browser will interpret them the same. Thus, the tags <Title>, <title>, and <TITLE> are identical to the browser. Some people think that tags in typed uppercase help the eye to distinguish them from predominantly lowercase content. Others prefer to use lowercase because they feel it's a lot faster to type tags without using the Shift key so frequently. Do whatever works best for you.

<head>...</head>

Every HTML file should be divided into two distinct sections, the first of which is the **head section**. The **<head>...</head>** tags delimit, or contain, the head information. Heads contain information that is pertinent to the entire document, including the title of the page and the color of the background, or relationships with other HTML documents. The best way to think about the differences between the head and the body sections (which are defined in a moment) is that the head section is mostly administrative stuff, and the body is the meat of what you display in the browser window. Let's take a look at the most common element in the head, the **<title>...</title>** tags.

<title>...</title>

The title of your document is not only what you call it, but what Netscape shows in the title bar of its display window when it opens your document as a Web page. Although the title of your HTML document isn't subject to the 31-character limit that the MacOS imposes on file names, it's a good idea to keep it under 45 characters so that it will then fit comfortably within the width of a standard Netscape browser window.

When you specify a title, make it something descriptive, not something generic. Don't, for example, use "Home Page," use "*Your Name* Home Page." This is important because if you choose to make a bookmark for this page, Netscape saves both the document's title and URL (the document's location on the Web) in the bookmark file. Of course, not quite following our own rule, our document's title at this early stage is the not very descriptive "xxxxx," which we used just to demonstrate the basic concepts of tag behavior.

As we close off our head information with the end tag </head>, we've created a head element. Now we can move on to the major portion of our HTML text file.

<body>...</body>

This is where the action is. The **<body>...</body>** tag contains the content of your page, and it always begins with the tag <body>. The body of your document could be a short paragraph about your company, or it could be several megabytes of meaningful discourse on Shakespeare. The sum total of our content is the line that reads "yyyyy." (We were going to make it "Why? Why? Why? Why? Why?" but we thought better of it.)

We know. It's not exactly the great American novel, but it's enough to make our point about the body element. To let the browser know that we've completed our content, we need to include the end tag </body>. Just as it did with the head, the section's closing tag completes the creation of the body element.

</html>

Let's wrap up this document—such as it is. There's one tag that is still open. Do you see it? It's the <html> tag at the very top of the `minimum.html` text file. We add the companion </html> tag, and we're done.

Before we actually show you this page, think for a moment about how you think it might look. Then launch Netscape and open `minimum.html` to see what it actually looks like (Figure 2.2).

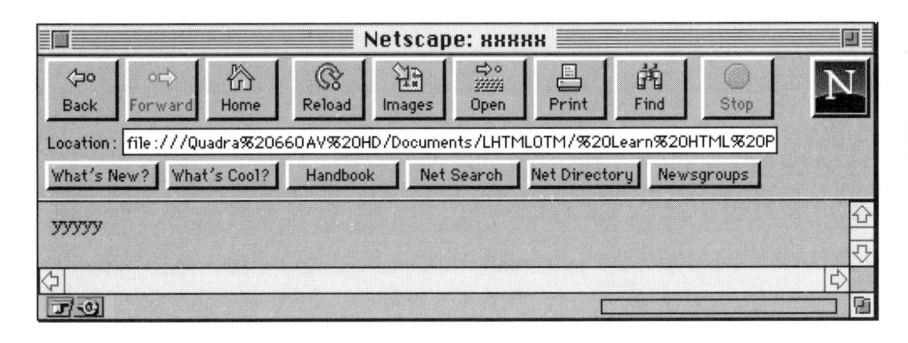

Figure 2.2
Viewing the sample Web page in Netscape.

> **By the Way...** Here's a shortcut you can use: In BBEdit Lite, go to the **Extensions** menu and use the **Preview** command to automatically launch (or switch to) Netscape to see what your source will look like when browsed. BBEdit Lite is smart enough to ask which browser to use if it doesn't already know.

The Paragraph Tags: <p>...</p>

We're on our way. Creating a one-line display is just the beginning. We need more, though, to do anything really interesting with HTML. That means creating paragraphs. The **<p>...</p>** element is the cue to the browser that we've created a paragraph. That's all there is to it: begin each paragraph with <p>, and end it with </p>. In fact, we could have enclosed our "yyyyy" display text in <p> and </p>, but we don't really need to since we have only one line of content. If you like, try it to see if it makes any difference.

> **By the Way...** Here are a few items to keep in mind about the <p>...</p> tags:
> - The end paragraph tag, </p>, is optional, and many people omit it from their Web pages. That will change with HTML 3.0, so get used to it and use it.
> - The opening <p> tag can be used by itself to insert blank lines in Web pages. We don't necessarily recommend doing this, and we'll show you a better way of adding blank lines later on.
> - Web browsers will generally assume that a <p> tag is present before and/or after a number of tags, such as the heading tags below, whether the <p> tag is actually there or not. It means that you will have a blank line immediately following the tags where inclusion of the <p> tag is assumed.

The Heading Tags: <h1>...<h6> and </h1>...</h6>

So far we have a simple page containing one line of text, and we've just seen how to create paragraphs. But before we do, let's add one more tag to our repertoire so that we have the ability to create sections with their own headings. For this, we need the **<h>...</h>** tags.

The <h> tag is called the **heading tag**. *Be careful not to confuse this tag with the head tags used in the head section of your HTML text file.* The heading tags display the text enclosed within in various formats different from the body text to make them stand out, such as boldface, underlined, larger size, centered, or capitalized. The format in which the heading is displayed depends upon the browser in which the user views your Web pages.

There are six levels of headings, graduated to indicate order of importance. You simply add the numbers 1 to 6 after the h to create each level; thus, <h1> is used first on a Web page, and <h6> is the last heading. Be careful when using the heading tag pair that you use the close heading tag and that it has the same level number that you used to open it. You should also use the heading tags in order—first the <h1> down to the <h6> tag—on a Web page. Using them out of order, such as using an <h3> tag before an <h1> to emphasize text is considered bad form and may look strange in some browsers.

> For future reference, note that besides being used in their most obvious roles as titles and attention grabbers, because of their incremental nature, headings make it simple to create outlines, presentations, tables of contents, and other ordered, hierarchical documents.

Let's take a look at a more complex HTML document to get a clearer picture of how heading tags come into play in a Web page. Use BBEdit Lite to open the document in the Authoring folder called headings.html. The source should look like the following:

```
<html>
  <head>
    <title>Heading Levels-Version 1</title>
  </head>
  <body>
    <h1>A Level 1 Heading</h1>
    <p>This is the text that starts the first paragraph of this
    section. I'm going to fill this document with enough text to
    make sure the paragraph has at least a few lines of text.</p>
    <h2>A Level 2 Heading</h2>
    <p>This paragraph is incredibly succinct.</p>
    <p>Here's another paragraph in the same section. Blah, blah,
    blah. This could be your text - Just imagine that!</p>
    <h3>A Level 3 Heading</h3>
    <h4>A Level 4 Heading</h4>
```

```
        <h5>A Level 5 Heading</h5>
        <h6>A Level 6 Heading</h6>
    </body>
</html>
```

Figure 2.3
Viewing the file as a Web page.

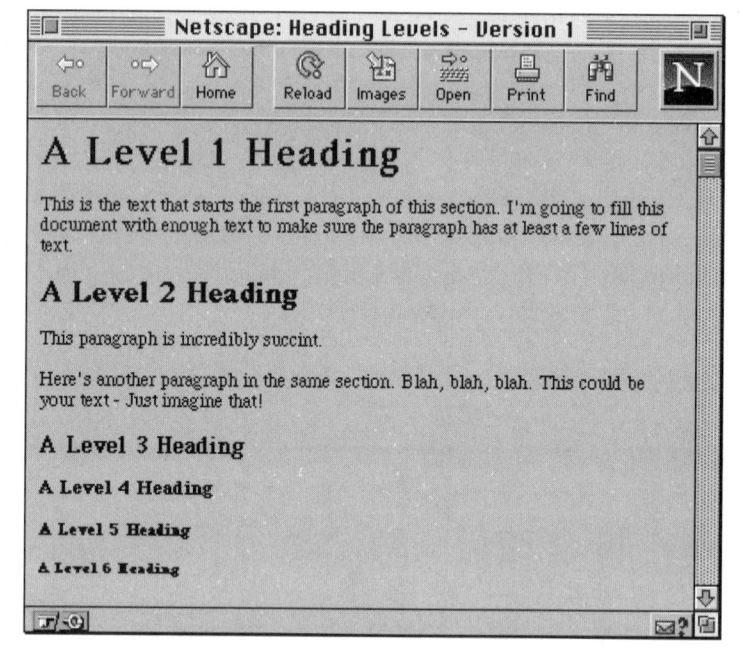

To use Netscape to view this document, either open the browser or, preferably, use the **Preview** feature in BBEdit Lite. Figure 2.3 shows what the sample page looks like viewed in Netscape where the heading delineations are easy to see.

Notice something else about the source for headings.html? We've indented lines within the head and body sections to make it easier to read. Just a few spaces make a world of difference, don't they? Note that indenting lines is for the benefit of the reader who wants to look at your source; browsers don't care if you make everything nice and readable or smoosh things together to conserve space. To illustrate this, we'll compress our sample page, taking out all the spaces and indents, even the carriage returns between lines. This compressed document, called smushed.html, looks exactly the same as the version in Netscape, but it is almost unreadable in BBEdit Lite, as follows:

```
<html><head><title>Smushed HTML Code</title></head><body><h1>A
Level 1 Heading</h1><p>This is the text that starts the first
paragraph of this section. I'm going to fill this document with
enough text to make sure the paragraph has at least a few lines of
text.</p><h2>A Level 2 Heading</h2><p>This paragraph is incredibly
succinct.</p><p>Here's another paragraph in the same section.
Blah, blah, blah. This could be your text - Just imagine that!
</p><h3>A Level 3 Heading</h3><h4>A Level 4 Heading</h4><h5>A
Level 5 Heading</h5><h6>A Level 6 Heading</h6></body></html>
```

As you can see, although spaces and indents mean nothing to your browser, they can make a big difference to someone trying to decipher or troubleshoot your source. And more often than not, that someone is you!

As a reminder, in general, we don't recommend that you forgo using end tags for element tags, because, in the future, browsers may require these tags. Better safe than sorry, we say.

What's Next

So far we've learned some background about HTML, and we've dissected a typical, albeit minimalist, HTML document to define the two major sections, called the head and the body. We've learned a few tags, including the title tag, the head *and* heading tags (don't confuse 'em!), the body tag, and the paragraph tag. We've also touched on some ways to make your pages a bit more readable. Finally, we created and tested our composing environment by using BBEdit Lite and Netscape simultaneously.

Next up: We dive much deeper into the HTML tag pool and explain how to customize tags to control more explicitly the presentation of our Web pages.

You've crossed the threshold, and there's no turning back now. Somewhere out there is a business card with the title Webmaster and your name on it.

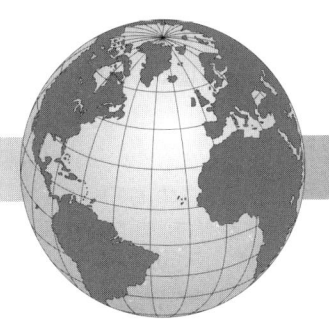

HTML Theory: A Must Read

In this chapter, we take the basic concepts that we just learned, rev the engine, and shift into high content gear. We introduce you to more of the HTML tags, describe how to customize them, and how they interact. We also do our best to further explain HTML version variations and browser variations. And we touch on that ethereal topic, white space—when it counts and when it doesn't. We also add a few "nit-picky" notes that we hope will make your HTML page design more trouble-free. In short, we prep you for the next two chapters, where it's tags, tags, and more tags.

Tag Structure

The tags we've introduced you to so far all follow the format *<tag name>*; that is, the tag name enclosed in angle brackets. But many tags include modifiers, called **attributes,** also enclosed within the same pair of brackets, as <tag *attribute…attribute*>. Attributes can be thought of as variables that contain values or are directions to the browser that a special logical condition exists within the element described by the tag. There can be one or more attributes included in a tag, and a value, several values, or no value for each attribute.

To illustrate this concept, let's look at **<img>**. In Chapter 2, we mentioned that the <img> tag lets you place images on your pages. It can contain several attributes that describe various options when displaying the image in your browser. Some of these attributes require values, some do not.

One of the most important attributes in the <img> tag is **src=** (for "source") because it indicates the image file that want to include on your Web page. The format is src = "URL" where the URL is the name of the file or the full Web address for the file if the file is in another directory or even on another machine. You must use the src= attribute each time you use the <img> tag.

Let's say that the name of our URL is floorplan.gif. Our tag will look like this:

```
<img src="floorplan.gif">
```

Next we'll add the **ismap** attribute, which tells the browser that this <img> is actually an **image map**—a special image that allows users to travel to different links based on where they click within the image. For instance, you could have an image map of a room in which each piece of furniture, when viewers click on it, will link them to a different page on your Web site. When viewers click on a bookcase, they link to your recommended reading list. When viewers click on the TV, they link to an episode guide to your favorite TV shows. And when they click on the couch, they link to a picture of a potato. (Hey, come on, work with me here.) The ismap attribute never has a value associated with it and is described as being "empty."

Now we'll combine <img> and ismap so that floorplan.gif is the URL of our image file, and the image contains a series of hotspots that will link to other Web pages or files when clicked on. (We'll learn how to create image maps very soon!)

```
<img src="floorplan.gif" ismap>
```

Two attributes common with the <img> tag are **height=** and **width=**. The values that you insert after the equal sign represent the image height and width in pixels. Some browsers (including Netscape) use those numbers to set aside space in which to insert the image after all the text has been placed. This precludes the browser repositioning the text after all pictures have been displayed. However, these attributes are not mandatory.

With these new attributes, our example might look like this:

```
<img src="floorplan.gif" height=300 width=400 ismap>
```

Another attribute that can be used with the <img> tag is **align=**. This attribute directs how a line of text will flow around an image. Three possible values of the align attribute are top, middle, bottom. Top aligns the top of the image with the highest item in the line of text; middle aligns the middle of the image with the baseline of the line of text; and bottom aligns the baseline of the image with the baseline of the line of text.

```
<img src="floorplan.gif" height=300 width=400 align=top ismap>
```

To summarize, we have discussed three values an attribute may contain: a quoted string such as "floorplan.gif", a number indicating height and width, and a predefined value such as top, middle, bottom.

We'll go into more detail about tag construction in the next two chapters, but for now, just keep these concepts in mind: Tags can contain attributes, which can subsequently hold further defining values.

> Don't use single quotation marks when delimiting a string; always hit that shift key and use doubles. And not "curly" quotes, or "smart quotes" like the ones you see in this sentence; they are not the same as "straight quotes" and cannot be read properly by any browser. Make sure that you don't turn on smart quotes in BBEdit's Preferences.

White Space

We all know the value of white space in documents, whether in printed version or on-screen. Without it, the legibility of everything we read would be seriously compromised. But that's because we're human beings. To machines, white space is meaningless. Well, Web browsers do the same thing, as we mentioned briefly in the previous chapter. Any extra spaces between words in the text in an HTML document will be discarded. Not surprisingly, the same is true for tags. Therefore, all of the following tag formats will give you the same result when displayed by your browser:

```
<img src = "floorplan.gif" height = 300 width = 400 ismap>

<imgsrc="floorplan.gif"height=300width=400ismap>
```

```
<img src="floorplan.gif"     height    =    300 width=400      ismap>
<img src="floorplan.gif"
    height=300
    width=400
    ismap>
```

The moral of the story: White space makes the HTML source more readable to the human eye, and although it's not mandatory, it's a good idea to use it.

HTML Comments

Like white space, comments in HTML source enable people to more easily understand what they're looking at. Comments are, essentially, "human-readable" statements, easy-to-interpret clues as to what a program is supposed to do. They provide valuable guidance for debugging purposes or to explain to a Web author what the source is meant to accomplish.

More importantly, comments in HTML documents can remind you, should you have to go back and revamp your site, what you did originally. Your audience won't see any of your comments—unless they view the source—so these notations in no way will impact the look of your Web pages.

Comments have a format all their own. Following the standard start angle bracket is an exclamation point, followed by two dashes, your comment, two more dashes, then the close angle bracket, like this:

```
<!--Comment goes here-->
```

Whatever is contained within comment tags is ignored by the browser. Additional white space between the text of the comment and the dashes is optional, but, again, it makes the text more readable.

> **Warning!** Many browsers aren't too happy when comments exceed one line, so keep them under 72 characters in length, including the tag delimiters. If you need a comment to be longer than 72 characters, use the comment tags on each line of text. For instance:

```
<!-- I need two lines of text to contain this massive, -->
<!-- long-winded comment that says nothing. -->
```

Also, a comment must not contain any other comments tags within its own tags. In other words, no nesting.

HTML Character Sets

The Web operates in the 7-bit world of UNIX (meaning that every character transmitted on the Internet must be made up of 7 bits). For us Mac users, this means that there are many typographic characters that cannot be represented directly by the characters themselves. Characters such as the yen sign (¥), the bullet (•), accented characters (Ü) and the like are not part of the basic 127-character set used on the Web. To represent all of the characters in the extended sets that we're used to using in most Macintosh fonts would require 8-bit representations, or 256 different characters.

There is a workaround, though. We can create **character equivalencies** using the ampersand (&) followed by the specific series of letters or numbers used to describe the characters and a semi-colon, which then are converted into the appropriate character when displayed by the browser. Let's say that we want our readers to see the actual tags that we used to create the elements that appear on the Web page (not just in BBEdit Lite or another text or HTML editor as would normally be the case, but in a Web page in Netscape). A simple sample will do. Let's use:

```
The format for the paragraph tag is <p>...</p>.
```

Normally, viewed in Netscape, this statement would appear as in Figure 3.1.

But if we want the tags to appear verbatim in Netscape, that is, we want to view the actual paragraph tag, we could use character equivalency. In this case, for the left angle bracket (the less-than symbol) we would use **<** for the right angle bracket, **>**. Thus, if we want people to see the <p>...</p> tags on a Web page, this is how we would type it:

```
The format for the paragraph tag is &lt;p&gt;...&lt;/p&gt;.
```

By the way, do you recall that we said there is a way to display the angle brackets that are usually reserved for tag names? Well, this is it. You would also use these equivalencies if, for instance, you needed to show the

Figure 3.1
A line of source. That doesn't look right, does it?

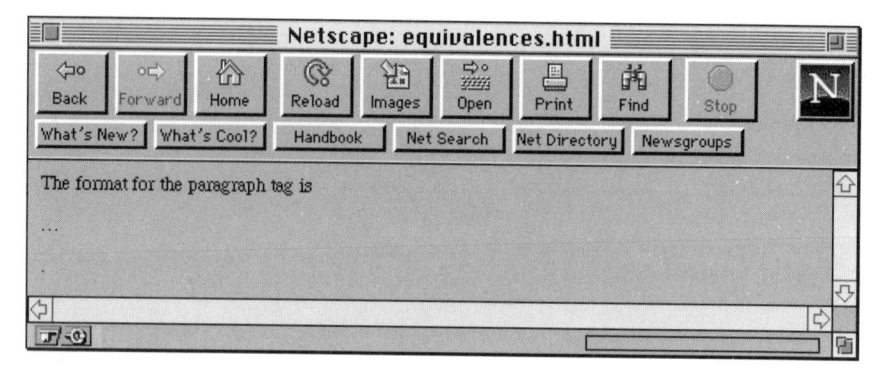

greater-than and less-than symbols in a mathematical equation. These and other HTML character equivalencies are listed in Appendix C.

HTML Versions

As noted, the current HTML standard is version 2.0, since version 3.0 has not been finalized yet. This version was agreed on by a committee of volunteers early in the summer of 1995. It consists of a basic set of tags that every browser should be able to handle. Certainly, Netscape Navigator handles HTML 2.0 tags very well. Unfortunately, the situation is much more complex than the preceding statement would make it seem.

Briefly, the problem is twofold: first, it took so long for the committee to finalize version 2.0 that discussions were already underway for HTML 3.0. At the same time, Netscape introduced a browser that handled not only HTML 2.0 tags, but also a series of tags that were unique to Netscape. And because Netscape's market share had reached an estimated 70–80 percent level for its browser, these tags had to be reckoned with: in essence, the standards were now being influenced and set by the marketplace rather than by academics.

We hope that by the time you read this, the contretemps will have been worked out; certainly, it is a positive indication that Netscape has two representatives on the HTML 3.0 committee.

In the meantime, what's a Web developer to do? Develop pages based on the agreed-upon HTML 2.0 standard? That would mean giving up some options that Netscape offers. Or should you develop pages according to Netscape's standard (known in some circles as N-HTML) but risk your pages showing up strangely in browsers that don't understand Netscape-specific tags?

In most cases, because a browser that can't interpret a tag will ignore it, we feel you should develop pages with an eye toward Netscape. That said, we also think it's a good idea to have a number of browsers on your Mac so that you can preview how your pages appear in both Netscape and non-Netscape browsers.

To see what we mean, we suggest you take a break from reading this book to look at some pages on the Web that are "Netscape enhanced," such as those on Netscape's home page <http://www.netscape.com>. Make note of the URLs as you go exploring so that you can then view those same pages using other browsers, such as America Online's (AOL) Web browser. You'll find there's usually a big difference. For example: the **<center>…</center>** tag (which centers the content between the start and end tags) is Netscape-specific, and AOL's browser ignores it; thus a lot of pages designed to be centered look pretty goofy in the current AOL browser.

The problem becomes clear when you consider that approximately 6 million people have Web access through America Online, some of whom you may be hoping to reach with your Web document. Clearly, then, you can't ignore the HTML 2.0 standard, nor can you avoid the impact of Netscape on the marketplace and, more important, on the Web. And don't think America Online isn't looking to its members. Rumor has it that they are making their homegrown browser fully Netscape-compatible. Plus, AOL will be making Netscape one of the browser options provided to its members.

Again, this all may become moot with the finalization of the HTML 3.0 standard, which will affect all browsers. However, there are already rumblings among vocal HTML designers that other browsers, such as Microsoft's Internet Explorer, have their own sets of proprietary tags, creating even more controversy.

Another important point to keep in mind on the browser issue: Many people don't have access to a graphical browser. Instead, they use a text-based Web browser such as Lynx to look at Web content. You should keep them in mind when designing your pages. As we go along, we'll show you how to do that by alerting you to the various text options available to you in tags that describe graphical images.

Version Breakdown

To make it easier to keep all the tag and version information straight, beginning in the next chapter, we've included tag tables that give not just definitions, but indicate whether tags are:

- part of the current HTML 2.0 standard and are considered universally accepted by all browsers;
- proposed as part of the standard for HTML 3.0 and may or may not be in some state of implementation by various browsers;
- considered proprietary to a particular browser's capability, such as the Netscape-specific tags just discussed;
- in various incarnations, a combination of two or more of the preceding.

To help differentiate between these implementations of HTML, we've included notations in the tag tables that will draw your attention to any proprietary information or implementation or browser-specific quirks.

Here is a sample table:

‹tag› ... ‹/tag›

Description: The description section outlines the purpose of the tag.

HTML 2.0 Attributes:

This section lists any attributes the tag may have in version 2.0 of the HTML standard.

HTML 3.0 Attributes:

This section lists any attributes the tag may have in version 3.0 of the HTML standard.

Netscape 2.0 Attributes:

This section lists any attributes the tag may have in N-HTML.

The top of each tag table has the start and end tags for element tags, or just the start tag for empty tags, and a description section. If there are attributes for HTML 2.0, HTML 3.0, or N-HTML, they are each listed separately, in their distinct sections.

Bear in mind that all of these various implementations of HTML are subject to change, so check in regularly at our Web site, http://www.spiderworks.com, for the latest updates and list of errata and corrections to this book.

Versions and Validators

A **validator** is a program that checks your source to make sure that it is compliant with whatever version of HTML you're using. If you have errors, the validator will show them to you. These validators rely upon what's called the **DOCTYPE** declaration to select which HTML version to check your pages against. Even if you have the option to choose a standard on the validator's Web site that's different from your DOCTYPE declaration, DOCTYPE will override that choice.

DOCTYPE is what's known as an **SGML declaration**; it's not an HTML tag per se. SGML, the Standard Generalized Markup Language, can be considered the "parent" of HTML; that is, HyperText Markup Language is a specific *type* of SGML. The DOCTYPE tag simply indicates that the document was written to a particular HTML standard. When it's used, the DOCTYPE tag always appears as the first item in the document (it precedes even the head section), and is one of the few items you'll put in your document that is not pure HTML.

If you're going to use tags that aren't part of the HTML 2.0 standard, such as some of the Netscape extensions or new tags that will be introduced as part of HTML 3.0, it isn't worth your while to use the DOCTYPE declaration. And because the standard for HTML 3.0 has not been finalized, validators would not be able to detect many possible errors in your source and may identify some aspects of the source as errors, even though they are not.

If, however, you are adhering to strict HTML 2.0 standards (and wouldn't that really impress the HTML purists out there who view your source?), it'll be worth your while to include the DOCTYPE declaration and run your Web pages through a validator. Here is the proper form for the DOCTYPE declaration in HTML 2.0:

```
<!DOCTYPE HTML PUBLIC "-//IETF//DTD HTML 2.0//EN">
```

> **By the Way...**
>
> There are two distinct camps in the Web design arena: constructionists and presentationists. Constructionists are the keepers of the SGML flame, who prefer to stick to so-called pure HTML and not extend it with special tags and attributes of their own making. If it's not a standard, they don't use it.
>
> Presentationists, on the other hand, prefer to treat HTML like PageMaker, and control as much as possible the way the viewer sees their documents. They welcome neat tricks and cool extensions to HTML.
>
> We're not advocating one over the other, and both have valuable and understandable viewpoints. By sticking to strict HTML, you are ensuring that the widest possible audience can read your pages, including the often-overlooked users of text-only browsers such as Lynx. You do, however, limit yourself to pedantic, methodical, lowest-common-denominator presentation. Conversely, being open to the latest in this field keeps you on top of the marketplace. It's your choice; only you can decide what is right for you and what you're trying to accomplish on the World Wide Web.

What's Next

Chapters 4 and 5 will show you all of the HTML tags for versions 2.0 and 3.0 (as the proposed standard currently stands), as well as the Netscape extensions, and we'll start putting together some useful Web pages as we go. Let's do it!

From the Neck Up: The Head Elements

Okay! Let's get this show on the road! We're going to set up a Web site for spiderworks.com, our creative services company, formed to write this book and to do other related projects. We feel that by stepping you through something we've done ourselves, we can more accurately describe the process of Web design. After all, we know what was going on in our heads (most of the time anyway!). In addition, because this is an actual Web site, all the URLs you see throughout these examples really exist; and for further comprehensibility, we've included a mirror image of the Web site (as it was at the date of publication) on the CD-ROM.

For now, though, think of spiderworks.com as your site—one you'll be building from scratch to learn all the elements that go into HTML coding and Web site design. If you see something you like—some HTML source, or the way things are arranged on the page—make a note of it for later use. We've included the source for each Web page on the CD-ROM, and if later you want to modify it to more accurately suit your company, your taste, or your goals, by all means edit it. We do it all the time: reuse HTML source here and there, alter it, tweak it.

Instant Replay

In this chapter, we're going to start by recapping some of the tag information we presented earlier, specifically the head elements, in order to put the "framework" around the bigger picture. (We move down to the body in Chapter 5.) You'll also see the first of the tag tables we promised you, which more succinctly define these all-important tags and amplify on their use. We saw the structure of a sample tag table in the previous chapter.

Remember that we said that the **<html>** tag begins all HTML files, and the </html> tag ends all HTML files. Again, in most browsers, you can get away with not using these tags, but because they serve to confirm the fact that the text within them is supposed to be HTML tagged text, we say use 'em. Here's the <html> tag table.

<html>...</html>

Description: Main container for HyperText Markup Language documents; begins and ends HTML documents.

HTML 2.0 Attributes:

None

HTML 3.0 Attributes:

Version="-//W30//DTD W3 HTML 3.0//EN"

URN=text	Universal Resource Name for document
Role=text	reserved for future use as definition of the role the document plays in the Web hierarchy

A few notes about the HTML 3.0 attributes listed above. The Version attribute is one suggested by the HTML 3.0 Internet draft on the W3 site http://www.w3.org. The Universal Resource Name (URN) is a persistent name for a resource, such as a document, on the Web. Unlike an URL, which also identifies resources on the Web, the URN is unchanging. The URL for a resource will change if the resource is moved to another Web site.

> **By the Way...** The HTML 3.0 attributes for <html> will be ignored by 2.0 browsers. There are no pure 3.0 browsers for the Mac at the time of this writing, but there should be soon.

Next in our little review session is the **<head>** element, which as you'll recall is one of the two main components of your HTML document, the other being the <body> element (which, again, we delve into in Chapter 5). The <head> element always appears in your document prior to the <body> element.

The <head> element itself does nothing special. It simply acts as a container for tags that *do* do something, such as the <title> tag. Here's the head tag table.

<head>...</head>

Description: Begins and ends the head section of the HTML document. Not to be confused with the <h1> through <h6> heading tags.

HTML 2.0 Attributes:
None

Next up for review is the **<title>** tag. Its role in HTML life is fairly simple: it contains the text that is used for the title of the HTML document. This title shows up in various ways, depending upon the browser you're using. In Netscape Navigator on Macintosh, the title is displayed in the title bar of your browser's window; in Mosaic (one of the earliest Web browsers, and the most popular prior to the advent of Netscape), you'll see it separately in a text box in the window's information bar.

> **By the Way...** The <title> tag has the distinction of being the only tag necessary for all browsers to interpret your document as a complete HTML document; <html>, <head>, and <body> are all considered optional!

More important, the document's title is what is captured when creating bookmarks in Netscape; therefore, a carefully crafted title will make it a lot easier for viewers to later interpret their bookmarks. Be aware, too, that the text string contained within the <title>…</title> tag will be reproduced on your Web page exactly as you type it, so make sure it looks the way you want it to—caps, lowercase, and so on. And keep it under 40 characters, as that's about the usual limit of characters that be viewed across the title bar of Netscape's default browser window.

> **By the Way…**
>
> The width of Netscape's default screen is 468 pixels, which sets the limit for most of the banner ads you'll see on Web sites that are feature advertising ("sponsored" sites). The designer creates ads that are 468 pixels wide (or less) so that the users don't have to resize their browser windows to see the whole ad. The height of the default screen depends upon the size of your monitor.

<title>…</title>

Description: Contains the title of the HTML document.

HTML 2.0 Attributes:

None

An Aside: The Short Version

Now that we've reviewed the basics, we think it's only fair to tell you about the "short version" of BBEdit Lite–based Web page design. No, this has nothing to do with standards versions—it is, in fact, a shortcut for creating the basic framework of a Web page. When you first open up BBEdit Lite (do so now, so you can follow along), you'll notice an item in the **Extensions** menu called **<> Document** (Figure 4.1).

If you click on it, it will insert your basic tags, including the <html>…</html> pair and the head and the body elements, and give you some other options as well. It's part of a really neat set of extensions to BBEdit Lite called HTML Tools, which comes to us courtesy of Lindsay Davies. Between those and Carles Bellevier's HTML Extensions further down the menu, you have the best of both worlds when it comes to using BBEdit

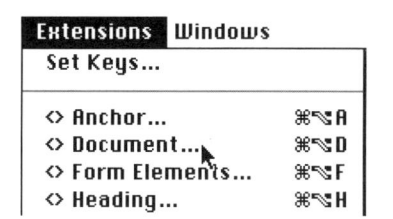

Figure 4.1
BBEdit Lite
<> Document
extension.

Lite as an HTML editor. Check out Figure 4.2 to see what appears in the basic BBEdit Lite document after you use invoke the <> **Document** command:

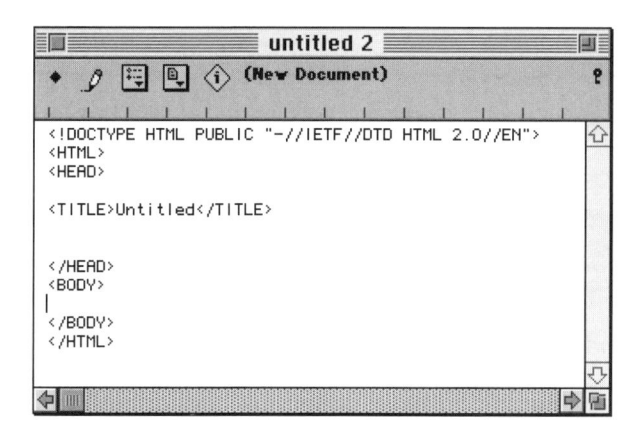

Figure 4.2
New document, prefilled by BBEdit Lite <> Document extension.

In the <> **Document** dialog box, you can fill out some things ahead of time, such as the title of your document, and decide whether you want the SGML prologue—DOCTYPE declaration. You can even customize <> **Document** further to include some comment lines or other template elements. A little later in this chapter, we'll be using this dialog box to begin building our page.

Planning the Site

Let's begin building the spiderworks site. As you become proficient, and depending on what you need to accomplish, you will find that you can create Web sites either according to very detailed plans or in a more abstract fashion. For beginners, though, it's best to stay within a structure. The basic structure we're going to use here is to develop a series of nested directories or folders to contain all the Web pages and support resources to be found on the spiderworks.com site.

A Little Background

Before we get down to brass tacks in building our site, let's look at how the average Web site is constructed. As you probably know from your own forays on the Web, Web sites are generally a collection of files, consisting of HTML pages and other resources, such as graphics, sound files, and video files. A Web site can also include programming scripts for accomplishing specific tasks, such as processing forms that visitors to your site fill out, like a guestbook, but we'll talk more about that later in the book.

All HTML files are served to Web browsers by a piece of software known as an **HTTP server** or a Web server. Generally the files that comprise your Web site reside on the same machine that hosts the Web server.

> **By the Way...**
> HTTP is the HyperText Transfer Protocol, and it's the standard that allows clients, such as Web browsers, and servers, such as a Web server, to interact with one another. For more information on HTTP, see Chapter 6. For an extremely detailed explanation of this protocol, point your Web browser to http://www.w3.org/hypertext/WWW/Protocols/.

Many companies and organizations have chosen to set up their own machine and Web server to host their Web sites. However, many individuals and organizations don't have the resources needed to do this, such as an adequate Internet connection with enough bandwidth that they can keep operational 24 hours a day. So we're assuming in this book that your Web site will reside on a machine at your Internet service provider or ISP. In some cases, the ISP who is providing you with an Internet connection to browse the Web or to send e-mail can also host your Web site.

> **By the Way...**
> While it's possible to set up a Web server like StarNine's WebSTAR on your own Mac, that is beyond the scope of this book. If you're interested in setting up your own Mac-based HTTP or Web server, you should look at *Planning and Managing Web Sites on the Macintosh: A Complete Guide to WebSTAR and MacHTTP* by Jon Wiederspan and Chuck Shotton (Addison-Wesley, 1996) or, if you're interested in providing a full complement of Internet services for users in addition to Web pages, look at *Providing Internet Services via the Mac OS* by Carl Steadman and Jason Snell (Addison-Wesley, 1996).

The files that comprise a Web site are linked together via hypertext links, and generally they are physically grouped together as well, in directories or folders on a hard drive of a computer. Most if not all of these directories will be nested, one within another, and the top directory will serve as the main HTML document directory. This directory will be the one that users will probably access the most because it generally contains the primary page, or home page, for a Web site. However, there will be times when pieces of your Web site will be in directories separate from those where the majority of your files reside. We'll cover that later.

An URL for a particular Web page lists both the name of the HTML file that the user is accessing and the hierarchy of directories that this file is nested in. For instance, in the URL http://www.spiderworks.com/info/support/help.html, the HTML file for the Web page "help.html" can be found in the support directory, which is turn is in the info directory, which is within the main HTML document directory on the www.spiderworks.com Web site. Generally, if an URL ends in a slash, you are accessing a directory on a Web site. If it doesn't end in a slash, you are usually accessing a file. More about this in Chapter 6.

Getting Started

This should give us enough background to start creating our own Web site. We're going to group all of our files together in a series of nested directories or folders and call our top level or main HTML document directory for our sample Web site `spiderworks web site`. Go ahead and create this folder on your desktop. It'll serve as the repository for all of your files for this site, and it will be where you create, test, and perfect your pages before letting the world see them (Figure 4.3).

The primary document in a Web site is the `index.html` file in the main HTML document directory. All browsers recognize this as a special file name, the one that is opened first when the browser scans the Web site's main group of documents.

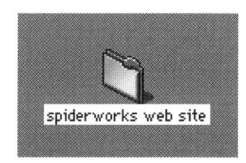

Figure 4.3
The spiderworks folder can be put anywhere, but a good place is on your desktop.

> **By the Way...** When you see an URL that ends with something other than .html or .htm, the browser is going to go looking for the index.html file within the last directory in the path of the URL. For instance, if you point your browser to http://www.spiderworks.com/info/support/, the browser will automatically call up the index.html file that should reside there.

Here's how to create the `index.html` page in the main document directory for your Web site on your hard drive.

1. Launch BBEdit Lite. You will see a new, untitled document.
2. Choose <> **Document** from BBEdit Lite's **Extensions** menu. Fill in the information as it appears in Figure 4.4: Check the SGML Prologue, HTML, Head, Body, and New document boxes; and fill in the title, which is simply spiderworks Home Page. Leave the rest of the dialog box alone for now.
3. Save the document as `index.html` in the `spiderworks Web site` folder.

We'll discuss the other options on this screen as we progress. The BBEdit Lite screen should look like Figure 4.5 after you save the document. Congrats! You've just created your first fully functional Web page, albeit a little thin on content. We promise, it will fill out as we continue.

Figure 4.4 The BBEdit Lite <> Document dialog box.

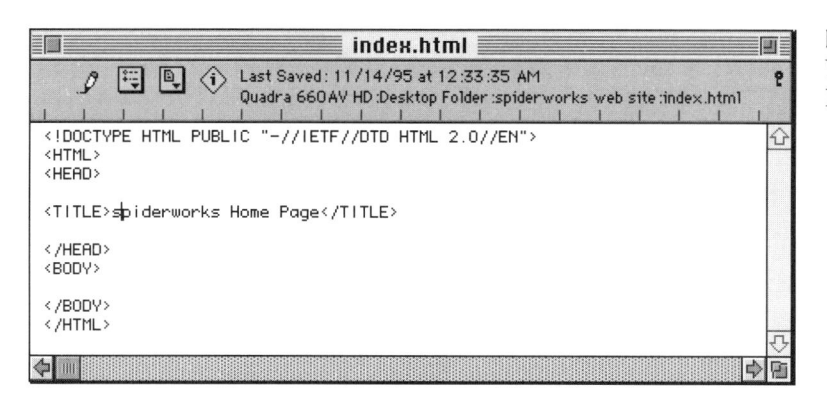

Figure 4.5
Your first HTML page!

```
<!DOCTYPE HTML PUBLIC "-//IETF//DTD HTML 2.0//EN">
<HTML>
<HEAD>

<TITLE>spiderworks Home Page</TITLE>

</HEAD>
<BODY>

</BODY>
</HTML>
```

Other Head Element Tags

We've covered the basic head element tags that you will routinely use in your Web pages. There are, however, head tags that are not mandatory and thus are not as commonly used. Still, they can be useful. We'll cover them below, although you might want to skip over them now and return to them later in order to start working with the next major group of tags—body tags—that are vital to the construction of a Web site. We cover the body tags, including both the essential ones and the more esoteric ones, in the following chapter.

Home Base

Any successful structure requires looking ahead to the finished product. In Web design, the **<base>** tag gives you the opportunity to do some advance planning for your Web site. If you know the URL, or address, at which your Web pages are going to reside on your ISP's site, you can place the URL within this element. It might be as easy as calling or e-mailing your ISP for your URL right now—or you might have to wait until your Web site is complete to add this tag to your Web pages.

When you use the <base> tag in a Web page, the page in a sense declares its own URL in Netscape and in some other browsers, which aids in locating the page for operations such as reloading and linking. Not every browser makes use of this tag, but for those that do, you'll see a significant increase in speed of access.

<base>

Description: Contains the intended Uniform Resource Locator for the HTML document.

HTML 2.0 Attributes:

href="URL"   actual address on the Web

The <base> tag also allows you to move a document, say, to another server or directory without breaking any of the relative links to resources, such as Web pages or other files, that the document may contain. For example, suppose you find a Web page that contains relative links. A relative link will not contain an entire Web or HTTP address—starting with the top directory of a Web page and working its way down through directories until the file is reached—for the resources that it's pointing to. Instead it contains a pathname or a listing of directories pointing to the resources that is relative to the directory that the Web page is in. A link, or an URL, is absolute when it contains the full HTTP address, including a directory structure starting with the top level of the Web site.

If you copy the Web page to your hard drive by saving the HTML source and then open the source with a Web browser, links that are relative, or do not contain an entire HTTP address but simply refer to files as if they exist in the same directory, will be dead. If, on the other hand, the document contains the <base> tag, your browser will treat all of the relative links as complete, because it will then have some idea of where to find them, based on the URL of the original document. If, for example, we include

```
<base href="http://www.spiderworks.com/index.html">
```

in our document, then users who save the source file to their hard drives will be able to access any relative links we put on the page. This assumes, of course, that the users' Internet connections, or HTTP connections, are active when you browse the document. For more information on relative and absolute URLs, see Chapter 6.

> By the Way...
>
> HREF is an attribute you'll see used with tags besides <base>. HREF stands for Hypertext Reference, and it specifies a link to another resource on a Web site, such as file or an URL for an HTML document or a graphic.

Let's add the base tag above to the `index.html` document on the line below the <title> tag. It should look like Figure 4.6.

Search Me

This section is "for future reference," but we thought you should know about it so that you can implement it when you're ready. Many Web pages have a region in the head section that looks like Figure 4.7. This feature is created using the **<isindex>** tag, which is an empty tag. This tag can now be placed anywhere on a Web page, including the body of the page, but usually it's at the top in the head section because HTML 2.0 specified that was where it belonged.

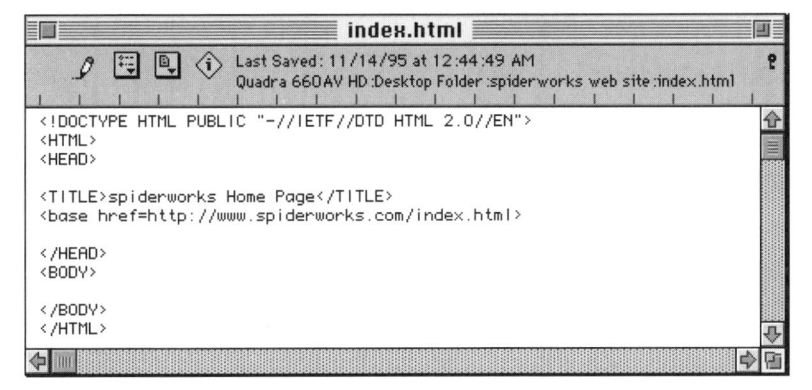

Figure 4.6
The <base> tag.

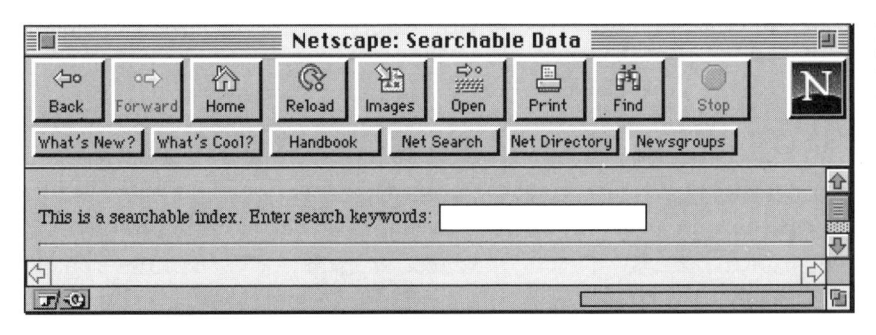

Figure 4.7
HTML document with <isindex> tag.

The <isindex> tag tells the browser, "Treat this document as a searchable index, so that users can look for a particular text string." Sounds simple enough: just declare the document to be searchable, and it is, right? Wrong. You need to take advantage of something called cgi-bin for this to take effect.

CGI, the Common Gateway Interface, is a standard that tells compatible servers how to access external programs so that the data is returned as an automatically generated Web page. For example, when you click on an image on a Web page "hotspot," a cgi-bin program does the actual translation between the coordinates on the screen of your mouse click and the appropriate action to take.

Your ISP may very well have a search engine within the service's `cgi-bin` directory. Check with their support staff to find out if one exists and how to use it, so that you can utilize the <isindex> tag.

<isindex>

Description: Declares the HTML document to be a searchable index.

HTML 2.0 Attributes:
None

Netscape 2.0 Attributes:
prompt=text   author-specified prompt text

Also be aware that Netscape allows you to create custom messages instead of the default, "This is a searchable index. Enter search keywords:". We won't be including this tag in the spiderworks.com site, but keep it in mind as you develop expertise—you'll want to take advantage of it.

Hitting the Links

The **<link>** tag sets up a relationship between your document and another HTML document. It is not the most common way to add links on your Web page to other Web pages: the anchor tag <a>...</a> in the next chapter is the tag that is used most often for this.

But the <link> tag has its uses, as you'll learn. An empty tag that belongs in the head section, the <link> tag connects one HTML document to another as a whole. Typically, it is not a viewable link.

Look at its accompanying tag table, and you'll see that this tag defines the address of the "linked to" HTML document by using the **href="URL"** attribute. The **name=** attribute refers to the name of an item, be it a style sheet, a banner, or another special item specified by the author of the linked document.

The <link> tag can set up a relationship between a number of items simultaneously; therefore, you can have more than one <link> tag. Relationships can also be set up in reverse, whereby your document is the linked-to document, by using the **rev=** attribute. You can also use the URN, or Uniform Resource Name, to describe an identifier separate from the URL.

The **methods=** attribute is used to describe the service under which your document is supposed to contact the linked document, whether it be HTTP for Web documents, FTP for executable files, gopher for gopher documents, or any other available UNIX service.

<link>

Description: Defines a relationship between this document and another. Rarely used.

HTML 2.0 Attributes:

href ="URL"	address of the linked document
name=text	anchor name
title=text	title of the linked document
rel=text	description of the relationship between the two documents
rev=text	description of the reverse relationship between the two documents
URN=number	Uniform Resource Number
methods=HTTP	link via HyperText Transport Protocol
FTP	link via File Transfer Protocol
gopher	link via gopher search
WAIS	link via WAIS search
mailto	link via e-mail

The <link> tag and its attributes are usually used by software that generates HTML documents on the fly, which means software that creates HTML pages out of a text repository, such as a database, based on user queries. Thus <link> isn't the most common tag on the block. Nevertheless, it's important to know what it does so that if you encounter it, you'll know what you're seeing. In addition, the <link> tag will probably be more widely used once HTML 3.0 becomes the law of the land. One very important way it probably will be implemented is as a way to include style sheets in your documents.

The <link> tag is also finding use in browsers that support the creation of on-the-fly toolbars—toolbars that are created by the user as needed. For instance, Prodigy's Web browser uses a particularly striking implementation of this feature, allowing users to create Web documents that feature self-designed toolbars, floating above the browser window. The **rel=** attribute defines how the toolbar will be built.

Certain common values have been reserved for the rel= attribute:

- **Bookmark:** to reference different points in long documents. The title attribute is used to label the bookmark. You can have more than one bookmark (contained in separate <link> tags). This would be useful for a frequently asked questions document (a FAQ) or a long list of items in an ordered directory, such as an address listing.
- **Copyright:** for copyright statements.
- **Glossary:** for glossaries.
- **Help:** for help documents.
- **Home:** for link points to a home page. The location of the home page would be the value of the href= attribute.
- **Index:** for indexes.
- **Next, Previous:** for referencing the next or previous document in a series of documents, such as a step-by-step lesson.
- **ToC:** for tables of contents. Again, the location of the home page would be the value of the href attribute.
- **Up:** for referencing the parent document; that is, this document is called by another document.

Going Behind the Scenes

In the Internet publishing world, you'll hear the term **meta-information.** It refers to information about files that is "behind the scenes," such as modification date, file size, language the file is written in, and site administrator. The **<meta>** tag is used for placing such information in your document header. There are two main uses of the <meta> tag to consider.

<meta>

Description: Provides meta-information, or user-defined information, about the HTML document.

HTML 2.0 Attributes:

http-equiv=text   defines HTTP header of content='s value
name=text   defines keyname of content='s value
content=varies   value for http-equiv= or name=

The first is a simple denotation of the keywords you want a Web indexing tool or a search engine such as WebCrawler (Figure 4.8), Lycos, or Yahoo to find when they come across your Web page. As you're probably aware, a search engine permits users to search a wide variety of Web sites, generally using keyword searches.

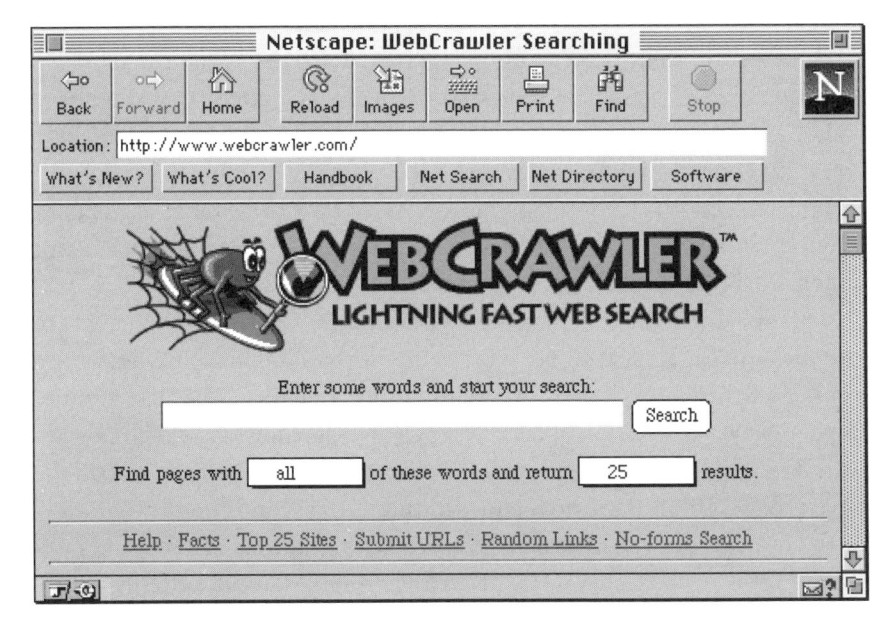

Figure 4.8 WebCrawler, an Internet search engine for locating World Wide Web documents.

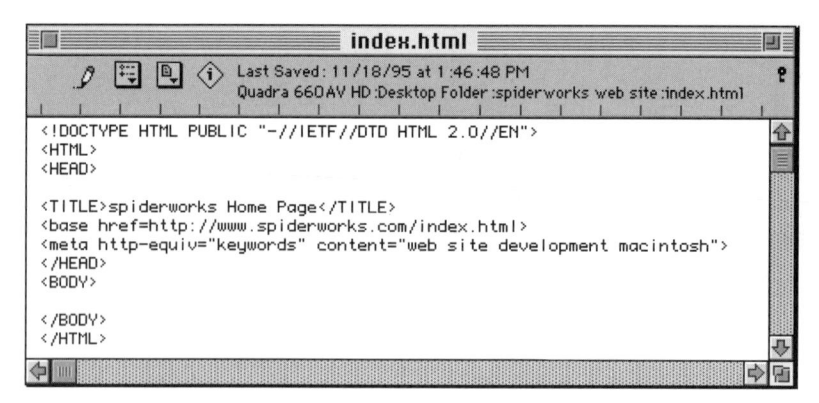

Figure 4.9
Inserting the <meta> tag.

```
<!DOCTYPE HTML PUBLIC "-//IETF//DTD HTML 2.0//EN">
<HTML>
<HEAD>

<TITLE>spiderworks Home Page</TITLE>
<base href=http://www.spiderworks.com/index.html>
<meta http-equiv="keywords" content="web site development macintosh">
</HEAD>
<BODY>

</BODY>
</HTML>
```

We use the http-equiv= attribute to specify the HTTP head. We use the name= attribute to indicate the type of information—keywords, authors, titles, etc.—that we want to provide to searching and indexing programs, and the content attribute to indicate the value of the information. So if we want spiderworks.com to come to the attention of people looking for tips on developing a Web site on the Mac, we could use the keyword "Web site development macintosh" with the <meta> tag:

```
<meta name="keywords" content="Web site development macintosh">
```

We're going to put the <meta> tag "keywords" in our document (Figure 4.9).

The second use of the <meta> tag is specific to the Netscape browser. Suppose, for one reason or another, you decide to move your Web page from one server to another. But because there are a lot of folks out there who have your old URL, you want to leave the Web equivalent of a forwarding address. To accomplish this, you would use the <meta> tag in conjunction with what's called the **client pull** feature of Netscape Navigator (which we'll discuss in depth later in the book).

Netscape uses the <meta> tag's http-equiv= value of "refresh" to reload the page. First it looks for a value in the content= attribute for a number and URL, separated by a semi-colon. The number is the number of seconds before the reload occurs, and the URL indicates which page to load. If no URL is specified, Netscape assumes that you want to reload the current page. Be sure to allow enough time—10 seconds ought to do it—for the user to read the information about your new location, before loading the page at your new URL. The following is sample code using the <meta> tag to indicate a forwarding address:

```
<head>
<title>We've moved!</title>
<meta http-equiv="refresh" content="10;
url=http://new.com/index.html">
</head>
<body>
I've found a <a href="http://new.com/index.html">new home</a> for
my page. If you're using Netscape, this page will automatically
transport you there in a moment. The rest of you? Click on the link.
</body>
```

The <meta> tag has other uses that you'll want to learn as your sites become more sophisticated, but for now, these are the two to keep in mind.

> The following tags have been proposed for HTML 3.0 but have not been implemented in any browser as of the date of publication. They're here for your information only, not to use in your page design…yet.

By the Way…

Ranger Spot

The **<range>** tag, another empty tag that is put in the head section of a Web document, is used to section off a segment of content in a Web page, with the from= attribute marking an element in the page as the beginning of the segment, and the until= attribute marking an element in the page as the end of the segment. The id= attribute defines the range and specifies the values of the from= and until= attributes, while the class= attribute defines the type of range.

<range>

Description: Describes a segment of the HTML document. Proposed HTML 3.0 tag that is not in wide use yet.

HTML 3.0 Attributes:

id="text"	user-defined range name
class=text	user-defined name of class
from=text	name of beginning marker
until=text	name of ending marker

Perhaps you want to allow viewers to search for a particular Web address on a Web page that contains tons of links to cool sites that you've found on the Web, along with a considerable amount of text explaining why these sites are so cool. To speed up the search process, you'd use the <range> tag to mark off the URL-rich section of your document to be searched when the viewer starts looking for sites.

The **<spot>** tag is used to define different points within your document that you may want to refer to in other tags, such as the <range> tag. You can think of the <spot> tag as an electronic marker. Like <range>, it is an empty tag that is part of the HTML 3.0 working specification.

<spot>

Description: Designed to allow placement of user-defined identifiers, or names at random points within a document. Proposed HTML 3.0 tag.

HTML 3.0 Attributes:

ID=text   user-defined name

Although these tags have not been finalized, assuming that they will, they should serve to provide an effective on/off switch for sorts, searches, formatting, and accessing certain parts of a remote document. Watch the 3.0 standard as it evolves for more information on <spot>.

Doing It with Style

As you no doubt know from working with your word processor of choice, style sheets allow you to set up and save standard ways—styles—of displaying text to be used over and over in document creation. We used a style sheet created in Microsoft Word that allowed the quick formatting of body text, HTML samples, tech blocks, and figure captions in this book.

The **<style>** tag, if and when it's implemented in the 3.0 standard (there is some debate over whether it will be), will let you do this on the fly in your Web pages. You'll be able to use a third-party style sheet generator to create your styles, choose fonts, alignment, sizes, tab stops, highlighting and so on, then link them to your pages. Style sheets are a convenient way to achieve a consistent, and thus professional, look for your Web sites, which is why we're alerting you to this tag—sooner or later HTML will permit style sheets.

<style>

Description: Establishes style characteristics for a Web page. May or may not be implemented in HTML 3.0.

HTML 3.0 Attributes:

notation=integer   describes style format being used

We are finished with the head tags—for now. We'll come back to them from time to time, when something in the body of our document needs to reference a head tag or when we need to remind you of a basic concept.

Next, we look at the rest of the tags, the body tags, which comprise a great deal of material. We'll take it slow, though. When you're ready, turn the page!

HTML Body Language

A head is no good without a body, and in this chapter, we explore many of the tags that are used to contain the content of a Web page and that affect how the information looks and feels to the end user. Because we are focusing on text in this chapter, one important body tag is not covered until the next chapter: the anchor tag (<a>...</a>), which represents a hypertext link to another Web page or other resource. If you absolutely must learn how to use this tag now, skip ahead to Chapter 6 and bone up on it. Then hurry back here—the body tags covered in this chapter are important.

The Body Elements

HTML 3.0 introduces a new set of attributes that are applied, in part or in total, to almost all of the body elements.

- **id="text"** name and id for an element in a Web page. This is used to link to one or more elements in a Web page, such as an image or a block of text.
- **lang=text** language used by intended audience for a Web page. This is the standard ISO language abbreviation for a language and country code (i.e., "lang=en.us" is English as used in the United States).

- **class=text** indicates types or classes of element in a Web page. When used in a body tag, it indicates that the tag is rendered differently than standard HTML 3.0, as dictated by attached style sheets.
- **align=text** paragraph justification. Values for align are:
    left: render paragraph left justified (default)
    right: render paragraph right justified
    center: render paragraph center justified
    justify: render paragraph fully justified (not yet implemented in Netscape Navigator)
- **clear=text** specifies at what point in the margin that text will flow around an image or figure. Values for clear are:
    left: text starts when left margin is clear of image or figure
    right: text starts when right margin is clear of image or figure
    all: text starts when both margins are clear of image or figure
    "x en": text starts when x units are free next to an image or figure. If there aren't x number of units free in the margin next to an image before the bottom of the image is reached, the text will appear below the image.
    "x pixels": text starts when x pixels are free next to an image or figure. If there aren't x number of pixels free in the margin next to an image before the bottom of the image is reached, the text will appear below the image.
- **nowrap** prevents a browser from automatically wrapping text.
- **md=string** verification checksum string. "md" stands for message digest, and it's a security feature. The checksum is associated with tag attributes that point to a file via an URL. The checksum is calculated each time the URL is invoked to ensure that the target file is always the same. If it isn't, the checksum returned to the browser will be invalid, and the browser should notify the user. This is primarily designed to work with the src= attribute for the <img> tag.

The tag tables in the rest of this book will refer to these attributes by name and an abbreviated definition. To refresh your memory as to what each attribute means, refer back to this section, which contains a fuller definition.

Bodyworks

The **<body>** tag, covered in Chapter 2 and as specified in the HTML 2.0 specification, is none too exciting—it indicates where to begin and end the content of a document. Netscape, however, has made it a little more interesting by making it a color commentator as well. In Netscape, you can now specify a color for the document background and display text with the <body> tag; you can also use it to define the colors of your links in their unvisited, activated (the user has just clicked on the link), and already visited states.

> There is no hard and fast rule for the colors of link states, but it has become common practice to put unvisited links in blue, activated links in red, and already visited links in purple, which are all also the default colors. Because readers are used to these color conventions, you should consider the value of maintaining them as one way to make your pages more user-friendly.

By the Way...

<body>...</body>

Description: Begins and ends the displayed content of the HTML document.

HTML 2.0 Attributes:

None

Netscape 2.0 Attributes:

background="URL"	Web address of GIF or JPEG file to be used as tiled background image
bgcolor=#rrggbb	hexadecimal triplet representing selected background color
text=#rrggbb	hexadecimal triplet representing selected text color
link=#rrggbb	hexadecimal triplet representing selected unvisited link color
alink=#rrggbb	hexadecimal triplet representing selected activated link color
vlink=#rrggbb	hexadecimal triplet representing selected visited link color

`<body>` (continued)

HTML 3.0 Attributes:

id="text"	name and id for Web page elements
lang=text	language used by intended audience for a Web page
class=text	indicates types or classes of element in a Web page
align=text	paragraph justification
clear=text	specifies at what point in the margin that text will flow around an image or figure
md=string	verification checksum string

Background color can be anything in the color spectrum between black and white, but you'll notice in your Web travels that it is often gray, which is the default color the Netscape browser will show if no background color is specified. If you decide to make it another color, remember to then make your text color something complementary.

Color Commentary

Before you read this section, take note in the <body> tag table of the term **hexadecimal triplet** in the Netscape 2.0 Attributes section. Before you utter the words "I don't do math," rest assured that you won't actually have to get out the calculator for this, but some background understanding of this concept will help you to better define colors for your Web document.

The numbers and letters you see in the example in this section are called hexadecimal triplets. They describe the color in the RGB model, which refers simply to how much red (R), green (G), and blue (B) is used to create the color. The hexadecimal system is a way of counting based on 16 digits, 0 through 9 and A through F, as opposed to the decimal system of 0 to 9, or the binary system 1 and 0. Triplet refers to the three sets of two digits each in the string that describes the color. The first set of digits in the hexadecimal triplet describes the red component of the color, the second the blue component, and the third the green component. The lower the hexadecimal number, the less of the color in the mix; the higher the number, more color in the mix. Thus, 00 means none of the color, and FF means the fullest amount of the color.

A few extreme examples of hexadecimal triplets should help illustrate the model. The color black is a complete absence of red, green, or blue; hence, its hexadecimal triplet is, as you might expect, 000000; white then is FFFFFF. Gray, in the middle of these two extremes, is 0F0F0F. Pure blue is 0000FF; pure red is FF0000. Purple, a mix of blue and red with no green, is FF00FF. These colors not coincidentally are also the default colors in the Netscape window: background (Netscape gray), text (black), unvisited link (blue), activated link (red), and visited link (purple).

Easy Color   Now that you have that under your belt, we're happy to tell you that this process is much easier with a piece of software called HTML ColorPicker by David Christensen (Figure 5.1), available at <http://hyperarchive.lcs.mit.edu/HyperArchive/Archive/text/html/html-color-picker-203.hqx>. It takes advantage of Apple's system software to give you the hexadecimal triplet of whatever color you want.

This utility is as easy as a pie chart to use: Simply click on the Picker button to use the Apple Color Picker to select any color you want, as shown in Figure 5.2. HTML ColorPicker will convert the red, green, and blue values that make up the selected color to their respective hexadecimal equivalents. Then, it will combine them into the triplet, add the requisite # symbol that tells Netscape it's a number, and let you place it on the Clipboard, ready for pasting into your HTML document.

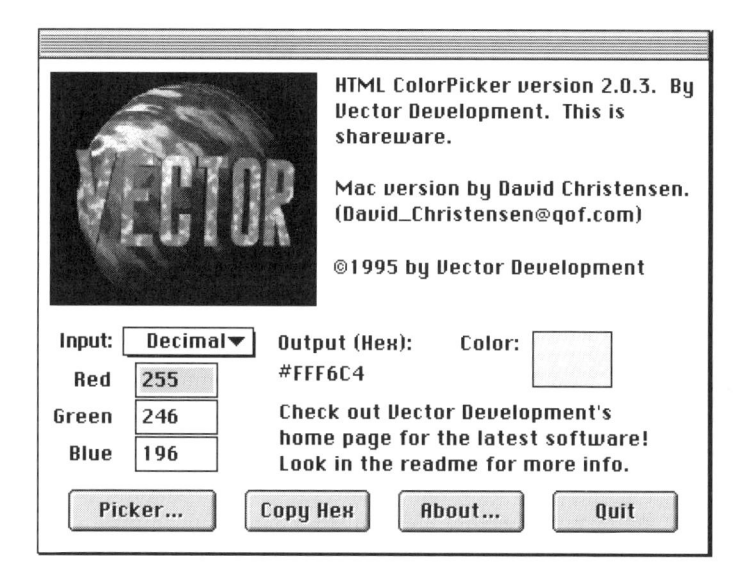

Figure 5.1
HTML ColorPicker.

Figure 5.2
The Apple Color Picker.

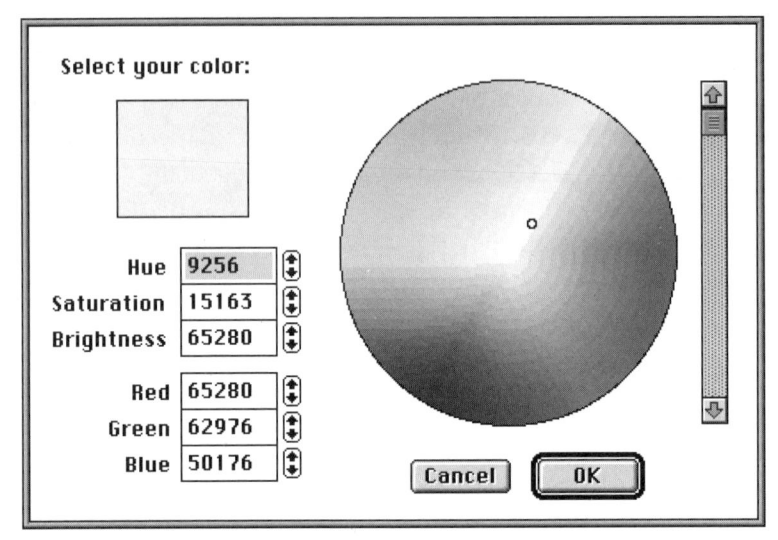

As a starting point, let's set the colors for our page to the default colors for all of the text attributes (which means we don't have to refer to them in the tag), and use HTML Color Picker to find a light tan for the background color. We'll use FFF6C4, which the Color Picker calls "wheat." Here's how to modify the <body> tag:

```
<BODY bgcolor="#FFF6C4">
```

Using BBEdit Lite, add this line to your `index.html` document, which should then appear as in Figure 5.3.

To preview what our document looks like so far, follow these steps:

1. Be sure to save the changes to your hard drive.

Figure 5.3
Now we have a background color—wheat.

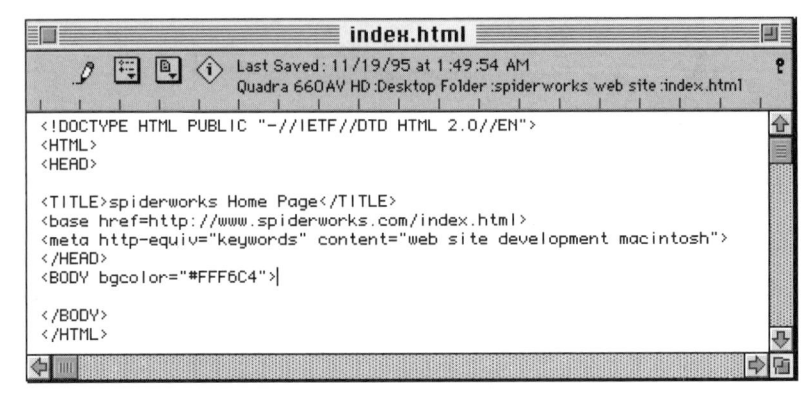

2. Hold down the Command and Shift keys and hit P. If you're using HTML ColorPicker for the first time, it will prompt you to specify the browser you want to use to preview your pages; thereafter, it will automatically launch the specified browser, then load the page for your viewing pleasure.

You should see a solid background of light tan, and no text. Pretty dull, right? Let's add some text now. (A word of caution: Don't forget what we said earlier, that browsers ignore spaces, returns, tabs, fonts, and other styled text features, so don't be surprised at the first display after adding text.) At this point, either type in some text of your own (be sure it begins after the open <body> tag) or open the `bodytext.txt` document in the `Authoring` folder and copy what you find there, pasting the content between your <body> tags. If you do the latter, the result will look like Figure 5.4. Just for grins, let's preview the document in Netscape, too, which is shown in Figure 5.5.

Not exactly easy to read, is it? To recap, this is what happens: when we type, we automatically include returns at the ends of lines, spaces, or tabs, and so forth. Netscape and all other browsers ignore those spaces and mush the whole thing together in one big textual mess. It wraps lines when

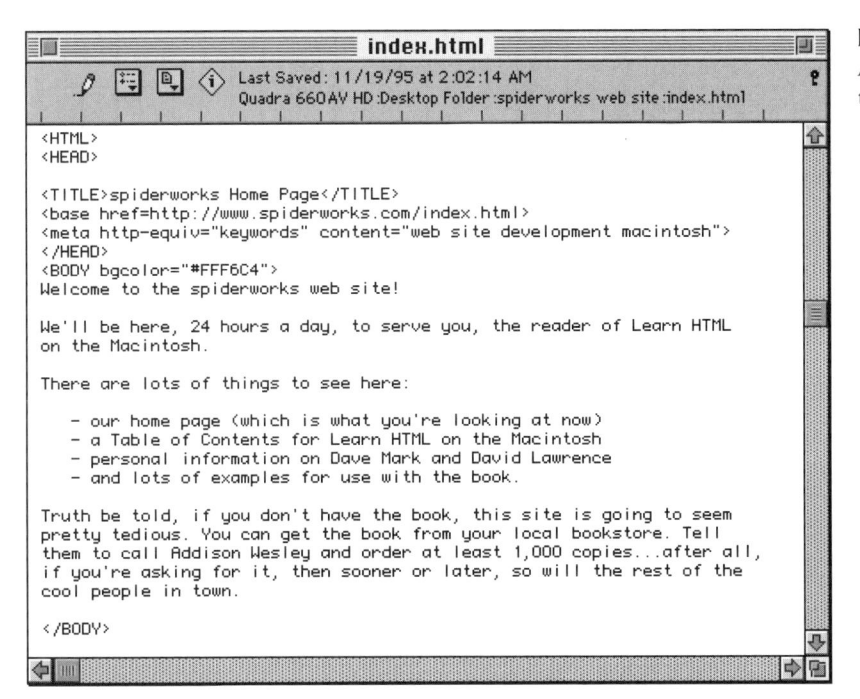

Figure 5.4
Adding some text.

it reaches the designated width of the window, and displays the text in 12 point Times, its default proportional font and size.

Figure 5.5
Oops!

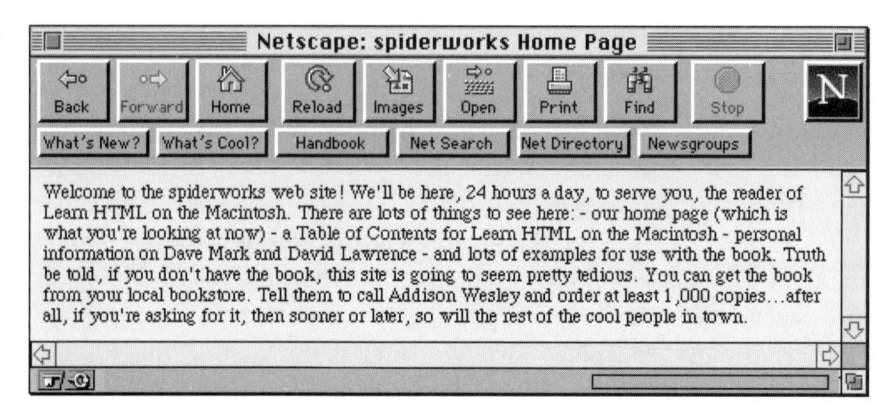

By the Way... If your Netscape doesn't look like Figure 5.5, go to the **Fonts and Colors** item in **Preferences** from the **Options** menu. Then, so you can follow along in this book, use the settings shown in Figure 5.6.

Figure 5.6
Fonts and Colors Preferences.

In spite of how our text looks at this stage, it's actually a good thing, because it gives us a baseline from which to go about specifying exactly how we want our text displayed using HTML tags. Let's start to make some sense of all this by adding some line breaks.

Gimme a Break!

Description: Line break.

HTML 2.0 Attributes:

None

HTML 3.0 Attributes:

clear=text   specifies at what point in the margin that text will flow around an image or figure

The **
** tag tells the browser to break to the next line, with no line space in between, when displaying text. Let's take a look at a quick example using <br>. If your code reads:

```
Line 1<br>
Line 2<br>
Line 3<br>
```

your document will browse as shown in Figure 5.7.

We use the <br> tag to separate the lines in a document so that they are legible and for styling purposes. Therefore, we'll put the <br> tag at the ends of the lines in our `index.html` document that we want to stand on

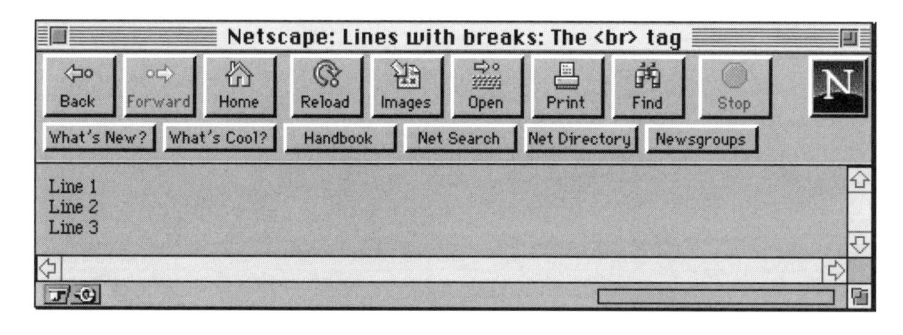

Figure 5.7
Break tags as rendered in Netscape.

Figure 5.8
The <br> tag at the end of major lines of text.

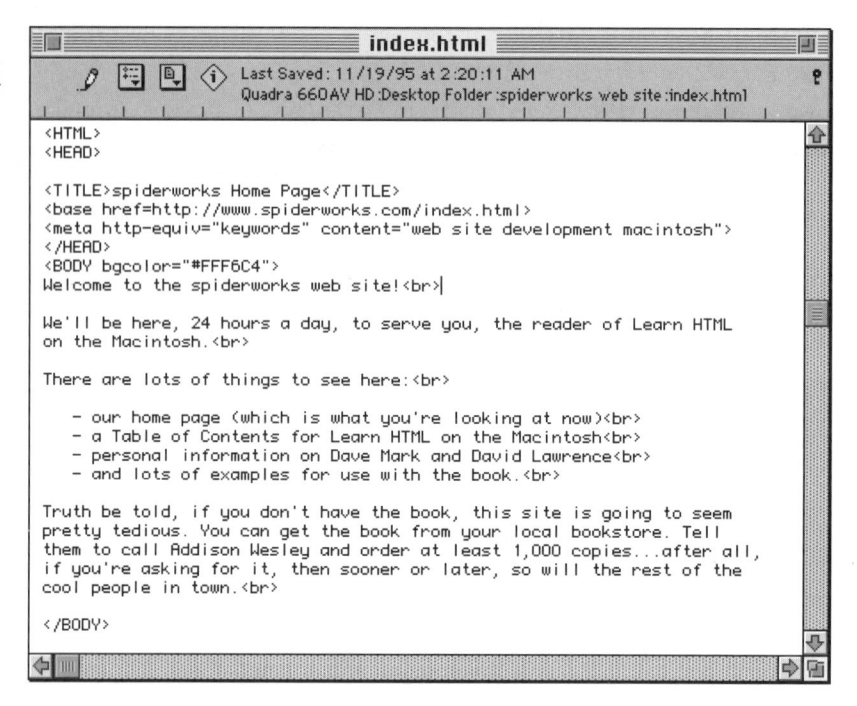

```
<HTML>
<HEAD>

<TITLE>spiderworks Home Page</TITLE>
<base href=http://www.spiderworks.com/index.html>
<meta http-equiv="keywords" content="web site development macintosh">
</HEAD>
<BODY bgcolor="#FFF6C4">
Welcome to the spiderworks web site!<br>

We'll be here, 24 hours a day, to serve you, the reader of Learn HTML
on the Macintosh.<br>

There are lots of things to see here:<br>

    - our home page (which is what you're looking at now)<br>
    - a Table of Contents for Learn HTML on the Macintosh<br>
    - personal information on Dave Mark and David Lawrence<br>
    - and lots of examples for use with the book.<br>

Truth be told, if you don't have the book, this site is going to seem
pretty tedious. You can get the book from your local bookstore. Tell
them to call Addison Wesley and order at least 1,000 copies...after all,
if you're asking for it, then sooner or later, so will the rest of the
cool people in town.<br>

</BODY>
```

their own, and let the text wrap in the last paragraph. Figure 5.8 shows how it looks after adding break tags, and Figure 5.9 shows the Netscape rendering.

Later, we'll learn how to more fully format that short four-item list in our document (the lines preceded by dashes), but for now, using the

Figure 5.9
Netscape-rendered breaks in text.

Welcome to the spiderworks web site!
We'll be here, 24 hours a day, to serve you, the reader of Learn HTML on the Macintosh.
There are lots of things to see here:
- our home page (which is what you're looking at now)
- a Table of Contents for Learn HTML on the Macintosh
- personal information on Dave Mark and David Lawrence
- and lots of examples for use with the book.
Truth be told, if you don't have the book, this site is going to seem pretty tedious. You can get the book from your local bookstore. Tell them to call Addison Wesley and order at least 1,000 copies...after all, if you're asking for it, then sooner or later, so will the rest of the cool people in town.

tag at the end of every entry assures that they will appear on separate lines with no spaces in between.

The <br> tag allows for a **clear** attribute with values of **left**, **right**, or **all**. It is used in conjunction with a left- or right-aligned inline image to direct that text appear to the left or the right when clear of the image.

As a Rule ...

The **<hr>** tag lets you include a horizontal rule across your document, and in Netscape, you can vary the thickness, width, and justification of the rule by using the attributes **size=**, **width=**, and **align=**, respectively. Other browsers ignore these attributes, and you must be satisfied with the default horizontal rule the browser provides.

<hr>

Description: Creates horizontal rules, or lines, across the page.

HTML 2.0 Attributes:

None

HTML 3.0 Attributes:

src="URL"	Web address of image to be used as the horizontal rule
id="text"	name and id for Web page elements
class=text	indicates types or classes of element in a Web page
clear=text	specifies at what point in the margin that text will flow around an image or figure
md=string	verification checksum string

Netscape 2.0 Attributes:

size=number	in pixels, the thickness of the rule
width=number	either in pixels or as a percentage of the screen's width, specifies the width of a rule on the screen
align=left	begins rule at left of screen right
=right	begins rule at right of screen
=center	begins rule in middle of screen
noshade	displays unembossed rule

Both the size= and width= attributes are given values in pixels. The default for size= is 2 pixels, which is also the smallest value permitted. Width= can also be specified as a percentage of the screen's width, such as width=25%. If you do not specify a width, implementation of the <hr> tag will result in a line that extends the full width of your browser window. The values for align= can be left, right, and center (center is the default).

Here are a couple of examples using the <hr> tag; the resulting rules are shown in Figure 5.10.

```
<hr>
<hr size=80 width=20>
<hr width=200>
<hr size=60 width=60 align=left>
<hr size=60 width=60 align=right>
<hr noshade>
```

> **By the Way...** Don't be surprised if when you're using another browser—such as the old OmniWeb browser on NeXT computers—that your <hr> tags result not in simple horizontal lines but in some rather, shall we say, decorative rendering. The OmniWeb browser rules are curlicue affairs that resemble wrought iron gatework.

Figure 5.10
Horizontal rule variations.

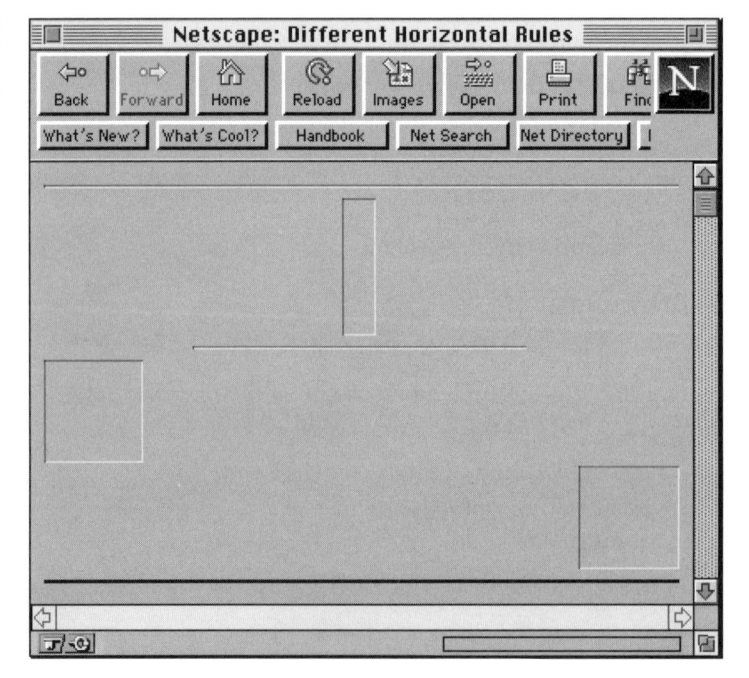

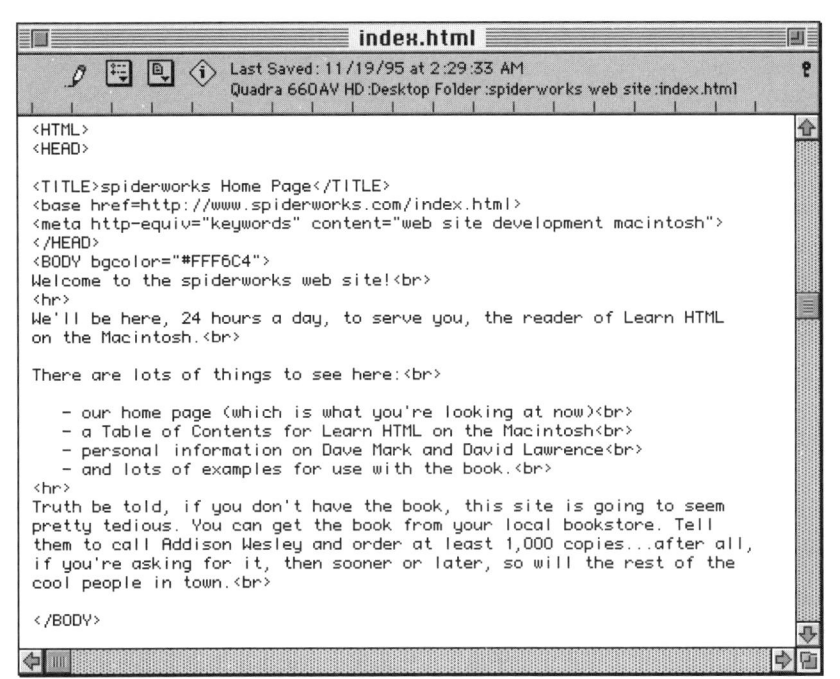

```
<HTML>
<HEAD>

<TITLE>spiderworks Home Page</TITLE>
<base href=http://www.spiderworks.com/index.html>
<meta http-equiv="keywords" content="web site development macintosh">
</HEAD>
<BODY bgcolor="#FFF6C4">
Welcome to the spiderworks web site!<br>
<hr>
We'll be here, 24 hours a day, to serve you, the reader of Learn HTML
on the Macintosh.<br>

There are lots of things to see here:<br>

    - our home page (which is what you're looking at now)<br>
    - a Table of Contents for Learn HTML on the Macintosh<br>
    - personal information on Dave Mark and David Lawrence<br>
    - and lots of examples for use with the book.<br>
<hr>
Truth be told, if you don't have the book, this site is going to seem
pretty tedious. You can get the book from your local bookstore. Tell
them to call Addison Wesley and order at least 1,000 copies...after all,
if you're asking for it, then sooner or later, so will the rest of the
cool people in town.<br>

</BODY>
```

Figure 5.11
Two horizontal rules to separate the text a bit.

Let's add a rule or two to our expanding document. We'll put one after the welcome line and one following the four-item list. Figure 5.11 shows the source; Figure 5.12 shows the Netscape rendering.

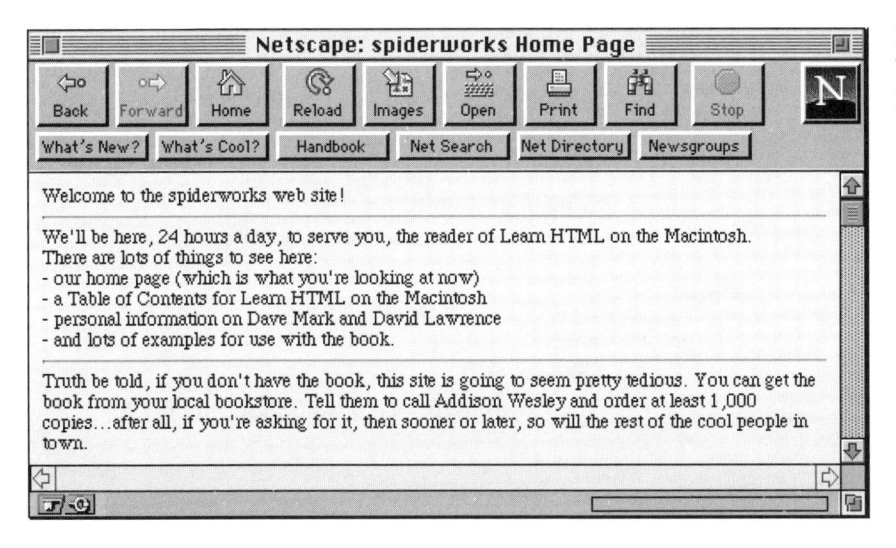

Figure 5.12
Two rules in place.

Image Is All

We know: It seems like we're all talk and no action, right? Well, we agree. Time for some visual content! Let's add the spiderworks logo, shown again in Figure 5.13, to our page to ground you more thoroughly in the uses of the important **<img>** tag.

<img>

Description: Displays inline images in the HTML document.

HTML 2.0 Attributes:

src="URL"	Web address of graphic; it can be a file name in the same directory as the Web page (a relative URL) or a relative or absolute pathname or URL
align=top	align top of graphic with tallest item in the displayed line
=middle	align middle of graphic with text baseline
=bottom	align bottom of graphic with text baseline
alt="text"	text displayed in the place of the graphic if the graphic is not available, is not viewable (for instance, in a text-only browser) or is not loaded
ismap	identifies the graphic as an imagemap

Netscape 2.0 Attributes:

align=left	align graphic to left margin, flow text along right edge of graphic
=right	align graphic to right margin, flow text along left edge of graphic
=texttop	align top of graphic with tallest text in the displayed line
=absmiddle	align middle of graphic with text midline
=baseline	align bottom of graphic with text baseline; exactly the same as align=bottom
=absbottom	align bottom of graphic with bottom of text, including descenders
width=integer	width of image in pixels
height=integer	height of image in pixels

<img> (continued)	
border=integer	width of the border around image in pixels; can be zero for no border
hspace=integer	adjacent space on either side of image in pixels when wrapping text
vspace=integer	adjacent space above and below image in pixels when wrapping text
lowsrc="URL"	Web address of lower-resolution image to be loaded before the image that is loaded by the src attribute
usemap="URL"	specifies URL that contains <map> container for image

HTML 3.0 Attributes:

id="text"	name and id for Web page elements
lang=text	language used by intended audience for a Web page
class=text	indicates types or classes of element in a Web page
align=text	paragraph justification; possible values are left, right, top, middle, and bottom
clear=text	specifies at what point in the margin that text will flow around an image or figure; Netscape does not support this attribute for this tag
md=string	verification checksum string

The <img> tag allows us to place inline images, which are simply graphics that are displayed in the midst of the text of the Web page. (You can also have external images that users can link to, but more about that later.)

The <img> tag lets us specify the source of the graphic, its alignment, and, if the document is accessed by a text-only browser, the text describing the graphic.

The graphics themselves are either GIF or JPEG files. Most of you are probably familiar with these two acronyms, but for those who need a quick reminder, here is a quick reprise: GIF stands for Graphics Interchange

Figure 5.13 Our beloved logo. **spider works**

Format, and is a system created by UNISYS and CompuServe that reduces the size of graphics files to allow for the use of a specially created plain text file to describe 8-bit, 256-color images that are viewable on any computing platform. Theoretically, a file saved as a GIF file will look the same on a Macintosh and a Windows machine. (We say theoretically, because no conversion is ever foolproof.) JPEG, for Joint Photographic Experts Group, is a different compression method that can reduce the size of graphics even further, in many cases to one-third the size of a GIF image. JPEG images are 24-bit and millions of colors. The drawback to JPEG is that the greater the compression used to make a line drawing, diagram, or other art a JPEG image, generally the greater the loss of image quality. Photos, however, can usually be made smaller in JPEG than in GIF without severely compromising the quality. Not all browsers support JPEG graphics, although Netscape does.

The options we have for specifying how we want an image displayed are greatly varied. We can make the image appear above words, next to a paragraph, even between the letters of a word, for example. Let's look at the attributes of the <img> tag, and figure out what makes sense for us on this page.

In building the <img> tag, we need to give the browser specific directions, the first of which is where to find the graphic. Let's create a folder called `resources` to hold our graphic in the main document directory of our Web site.

1. Open the `spiderworks web site` folder on your desktop.
2. Create a new folder by selecting **New Folder** from the **File** menu.
3. Call that folder `resources`.
4. Open the `resources` folder.
5. Create another new folder by repeating step 2.
6. Call that folder `images`.
7. In the `Authoring` folder, look for the file `spiderworks.gif`. Use the **Find** command from the **File** menu if you need to. Drag `spiderworks.gif` to the `images` folder you just created.
8. Bring the `spiderworks web site` folder to the front.
9. Select by **Name** from the **View** menu.

10. Click on the triangle next to the `resources` folder to show the `images` folder, and then do the same for the `images` folder.

Your main document directory in `spiderworks web site` should look like Figure 5.14. You should see the `index.html` file we've been working on, as well as the new folders we've just created. The `images` folder contains the GIF file we want to display on our Web page.

To build our <img> tag, let's start with the location of the source image in the Web site. The src= attribute takes care of that. We'll need an URL for the browser to locate the graphic. Note that this URL won't start with http:// since the graphic is within our Web site; it is a relative URL. Therefore, all we need is the path to the graphic, detailing the folders or directories that the file is nested in, relative to the main document directory (`spiderworks web site`). The path, or directory hierarchy, should be in quotes:

```
<img src="resources/images/spiderworks.gif">
```

This tells the browser that it can find the file `spiderworks.gif` in the folder (directory) `images`, which in turn is in the folder `resources`, which is found in the main document directory: `spiderworks web site` (the same folder that `index.html` is in). Be sure to separate the directories in your directory hierarchy of your URL with slashes (forward slashes, *never* back slashes).

Type the <img> tag exactly as you see it above, in the `index.html` file directly below the <body> start tag. Then, the next time we load `index.html` in our browser, we'll be able to see the logo. If you read the <base> tag description in the last chapter instead of skipping ahead to the body tags in this chapter, you've probably added the <base> tag to your `index.html` file. Because we're modeling the Web site on our Macintosh and we don't want the browser to go looking for the image on the actual server you've designated in the <base> tag (this is probably the address for

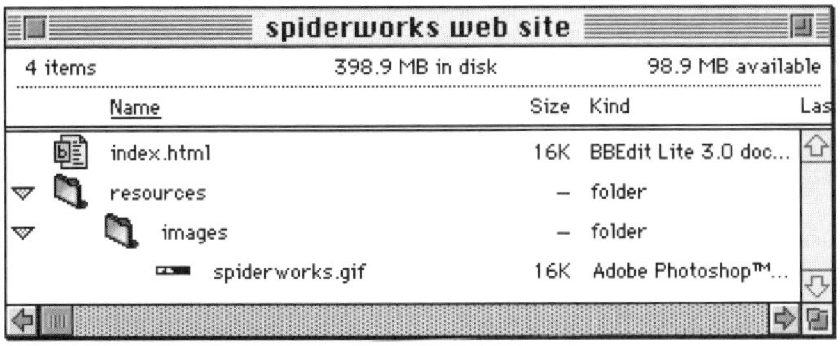

Figure 5.14
A basic approach to Web site hierarchy.

Figure 5.15
Commenting out the <base> tag.

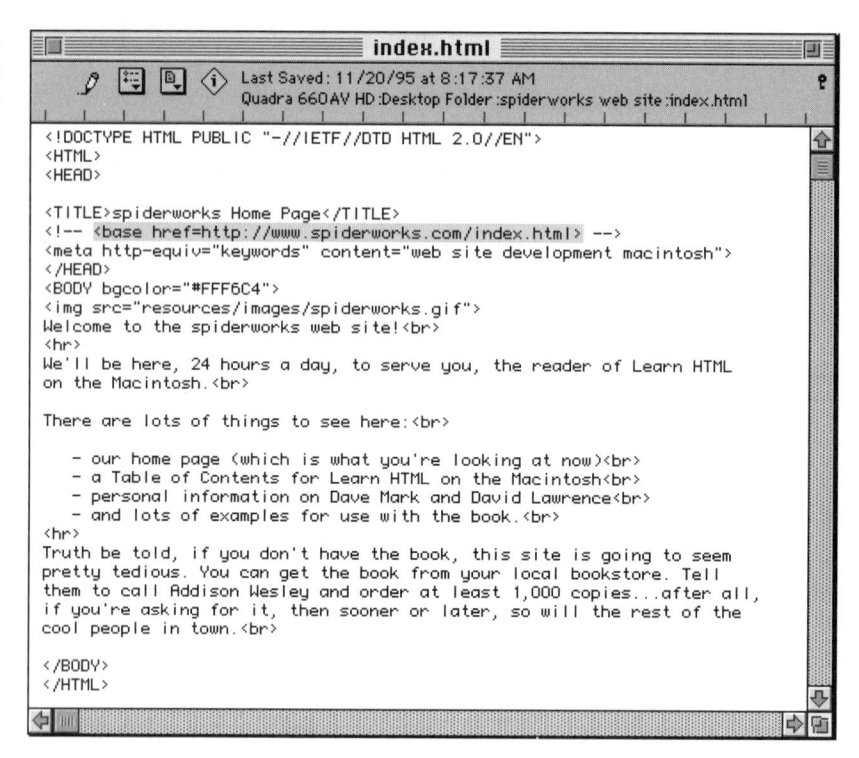

```
<!DOCTYPE HTML PUBLIC "-//IETF//DTD HTML 2.0//EN">
<HTML>
<HEAD>

<TITLE>spiderworks Home Page</TITLE>
<!-- <base href=http://www.spiderworks.com/index.html> -->
<meta http-equiv="keywords" content="web site development macintosh">
</HEAD>
<BODY bgcolor="#FFF6C4">
<img src="resources/images/spiderworks.gif">
Welcome to the spiderworks web site!<br>
<hr>
We'll be here, 24 hours a day, to serve you, the reader of Learn HTML
on the Macintosh.<br>

There are lots of things to see here:<br>

   - our home page (which is what you're looking at now)<br>
   - a Table of Contents for Learn HTML on the Macintosh<br>
   - personal information on Dave Mark and David Lawrence<br>
   - and lots of examples for use with the book.<br>
<hr>
Truth be told, if you don't have the book, this site is going to seem
pretty tedious. You can get the book from your local bookstore. Tell
them to call Addison Wesley and order at least 1,000 copies...after all,
if you're asking for it, then sooner or later, so will the rest of the
cool people in town.<br>

</BODY>
</HTML>
```

your ISP's server), let's turn that line, temporarily, into a comment. To do this, highlight the line containing the <base> tag in BBEdit Lite:

`<base href="http://www.spiderworks.com/index.html">`

and then use the HTML **Comment** command from the **Extensions** menu. Using this command places the comment delimiters, <!-- ... -->, which we described earlier, around the line. This will turn our <base> tag line into a comment and will cause the browser to ignore it. Figure 5.15 shows how this looks.

Now let's reload the `index.html` file to see how our first inline image looks. Check it out in Figure 5.16. Oops. Obviously, we forgot something. Remember, HTML mashes everything together unless directed otherwise; so, as you can see in the figure, the first line of text begins on the same line as the spiderworks logo. Let's add a <br> tag to that line:

`<img src="resources/images/spiderworks.gif"><br>`

The result is in Figure 5.17.

This page is looking pretty good, but it's only the beginning. There are many options for the <img> tag, which we explore in Chapter 6.

Chapter 5   HTML Body Language   77

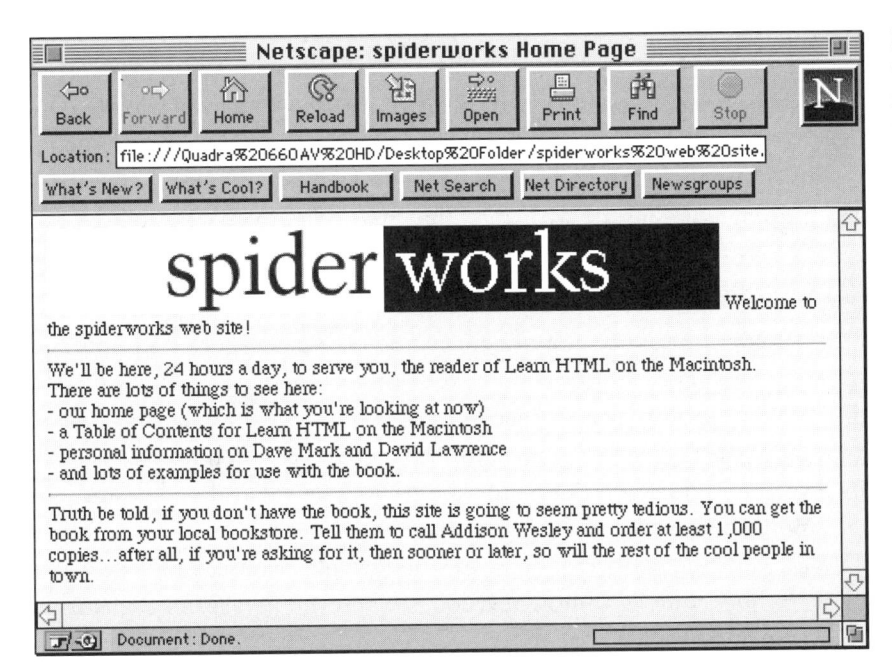

Figure 5.16
Our first inline image, but with an oversight.

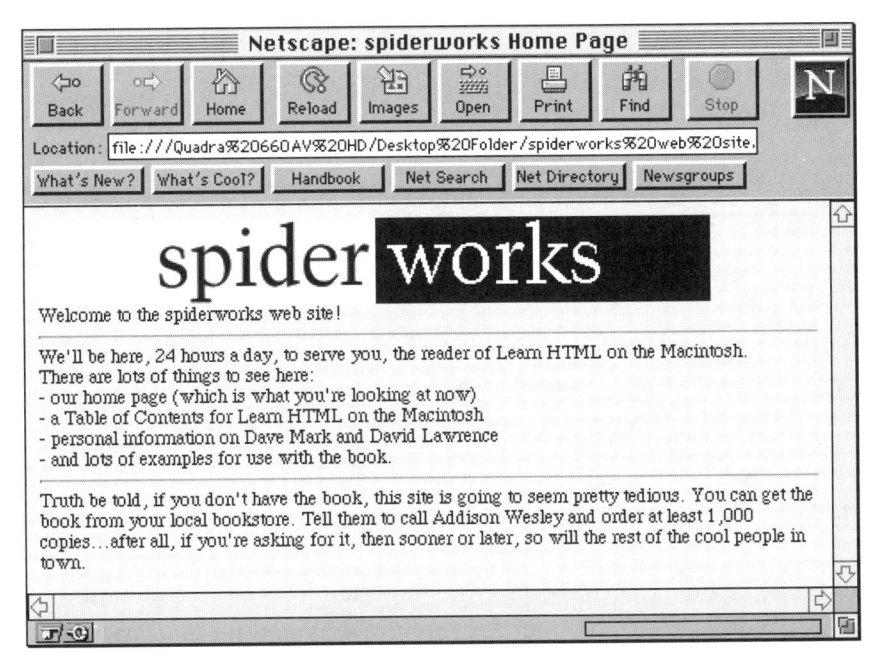

Figure 5.17
Better!

Block Party

The block elements, as you might suspect, are used when you want to contain, section off, or highlight sections—blocks—of text, such as paragraphs of content, lines of source code, an address, a lengthy quotation, and headings. We'll start with an oldie but goodie, the paragraph tag.

Back to Paragraph

The paragraph tag is one of our former acquaintances, but it's important to discuss it again within the context of other block tags. Sometimes the differences are not easy to see; indeed, sometimes you can use one or another of the tags to accomplish the same effect, but technically, each has its own role. First we'll define the differences between the <br> and <p> tags more specifically.

We've just seen how text behaves when we place a break tag at the end of every line. And recall how text looks when the paragraph tag is used. Lines typed as follows:

```
<p>Line 1</p>
<p>Line 2</p>
<p>Line 3</p>
```

result in what's shown in Figure 5.18.

Figure 5.18 Paragraph tags rendered in Netscape.

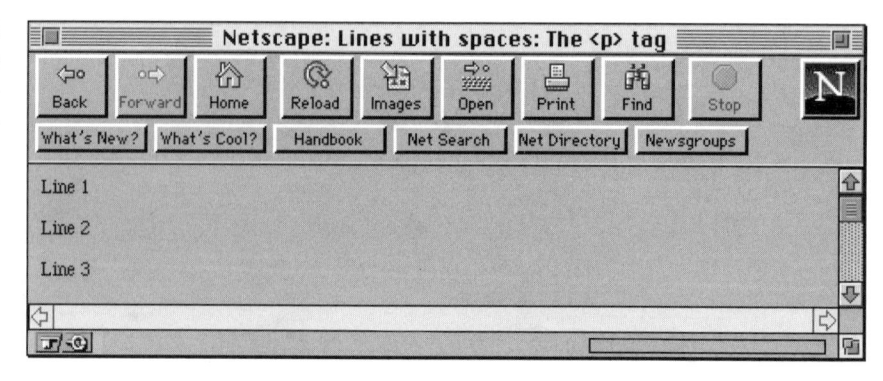

If it's still not clear to you how these two tags differ, think of it this way: a break is similar to a hard return; use it when you want to or have to for design purposes to "force" a line to break. Paragraph tags are for multiline blocks of content in which you want the lines to wrap until the end is reached and then skip a line to the next bit of text.

`<p> ... </p>`

Description: Describes the boundaries of display text that form a distinct paragraph. The end tag, </p>, is optional.

HTML 2.0 Attributes:

None

HTML 3.0 Attributes:

id="text"	name and id for Web page elements
lang=text	language used by intended audience for a Web page
class=text	indicates types or classes of element in a Web page
align=text	paragraph justification
clear=text	specifies at what point in the margin that text will flow around an image or figure
nowrap	prevents browser from automatically wrapping text

Netscape 2.0 Attributes:

align=left
    =right
    =center

With that in mind, let's adjust our document by placing paragraph tags (start and end) around three blocks: the opening paragraph, the line preceding the list, and the last paragraph. Remember to remove the <br> tags from the ends of these paragraphs. The code should now look like Figure 5.19.

Lining 'Em Up Before we view in Netscape what we've achieved by adding paragraph tags, let's also consider how we want those paragraphs aligned. The **align=** attribute is just beginning to be implemented, and its values will no doubt be some of the first HTML 3.0 standards adopted, so it's essential to learn them.

Let's take a sample paragraph and see how we can align the text in Netscape. Open document `justification.html` on your hard drive in the `Authoring` folder. There, the same paragraph is repeated four times, but with different values for the align= attribute: left, right, center, and justified. These samples, as browsed in Netscape, are shown in Figure 5.20.

Figure 5.19
Replacing
<b> tags with
<p> tags.

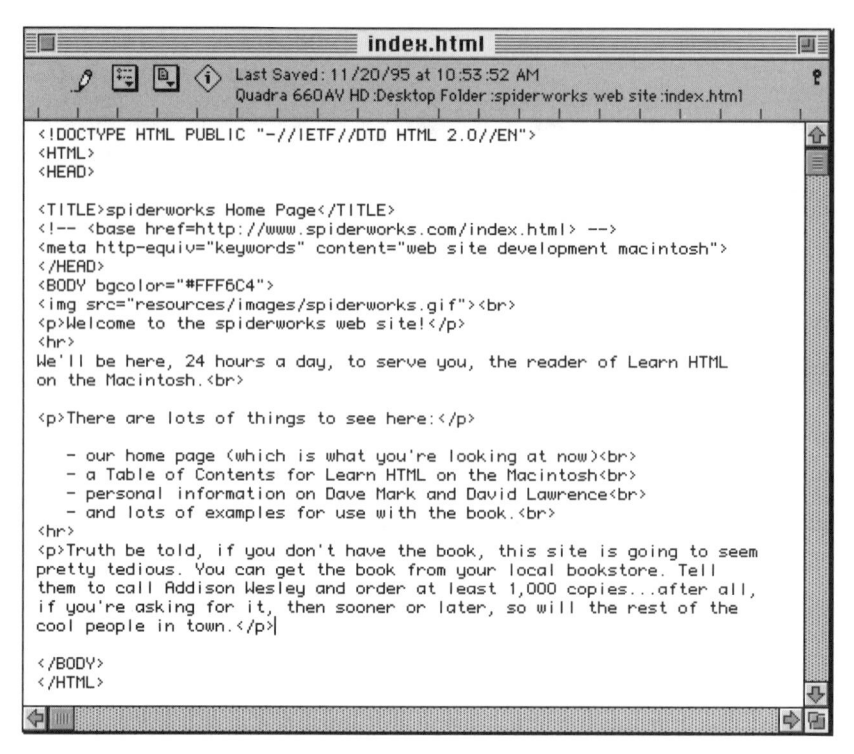

```
index.html
Last Saved: 11/20/95 at 10:53:52 AM
Quadra 660AV HD:Desktop Folder:spiderworks web site:index.html

<!DOCTYPE HTML PUBLIC "-//IETF//DTD HTML 2.0//EN">
<HTML>
<HEAD>

<TITLE>spiderworks Home Page</TITLE>
<!-- <base href=http://www.spiderworks.com/index.html> -->
<meta http-equiv="keywords" content="web site development macintosh">
</HEAD>
<BODY bgcolor="#FFF6C4">
<img src="resources/images/spiderworks.gif"><br>
<p>Welcome to the spiderworks web site!</p>
<hr>
We'll be here, 24 hours a day, to serve you, the reader of Learn HTML
on the Macintosh.<br>

<p>There are lots of things to see here:</p>

   - our home page (which is what you're looking at now)<br>
   - a Table of Contents for Learn HTML on the Macintosh<br>
   - personal information on Dave Mark and David Lawrence<br>
   - and lots of examples for use with the book.<br>
<hr>
<p>Truth be told, if you don't have the book, this site is going to seem
pretty tedious. You can get the book from your local bookstore. Tell
them to call Addison Wesley and order at least 1,000 copies...after all,
if you're asking for it, then sooner or later, so will the rest of the
cool people in town.</p>

</BODY>
</HTML>
```

Figure 5.20
Netscape 2.0
alignments.

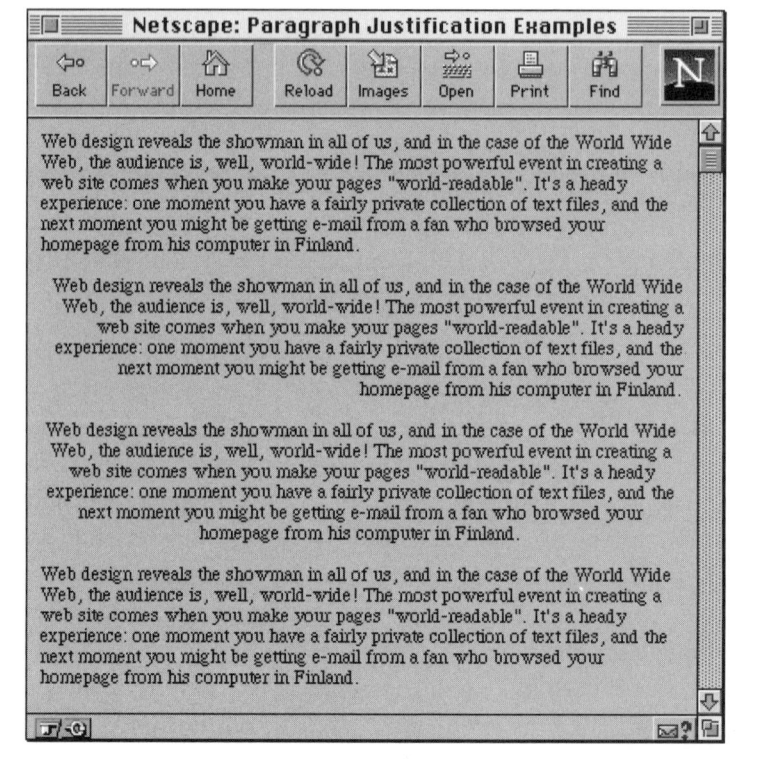

Netscape: Paragraph Justification Examples

Web design reveals the showman in all of us, and in the case of the World Wide Web, the audience is, well, world-wide! The most powerful event in creating a web site comes when you make your pages "world-readable". It's a heady experience: one moment you have a fairly private collection of text files, and the next moment you might be getting e-mail from a fan who browsed your homepage from his computer in Finland.

Web design reveals the showman in all of us, and in the case of the World Wide Web, the audience is, well, world-wide! The most powerful event in creating a web site comes when you make your pages "world-readable". It's a heady experience: one moment you have a fairly private collection of text files, and the next moment you might be getting e-mail from a fan who browsed your homepage from his computer in Finland.

Web design reveals the showman in all of us, and in the case of the World Wide Web, the audience is, well, world-wide! The most powerful event in creating a web site comes when you make your pages "world-readable". It's a heady experience: one moment you have a fairly private collection of text files, and the next moment you might be getting e-mail from a fan who browsed your homepage from his computer in Finland.

Web design reveals the showman in all of us, and in the case of the World Wide Web, the audience is, well, world-wide! The most powerful event in creating a web site comes when you make your pages "world-readable". It's a heady experience: one moment you have a fairly private collection of text files, and the next moment you might be getting e-mail from a fan who browsed your homepage from his computer in Finland.

As you can see, the first sample is flush left, the default; the second option is flush right; the third, center. Notice, though, that the fourth sample is flush left again. Why? Because full justification (flush right and left) has not been implemented yet by Netscape, so the browser resorts to its default of flush left.

There's still more to the <p> tag, which we'll show you later. For now, we'll move on to another new block tag.

Putting Up Preserves

The human animal is nothing if not contrary, and just as we wanted to be able to define our line and paragraph breaks, sometimes we would like just the opposite—the ability to type or paste in a passage of text, preserving its line breaks, white spaces, and indents, without regard to breaks of any kind. Suppose, for example, you are constantly updating a page with large amounts of text, where it would be tedious to go through and add paragraph or line break tags by hand. Or perhaps you are constantly cutting and pasting content from other sources that have their own formatting, and you want to keep the line spacing intact. The **<pre>** tag—for preformatted text—lets us do that. Just put up the <pre>…</pre> tags, and paste your preformatted text in between.

One important limitation of the <pre> tag that you should keep in mind is that all body text contained within the <pre> and </pre> tags will be rendered by the browser in a monospaced font (Courier is the default), where the width of the typed characters is the same, as opposed to proportional fonts in which the width of the type characters varies (an "I" takes up less space than a "w," for instance).

A monospaced font clearly is ideal when you have to "line up" characters in columnar data, such as address lists, spreadsheets, numeric data, and file listings. E-mail messages, too, are usually best displayed in a monospaced font, since popular mail readers pad the To, From, and Subject lines with spaces so that the items on those lines line up. Lines of programming code, such as C, are usually rendered in a monospaced font, so the <pre> tag is good for this purpose, although we'll see later that programming code has a tag all its own.

Perhaps <pre>'s biggest advantage is that it lets you get large documents up and on the Web quickly. Say you have a 50-page white paper that has to be delivered to the press *now*. You can take the raw text, plop it between the <pre> and </pre> tags on a Web page, and you're off to the races. You can format the data for better readability later.

\<pre\> ... \</pre\>

Description: Allows you to use preformatted text and retain such features as white space, line breaks, and indentations, but renders text in a monospaced Courier font.

HTML 2.0 Attributes:

None

HTML 3.0 Attributes:

id="text"	name and id for Web page elements
lang=text	language used by intended audience for a Web page
class=text	indicates types or classes of element in a Web page
align=text	paragraph justification
clear=text	specifies at what point in the margin that text will flow around an image or figure
width=integer	number of characters in a line of text

Up Close and Personal

URLs give Web seekers addresses to locate us in cyberspace, but how do we set apart our physical contact information in our Web pages? (People still do want to meet in real life on occasion.) We use the appropriately named **\<address\>** tag.

\<address\> ... \</address\>

Description: Sets off physical address information

HTML 3.0 Attributes:

id="text"	name and id for Web page elements
lang=text	language used by intended audience for a Web page
class=text	indicates types or classes of element in a Web page
align=text	paragraph justification
clear=text	specifies at what point in the margin that text will flow around an image or figure

Chapter 5 HTML Body Language 83

You can add a horizontal rule, with a width of 2 inches and aligned to the left, to give a "footnote" feel to an address block. To do so, add the following code to the `index.html` document. (You can open the file called `address.txt` in the `Authoring` folder on your hard drive and cut and paste, if you prefer.)

```
<hr align=left width=150>
<address>
To contact us via mail or phone:<br>
spiderworks<br>
2816 Saddlebred Court<br>
Suite 200<br>
Glenwood, MD 21739-9740<br>
Phone: 301/854-5459<br>
</address>
```

The result is in Figure 5.21.

> **Important!** Text within an <address> tag still must have line breaks added at the end of each line. Otherwise, the browser will compress the text together in a continuous stream.

Currently, the default in most browsers is to show text contained within the address tag in italics. Be aware that this is not the same as adding the italics tag, <i>, which we'll learn about later.

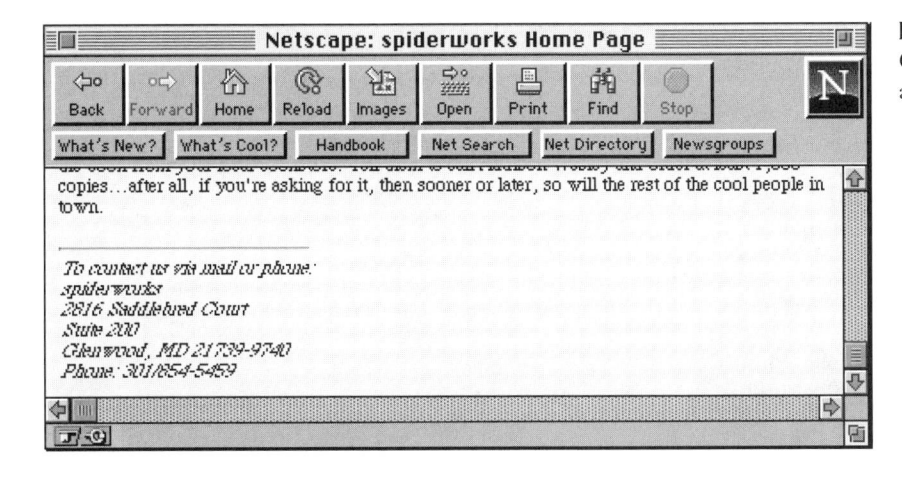

Figure 5.21
Creating an address block.

He Said, She Said: Quoting Someone

When you want to set off a lengthy quotation, **<blockquote>...</blockquote>** is your tag. (Happily, in HTML 3.0, you'll be able to abbreviate this tag name to <bq>...</bq>.)

<blockquote>...</blockquote> [bq]

Description: Sets off a continuous block of quoted material. In HTML 3.0, these tags are shortened to <bq>...</bq>

HTML 2.0 Attributes:

None

HTML 3.0 Attributes:

id="text"	name and id for Web page elements
lang=text	language used by intended audience for a Web page
class=text	indicates types or classes of element in a Web page
clear=text	specifies at what point in the margin that text will flow around an image or figure
nowrap	prevents browser from automatically wrapping text
credit	defines source of quote

To illustrate how this tag displays text in your browser, let's add the following text, found for your cutting and pasting pleasure in `blockquote.txt` in the `Authoring` folder, between our final paragraph and our address block, as follows:

```
One reader said:
<blockquote>
Terrific book. I only wish I had had this at my side when my
company shoved a Macintosh, our brochures, and a SLIP connection
in front of me and told me I was now the Webmaster. Thanks for
keeping the Macintosh flame.
<p>John Flint<br>
Columbus, Ohio
</blockquote>
```

Then look at the text rendered in Netscape in Figure 5.22.

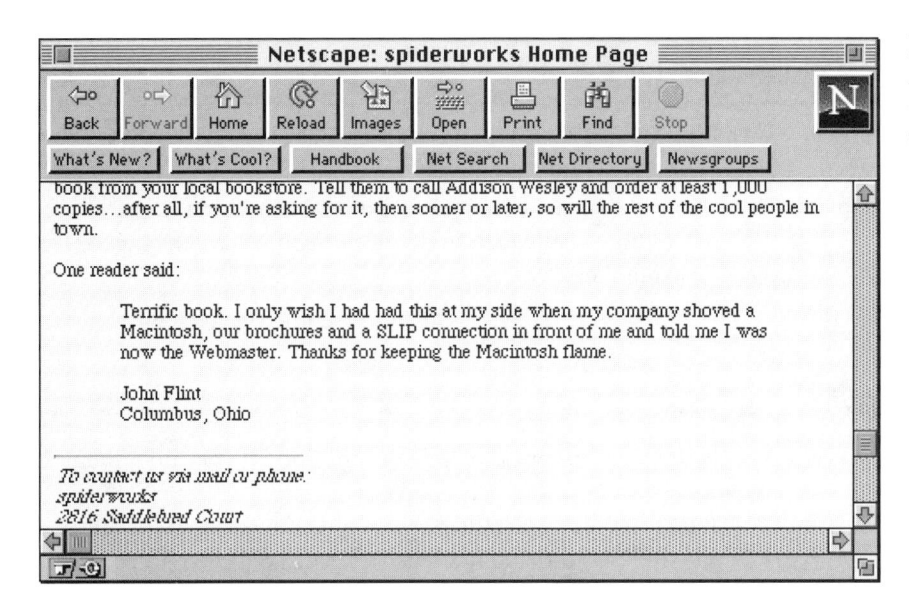

Figure 5.22
A <blockquote> tag in action.

It's All in Your Head

Headings also are old acquaintances. Remember, there are six levels that make up the entire set of heading tags: <h1> through <h6>.

<h*n*>...</h*n*>

Description: Displays text as variously formatted headings, from <h1> to <h6>.

HTML 2.0 Attributes:

None

HTML 3.0 Attributes:

id="text"	name and id for Web page elements
lang=text	language used by intended audience for a Web page
class=text	indicates types or classes of element in a Web page
align=text	paragraph justification
clear=text	specifies at what point in the margin that text will flow around an image or figure
nowrap	prevents browser from automatically wrapping text
md=string	verification checksum string

<hn> (continued)	
seqnum=integer	sequence number of heading relative to other heading(s) in the document
skip=integer	skips ahead in sequence number of heading when some headings have not been included in sequence numbers
dingbat="text"	icon displayed as a bullet preceding the heading
src="URL"	image preceding the heading

We'll try out the heading options now on our `index.html` document:

1. Select the first line of text in the document ("Welcome to the spiderworks Web site!") and make it a level 1 heading. (The end tag must contain the same level number as its start tag.)
2. Select the line above the list ("There are lots of things to see here:") and make it a level 2 heading.
3. Delete the paragraph tags in these lines now, because heading tags have line breaks implicit in their rendering.

Here's what the section of document code should look like:

```
<H1>Welcome to the spiderworks Web site!</H1>
<hr>
We'll be here, 24 hours a day, to serve you, the reader of Learn HTML on the Macintosh.<br>
<H2>There are lots of things to see here:</H2>
```

The Netscape version can be seen in Figure 5.23.

Is this beginning to look more like some of the pages you've seen on the Web? One more thing on these heading tags: the **nowrap** attribute prevents the wrapping of the heading within the browser window. As with all of the tags that have nowrap as an option, you can create your own line breaks by using <br>.

Heading into Version 3.0   (Read this with an eye toward the future of the HTML 3.0 standard.) As with most of the HTML 3.0 tags, headings are destined to have styles applied to them just like any other textual element—with some twists. The **seqnum=** attribute acts as a counter, starting with a default value of 1 (unless another value is specified) at the

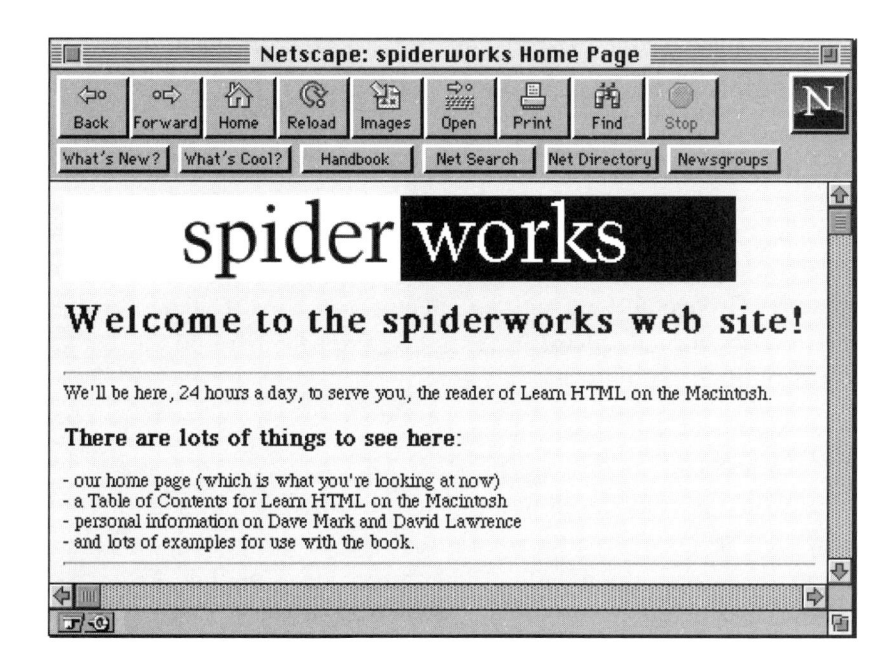

Figure 5.23
index.html with <h1> and <h2> headers.

beginning of each document with the first heading and increasing each time that level of heading is encountered. Whenever a heading of a higher value is encountered, the value is reset to the original value specified in the seqnum= attribute. For instance, if seqnum=2 is used for a h2 heading <h2 seqnum=2>…</h2>, the value is reset to 2 for that heading each time that a <h3> through <h6> heading is encountered. This attribute will allow you to keep track of the hierarchy of your headings. If, say, you always want the next heading subordinate to an <h2> heading to be a particular style, you'll be able to set that in 3.0.

In addition, HTML 3.0 will allow you to place images, small or large, on the same baseline as headings, with two new attributes, **dingbat=** and **src=**. You will be able to include either a small, icon-like dingbat similar to those in the Zapf Dingbat font with the dingbat= attribute or direct the browser where to find an inline image to place before the heading on the same line with the src= attribute. There is also a security feature proposed for the HTML 3.0 version of this tag; the **md=** attribute. When used in conjunction with the src= attribute, the md= attribute allows a checksum scheme to verify that the graphic associated with the heading is actually the graphic the author of the page intended you to see.

Let's step back for a moment and see where we are: We have display text, we've added line breaks and paragraphs, we've incorporated graphics, set off our address, and we've defined some headings. Ready for some more? Great! Let's work on that list in `index.html`.

List Elements

Three types of lists are used most often in the creation of Web pages: unordered, ordered, and definition lists. Each type shares some common tag features: an overall type tag that encompasses the list, item tags that denote individual entries in the list, and several appearance options that let you change the way the list looks.

In Order

We'll look first at an **ordered list,** which is distinguished by some sort of step-by-step, sequential pattern: 1 through 10, A through Z, i through xxvi, a table of contents, an outline, and others. The overall list type tag is **<ol>,** and the end tag is, of course, **</ol>.**

<ol> ... </ol>

Description: Displays items contained as an incremental list, one item to a line. Each item in the list is preceded by the empty tag <li>. The optional line heading <lh> defines a title for the list when used immediately after the <ol> tag.

HTML 2.0 Attributes:

None

Netscape 2.0 Attributes:

type=A	uppercase letters (A, B, C, D…Z; AA, AB…)
a	lowercase letters (a, b, c, d…z; aa, ab…)
I	uppercase Roman numerals (I, II, III, IV…)
i	lowercase Roman numerals (i, ii, iii, iv…)
1	Arabic numbers (1, 2, 3, 4…)
start=integer	numeric starting point for item numbers in list
value=integer	number that item number should be given; count continues sequentially until a new value is specified

\<ol\> (continued)

HTML 3.0 Attributes:

id="text"	name and id for Web page elements
lang=text	language used by intended audience for a Web page
class=text	indicates types or classes of element in a Web page
align=text	paragraph justification
clear=text	specifies at what point in the margin that text will flow around an image or figure
seqnum=integer	sets the starting sequence number for the first item
continue	continues numbering where last ordered list left off
compact	displays the list with less space between items

Let's look at an example of an ordered list. In the Authoring folder on your hard drive, you'll find a document called ordered.html. Open it in BBEdit Lite to see the source, then preview it in Netscape. It's a step-by-step list of instructions for that ancient art of playing vinyl records. As you can see from the code, the opening <ol> tag tells the browser that the list items that follow will be in sequential order. Each item in the list is preceded by the empty tag **\<li\>** for **list item** (see below for this tag table). The default numbering scheme in Netscape is Arabic numerals—1 through *n*, with *n* being the last number in the list. Figure 5.24 displays this list.

Obviously, an ordered list is the best choice here, because no step in the process can occur without the prior step being completed. But just for practice, let's specify an alternative numbering scheme by adding the **type=** attribute to the <ol> tag. Check out how the list looks by replacing the opening <ol> tag with any of these:

```
<ol type=A>
<ol type=i>
<ol type=I>
<ol type=a>
<ol type=1 start=5>
<ol type=A start=5>
```

Notice in the last two examples that we've also used the start= attribute, with a value of 5. This means that whichever type of ordered list we

Figure 5.24
An ordered list.

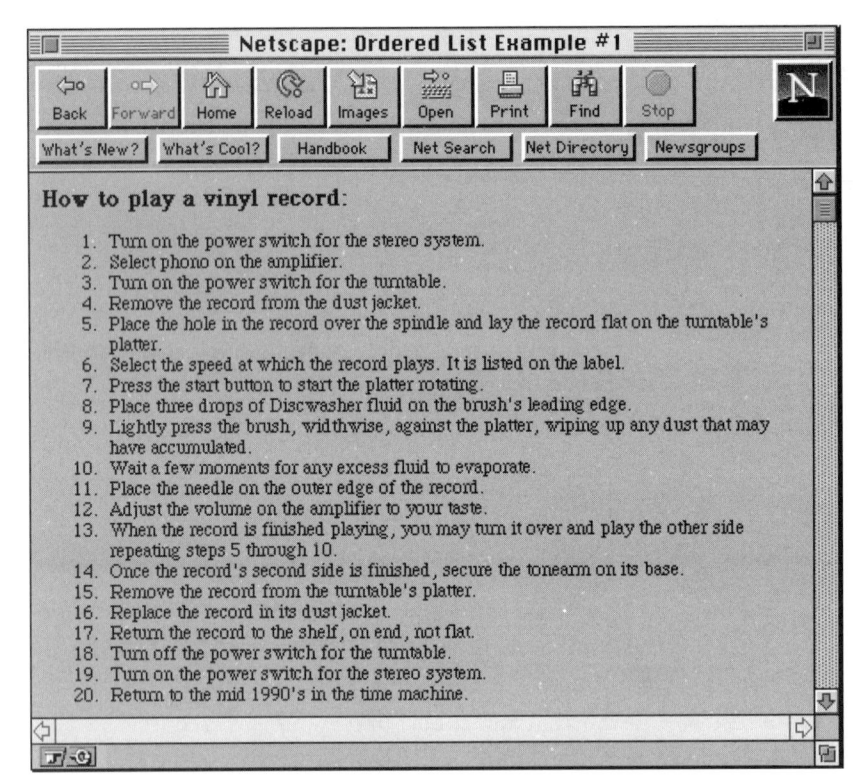

choose, the list will be ordered beginning with that value, whether the value is an Arabic number (5), an uppercase letter (E), an uppercase Roman numeral (V), and so on. Figure 5.25 shows the list reordered by capital letters.

Figure 5.25
Reordering the list.

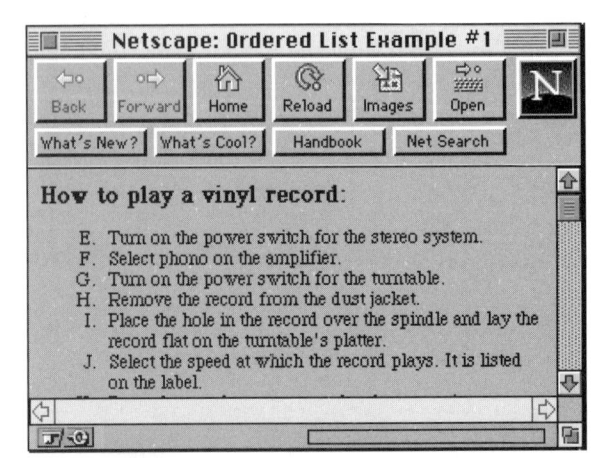

In Any Order

The unordered list, because its entries can appear in any sequence, do not require a numbering or lettering scheme. Its items instead are preceded with bullet characters, such as o, •, □. The unordered list tag pair is **<ul>...</ul>**.

<ul>...</ul>

Description: Displays items contained as a bulleted list, one item to a line. Each item in the list is preceded by the empty tag <li>. The optional line heading <lh> defines a title for the list when used immediately after the <ul> tag.

HTML 2.0 Attributes:

None

Netscape 2.0 Attributes:

type= circle	open circle at the beginning of each item
disc	filled circle at the beginning of each item
square	open square at the beginning of each item

HTML 3.0 Attributes:

id="text"	name and id for Web page elements
lang=text	language used by intended audience for a Web page
class=text	indicates types or classes of element in a Web page
clear=text	specifies at what point in the margin that text will flow around an image or figure
md="text"	verification checksum string
compact	displays the list with less space between list items
dingbat="text"	icon displayed as a bullet preceding the list item
src="URL"	specifies the image preceding the list item
plain	specifies that no bullets will be displayed
wrap=text	specifies that list will be displayed in one or more columns; the values are wrap=vert (items are displayed in vertical columns down the page) and wrap=horiz (items are displayed in horizontal columns across the page)

Figure 5.26
Changing bullets.

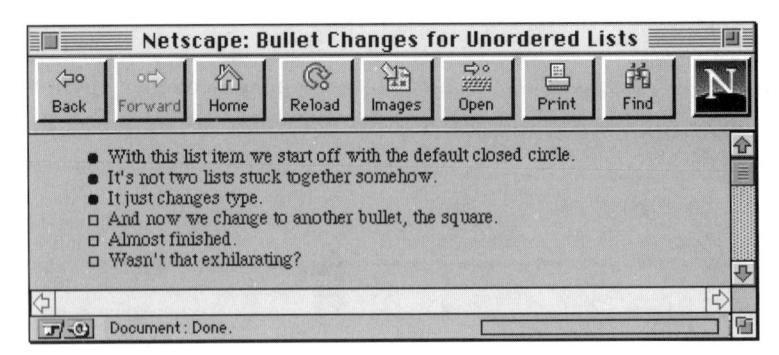

> Netscape: Bullet Changes for Unordered Lists
>
> - With this list item we start off with the default closed circle.
> - It's not two lists stuck together somehow.
> - It just changes type.
> ☐ And now we change to another bullet, the square.
> ☐ Almost finished.
> ☐ Wasn't that exhilarating?

Note that Netscape adds the type= attribute to <ul> as well, but instead of giving you a number scheme to choose from, it lets you pick between a filled bullet (**type=disc**), an open bullet (**type=circle**), and a square (**type=square**).

You can also use the type= attribute with the list item tag <li>, by changing the type of bullet displayed at the beginning of the list item's line. If you use it with the <li> tag, you have to add the type= attribute only once, and the rest of the list items will feature that new bullet type, as shown in the following source found in unordered.html in your Authoring folder, and in Netscape in Figure 5.26.

```
<UL>
<LI>With this list item we start off with the default closed
circle.
<LI>It's not two lists stuck together somehow.
<LI>It just changes type.
<LI type=square>And now we change to another bullet, the square.
<LI>Almost finished.
<LI>Wasn't that exhilarating?
</UL>
```

By the Way...

In Netscape, by default, no extra line spaces are inserted between list entries. But in other browsers, such as the one resident in Intercon's TCP Connect II and America Online's and eWorld's first Mac browser (which are, for all intents and purposes, the same Web browser), line spaces are automatically added between items. If you want to accommodate users of these other browsers, you can use the <br> tag at the end of every line to override the line-spacing feature.

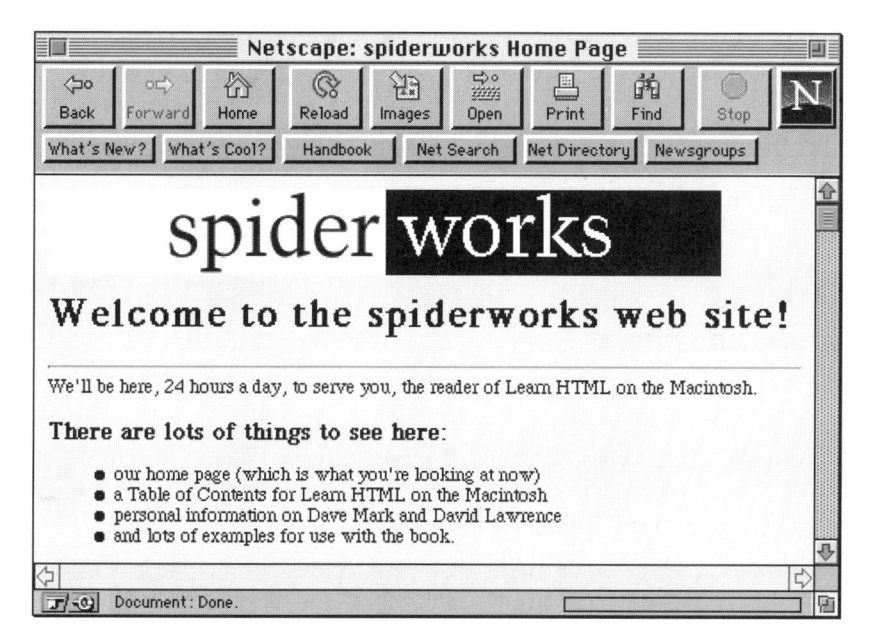

Figure 5.27
Adding an unordered list to our home page.

At this juncture, let's change the list in our `index.html` document to an unordered scheme. A quick way to do this is to highlight all of the text to be converted into a list in BBEdit, then choose **HTML Format** from the **Extensions** menu. Then, in the resulting dialog box, choose **Unordered List**. Pretty cool, huh? Here's what that code would look like:

```
<H2>There are lots of things to see here:</H2>

<UL>
<LI>our home page (which is what you're looking at now)<BR>
<LI>a Table of Contents for Learn HTML on the Macintosh<BR>
<LI>personal information on Dave Mark and David Lawrence<BR>
<LI>and lots of examples for use with the book.<BR>
</UL>
<hr>
```

See the finished product in Figure 5.27.

Itemized Lists

Each of the items in ordered and unordered lists is preceded by a list item <li> tag. This tag specifies a new item in the list, preceded by a number, letter, image, or bullet, depending upon the type of list.

<li> ... </li>

Description: Indicates individual items in an ordered <ol> or unordered <ul> list.

HTML 2.0 Attributes:

None

Netscape 2.0 Attributes:

type=A	uppercase letters (A, B, C, D...Z; AA, AB...)
a	lowercase letters (a, b, c, d...z; aa, ab...)
I	uppercase Roman numerals (I, II, III, IV...)
i	lowercase Roman numerals (i, ii, iii, iv...)
1	Arabic numbers (1, 2, 3, 4...)
circle	open circle at the beginning of each item
disc	filled circle at the beginning of each item
square	open square at the beginning of each item
value=integer	number that item number should be given; count continues sequentially until a new value is specified in an <ol> list

HTML 3.0 Attributes:

id="text"	name and id for Web page elements
lang=text	language used by intended audience for a Web page
class=text	indicates types or classes of element in a Web page
align=text	paragraph justification
clear=text	specifies at what point in the margin that text will flow around an image or figure
md="text"	verification checksum string
dingbat="text"	icon displayed as a bullet preceding the list item in <ul>; overrides src= or dingbat= attribute
src="URL"	image preceding the list item in <ul>; src= or dingbat= attribute
skip=integer	list counter is increased by value indicated; only used in <ol> when seqnum= or continue attributes are used

The Defining Factor

Finally, there is the **definition list, <dl>...</dl>**. This list, sometimes referred to as a dictionary list or a glossary list, is generally used to set off concepts and their definitions. These lists are usually composed of two entities per list item: a concept or term and its definition. Of course, the most obvious example of this type of list is a dictionary list.

But that isn't the only use for <dl>. Anytime you have a list of corollary information—material that has multiple parts, each requiring a bit of explanation—you have a prime candidate for a definition list.

<dl>...</dl>

Description: Displays items contained as a definition list, one term (indicated by the empty tag <dt>) and one definition (indicated by the empty tag <dd>) per entry.

HTML 2.0 Attributes:

None

HTML 3.0 Attributes:

id="text"	name and id for Web page elements
lang=text	language used by intended audience for a Web page
class=text	indicates types or classes of element in a Web page
clear=text	specifies at what point in the margin that text will flow around an image or figure
compact	displays the list with less space between items

The following is sample source for a definition list. Note that the subordinate empty tag <dt> precedes each term and the subordinate empty tag <dd> precedes each definition, which can span more than one line. Most browsers indent the definition and display the term as a hanging indent, left justified. The text of this list, which follows, can be found in definition.html in your Authoring folder. The Netscape rendering of this list can be found in Figure 5.28.

```
<h3>Some funny viruses from the Internet:</h3>
<DL>
```

```
<DT>Texas Virus
<DD>Makes sure that it is bigger than any other file.
<DT>Congressional Virus
<DD>The computer locks up, and the screen splits erratically with
a message appearing on each half, blaming the other half for the
problem.
<DT>Elvis Virus
<DD>Your computer increases its hard drive capacity, slows to a
crawl, and then self destructs, only to resurface at shopping
malls, service stations, and fast food restaurants across rural
America.
<DT>Politically Correct Virus
<DD>Never calls itself a "virus," but instead refers to itself as
an "electronic micro-organism."
</DL>
```

Figure 5.28
A definition list.

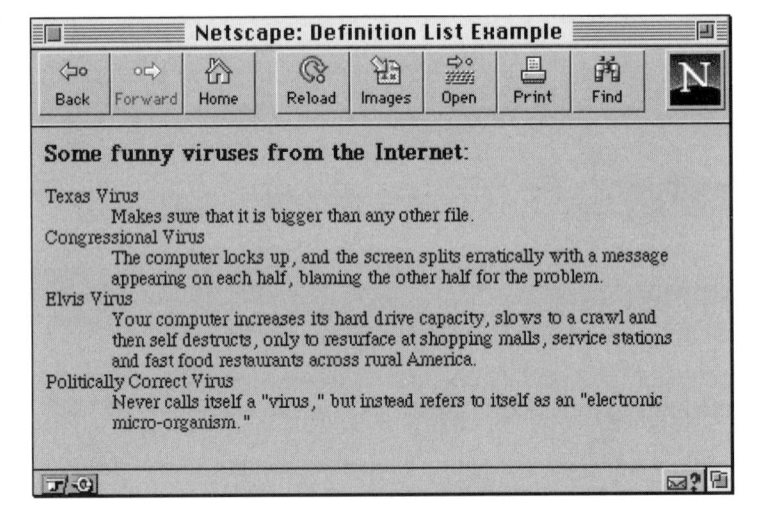

The Nesting Instinct

Before we leave this topic, you should be aware of another list capability for designing, and especially for giving order to, your Web pages. A nested list is a sublist contained within another list, such as an ordered list within an unordered list. Here's a nested list I use in my personal Web site:

```
<H3>People in Computers to Whom You Should Listen and Why</h3>
<UL>
<LI>Don Crabb
  <OL>
  <LI>He writes for MacWeek
  <LI>He teaches freshmen
  <LI>He's got the longest .signature in the world
  </OL>
```

```
<LI>Heather Champ
  <OL>
  <LI>She designed the Cool Site of the Week
  <LI>She's Canadian
  <LI>She balances great design with respect for current bandwidth
  </OL>
<LI>Penn Gillette
  <OL>
  <LI>He 'gets' computers
  <LI>He makes Teller bleed through his eyes
  <LI>He does the promos for Comedy Central
  </OL>
<LI>Leo Laporte
  <OL>
  <LI>He does a great radio show
  <LI>He uses Macs *and* PC's
  <LI>He's never treated me like a competitor
  </OL>
<LI>Guy Kawasaki
  <OL>
  <LI>He's an Apple Fellow
  <LI>He writes terrific prose
  <LI>He never forgets when you forget to turn the tape deck on
  </OL>
<LI>Robin Williams
  <OL>
  <LI>One of the nicest people you'll ever meet
  <LI>She wears hats like they've never been worn by anyone
  <LI>She's got Guy-s coming to her rescue at every turn
  </OL>
</UL>
```

Take a look at it in Netscape, in Figure 5.29.

Semantic Format Elements

There are two distinct sets of tags that determine the way text is displayed in browsers; one turns control over to the browser (**semantic**), the other keeps it firmly in your grasp (**physical**, which we discuss next). When you use one of the semantic tag pairs, any text you close within it will appear in the style defined for that tag by the developers of that browser. Initially, you might be put off by the thought that semantic tags interfere with your creativity, but think twice. We are in favor of using semantic tags, because you never know which browser your reader is using, and if you're interested in reaching the widest possible audience, it's smart to design so that your work appears the best everywhere, not just in one browser. It's important to keep in mind that what you design in Netscape may not be what

Figure 5.29
Nested lists.

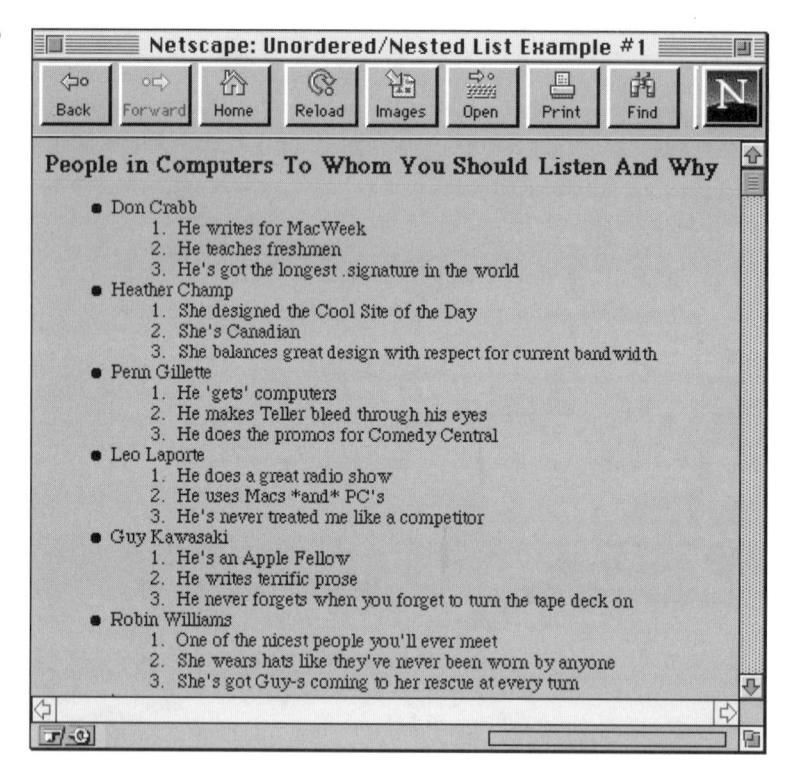

your reader will see in, say, Mosaic. Let's look at the set of semantic tags available to us. We've included the HTML files in the `Authoring` folder, each titled as `"tag".html`, where "tag" is the physical tag involved.

Issuing Citations

The **<cite>** tag is used to set off a citation, such as magazine article, a title of a book, an author's name, etc. Here's an example that uses this tag:

```
Throughout time, the level of butterfat in ice cream has been the
one single determining factor as to the creaminess of its texture.
"Butterfat content is what separates the storeboughts from the
standouts,"<cite>The American Ice Creamer (vol. 1, issue 7, pps.
7-22)</cite>
```

`<cite>`...`</cite>`

Description: Used to format a citation for quoted material.

HTML 2.0 Attributes:
None

In Netscape, <cite> italicizes the citation (see Figure 5.30). But other browsers may use a slightly smaller font, or even insert a footnote marker and display the source along the footer of the document.

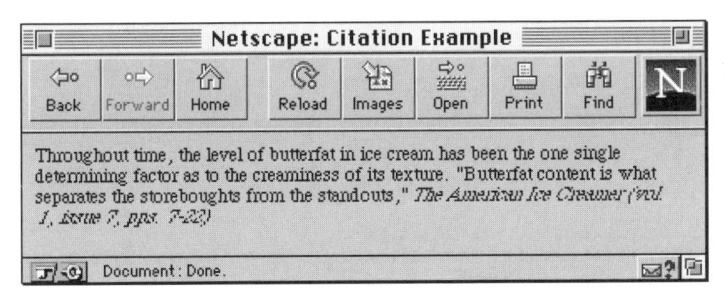

Figure 5.30
A citation in Netscape.

In Code

The `<code>`...`</code>` tag pair is very similar to the `<pre>` tag pair (remember we gave you a heads up to that in the `<pre>` section); it's used to display programming code. Courier is the default font for `<code>` in Netscape.

`<code>`...`</code>`

Description: Used to display programming code.

HTML 2.0 Attributes:
None

If you're wondering why not just use `<pre>` to display all monospaced text, the answer is that you can. By using `<code>`, however, you can more easily identify the sections of your HTML documents that contain programming code and more easily edit and maintain them. Also, you can use <code> to define a line of code within a paragraph, while <pre> is used to define the entire paragraph.

Here's an example using <code>:

```
<p>This is a sample BASIC program that prints the numbers 1 to 10
on a single line:
<p>
<code>
10 FOR I=1 TO 10<br>
20 PRINT I;<br>
30 NEXT I<br>
40 END<br>
</code>
<p>Type this in, then type LIST to make sure you've typed
correctly, then RUN your program.
```

Note that you do need to include the break tag in code to indicate where you want lines of code to end. The Netscape display for this code is shown in Figure 5.31.

Figure 5.31
A code sample in Netscape.

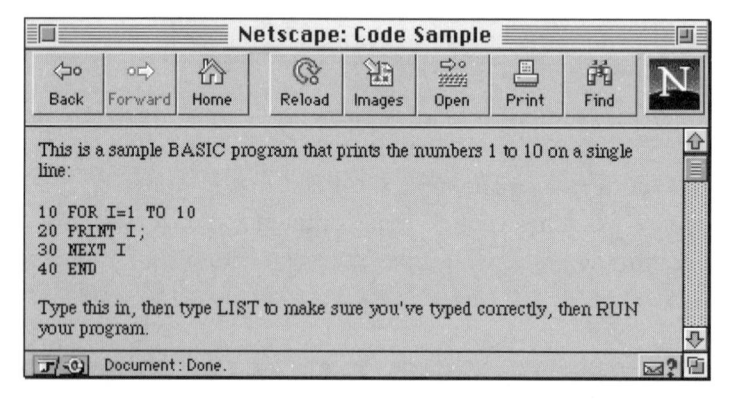

For <Em>phasis

The **<em>** tag is, for all intents and purposes, equivalent to italicizing text, because all of the major graphical browsers, including Netscape, render text contained between the <em>…</em> tag pair in italics. But, again, it is important to remember that not everyone uses graphical browsers, and that people with specialized needs may set up <em> styles that are far more complex than simple italicization.

`<em>...</em>`

Description: Describes enclosed text as emphatically stated. Usually equivalent to <i>talic but may vary from browser to browser.

HTML 2.0 Attributes:

None

If you're familiar with e-mail shorthand, you're used to seeing people emphasize a word or phrase by placing it between *asterisks*. You use <em> similarly, as shown in the following source and in Figure 5.32.

```
For all of the years Nick had known her, she had never <EM>once
</EM> worn anything but jeans and a t-shirt. Tonight was
different. <EM>Stunning</EM> was the word that came to mind as he
watched her float down the stairs towards the waiting car.
```

Figure 5.32
<Em>phasizing words.

Type This

The **<kbd>** tag pair (short for keyboard) is another tag whose enclosed text is often rendered in the monospaced font Courier. It's used to set off a list of instructions that direct the user to type certain characters or strings from their computers, as in this sample source:

```
<p>First, you will be asked for a user ID and password. Type them
in at the appropriate prompts. Here's a sample:
<p>
USER ID: <kbd>tamara</kbd>
<p>
PASSWORD: <kbd>hagged</kbd> <--- this will be hidden by bullets as
you type.
```

You can see this source viewed in Netscape in Figure 5.33.

<kbd>...</kbd>

Description: Used to display type that users are instructed to type on their keyboard; often used for tutorials.

HTML 2.0 Attributes:

None

Figure 5.33 Using <kbd> to direct users to type information.

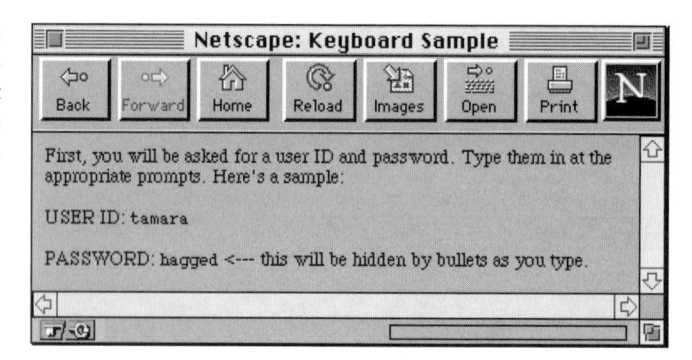

Sample

Another monospaced display tag, **<samp>,** is designed to call the viewer's attention to a separate segment of text, as shown here:

```
<p>Here's a sample of Marie's prose:
<p>
<samp>
There really isn't any need for people to get upset; there's not a
whit you can do about it once it's done.
</samp>
```

Check it out in Figure 5.34.

<samp>...</samp>

Description: Indicates that the enclosed content is to be displayed as sample text.

HTML 2.0 Attributes:

None

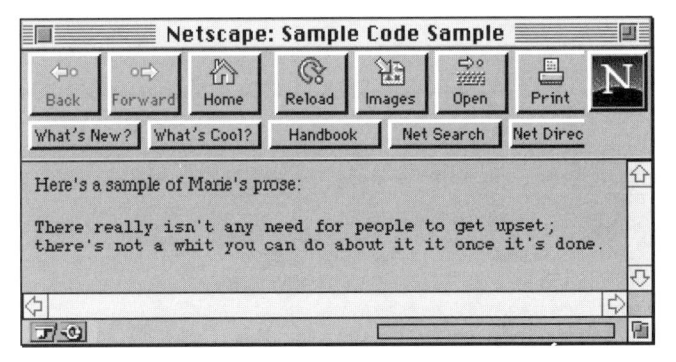

Figure 5.34
Sample text in Netscape.

Sometimes, You Gotta be Strong

When you want to get the viewer's attention, use **<strong>**. As you might guess, you'll usually see text contained within this tag pair rendered in bold, as it is in Netscape.

```
<h3>Horror Movie Actor Survival Rules:</h3>
<UL>
<LI>When it appears that you have killed the monster,
<STRONG>never check to see if it's really dead</STRONG>.
<LI>If you find that your house is built upon or near a cemetery,
was once a church that was used for black masses, had previous
inhabitants who went mad or committed suicide or died in some
horrible fashion, or had inhabitants who performed necrophilia or
satanic practices in your house, <STRONG>move away immediately
</STRONG>.
<LI><STRONG>Never</STRONG> read a book of demon summoning aloud,
<STRONG>even as a joke</STRONG>.
<LI><STRONG>Do not</STRONG> search the basement,
<STRONG>especially</STRONG> if the power has just gone out.
<LI><STRONG>Listen to the audience</STRONG> when they tell you not
to go in a particular room. <STRONG>Trust their judgement!</STRONG>
</UL>
```

When you view this source in Netscape (Figure 5.35), be sure to notice that you can place <strong>—and any of the other semantic or physical tags—within lists.

<strong>...</strong>

Description: Displays enclosed text for maximum effect or emotion, usually rendered by the browser in bold type.

HTML 2.0 Attributes:

None

Figure 5.35
Strongly recommended.

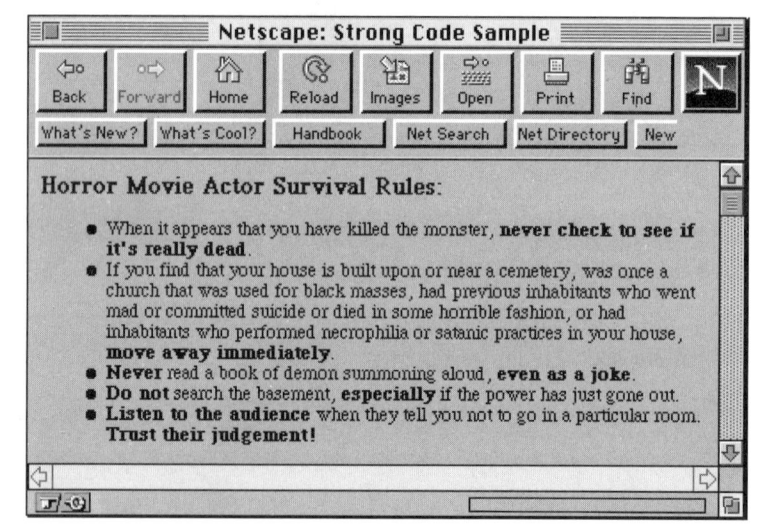

Varying Variables

The **<var>** tag is used to set off variable names in text-based equations and statements. For you non-programmers, a variable is a term that holds a value, such as an integer, a floating-point number, a text string, or some other value, that can change. In most browsers, <var> italicizes the variable it contains.

<var>...</var>

Description: Indicates that the enclosed text is a variable name; appears italicized in most browsers.

HTML 2.0 Attributes:

None

Here is a example of how to use <var>:

```
<h3>Variables used:</h3>
<UL>
<LI><VAR>loop</VAR> = number of iterations of the process
<LI><VAR>upper</VAR> = upper boundary
<LI><VAR>lower</VAR> = lower boundary
```

The source looks like Figure 5.36 when viewed in Netscape.

In summary, we're aware that many of the semantic tags seem to do the same thing. But keep in mind that it's not just the result that you need to focus on, but how the source is blocked out, as well. You may have, for example, a number of different sections in your Web page that are all monospaced, but for different reasons. Should you have to go back to rework the source, these apparently similar semantic tags will help you keep things straight.

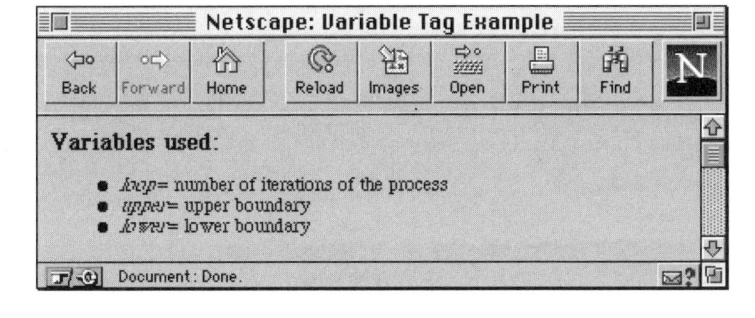

Figure 5.36
Differentiating variables.

Physical Format Elements

Let's get physical! The tags we discuss in this section are for use when you need to format something quickly and in exactly the way you intend. Before we begin using them, though, we want to reiterate the difference between semantic (logical) and physical tags: By implementing semantic tags, you let the user's browser, and, in turn, how that user may have configured that browser, stay in control of how a document's attributes will display on screen; by implementing physical tags, you force the browser to render the text the way you specify.

All Together, Now

Because you are familiar with most of the concepts that the tags in this section represent, such as bold, italics, and underline, in working with word processing programs, we're going to show you only one sample that includes these physical tags. We do include all the respective tag tables, however, for your convenience. You'll find the code for this in text-style.html in the Authoring folder.

The **<b>** tag renders the text in boldface. It is similar to the semantic <strong> tag, but it will always produce a boldface term or phrase, while <strong> may cause the term or phrase to be rendered in bold in one browser and underlined in another.

<b> ... </b>

Description: Displays text as bold.

HTML 2.0 Attributes:

None

The **<i>** tag italicizes the text that it contains. It is similar to the semantic tag <em>, except that the text contained in <em> may not be rendered in italics in all browsers.

<i> ... </i>

Description: Displays text as italic.

HTML 2.0 Attributes:

None

The **<tt>** tag, which stands for teletype, renders text in a typewriter-like monospaced font.

<tt>...</tt>

Description: Displays text as monospaced typewriter text.

HTML 2.0 Attributes:
None

HTML 3.0 Attributes:

id="text"	name and id for Web page elements
lang=text	language used by intended audience for a Web page
class=text	indicates types or classes of element in a Web page

---

The **<u>** tag renders its content as underlined, or in some browsers, as italicized. It is rarely used, but presented here so you'll recognize it if you encounter it.

> Although underlined text is supported by some browsers, it is not part of either the HTML 2.0 or 3.0 standard. Even Netscape ignores it for a very good reason: underlined text is usually an indication that the text is a link to somewhere else. You'll learn about designating links in Chapter 6.

<u>...</u>

Description: Displays text as underlined. Not implemented by all browsers.

As you might have guessed, the **<big>** tag displays the text it contains in a font size that is larger than normal text on the Web page.

<big> ... </big>

Description: Displays slightly larger than normal size display text.

HTML 3.0 Attributes:

None

If the **<big>** tag enlarges text, then the **<small>** tag must reduce the font size of its enclosed text so that it's smaller than the normal text on the Web page.

<small> ... </small>

Description: Displays slightly smaller than normal size display text.

HTML 3.0 Attributes:

None

The **<sup>** tag displays the text that it contains as superscript, so that it is above the normal baseline of the text in that line. In many browsers, superscript text is also displayed in a smaller font than normal text.

<sup> ... </sup>

Description: Displays text as superscript.

HTML 3.0 Attributes:

id="text"	name and id for Web page elements
lang=text	language used by intended audience for a Web page
class=text	indicates types or classes of element in a Web page

---

The **<sub>** tag displays the text that it contains as subscript, so that it is below the normal baseline of the text in that line. In many browsers, subscript text is also displayed in a smaller font than normal text.

<sub>...</sub>

Description: Displays text as subscript.

HTML 3.0 Attributes:

id="text"	name and id for Web page elements
lang=text	language used by intended audience for a Web page
class=text	indicates types or classes of element in a Web page

Here's the sample source, using all of these tags, followed by its Netscape rendering in Figure 5.37. Notice that although we use the <u> tag to underline a segment of text, Netscape does not recognize this tag. Therefore, the text will not appear as underlined to the user.

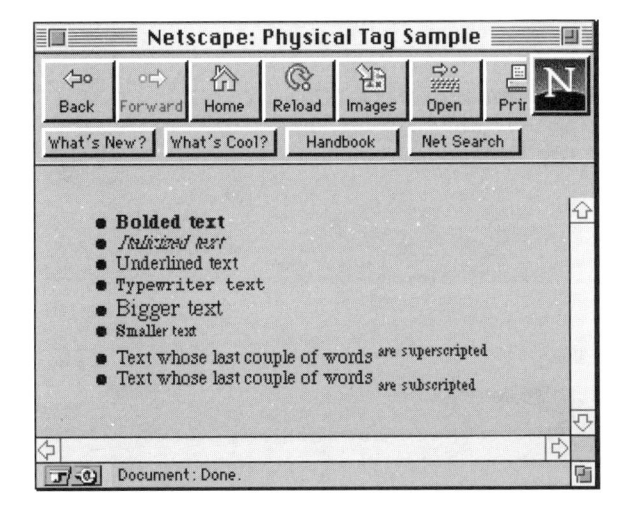

```
<UL>
<LI><B>Bolded text</B>
<LI><I>Italicized text</I>
<LI><U>Underlined text</U>
<LI><TT>Typewriter text</TT>
<LI><big>Bigger text</big>
<LI><small>Smaller text</small>
<LI>Text whose last couple of words <sup>are superscripted</sup>
<LI>Text whose last couple of words <sub>are subscripted</sub>
</UL>
```

Figure 5.37 Physical formatting samples.

Quote, Unquote

The **<q>** tag is similar in purpose to the semantic <cite> tag. It's used to set off short quotations that don't require the <blockquote> tag. The <q> tag pair also takes care of nested quotations, properly placing single quotes within double quotes, and indicating when the quoted source cites other sources. For example, the following source:

```
As Roger put it,<q>When someone says <q>Do it my way,</q>he or she
usually implies <q>the highway</q> as the unspoken alternative.</q>
```

would be rendered:

> As Roger put it, "When someone says 'Do it my way,' he or she usually implies 'the highway' as the unspoken alternative."

In Any Language

The **<lang>** tag is designed to be used for quoting text in a foreign language. It should not be confused with the lang= attribute for the body tag. The lang= attribute should be used to set language context for larger sections of the document, and often it's used to set the language context for the document as a whole. The <lang> tag is used to set apart small quoted sections of the document that are in a language that is different from the primary language used in the document as a whole.

<lang> ... </lang>

Description: Changes the language context for the contained text from the primary language used in the rest of the document.

HTML 3.0 Attributes:

name="text"   language desired

Author, Author!

HTML designers customarily "sign" their documents at the bottom of their Web pages, and this proposed tag is an attempt to formalize that process.

<au>...</au>

Description: Used to display the name of the author of a Web document.

HTML 3.0 Attributes:

id="text"	name and id for Web page elements
lang=text	language used by intended audience for a Web page
class=text	indicates types or classes of element in a Web page

In Person

This proposed tag's purpose is to allow easy extraction of proper names by automatic indexing programs; it would be a boon to all the folks out there who ask the question, "Isn't there a white pages for people on the Net?"

<person>...</person>

Description: Delimits the names of individuals.

HTML 3.0 Attributes:

id="text"	name and id for Web page elements
lang=text	language used by intended audience for a Web page
class=text	indicates types or classes of element in a Web page

---

By the Way...

As we went to press, Now Software had just introduced several cool products designed to integrate contact and calendar information into your web design. If you'd like to see what all the fuss is about, hit their website at http://www.nowsoft.com. We've also included demo versions of most of Now's popular personal information management and system utility software on the CD. Look for it in the goodies folder.

Doesn't Anybody Use Real Words Anymore?

People seem to use acronyms and abbreviations more every day. If you, like us, have trouble remembering how to find your way through that alphabetical jungle, you'll be glad when these tags are approved for use in 3.0. In conjunction with a style sheet, an acronym contained within **<acronym>...</acronym>** would be linked back to its full definition, as would any abbreviation contained within **<abbrev>...</abbrev>**.

<acronym>...</acronym>

Description: Marks up acronyms.

HTML 3.0 Attributes:

id="text"	name and id for Web page elements
lang=text	language used by intended audience for a Web page
class=text	indicates types or classes of element in a Web page

<abbrev>...</abbrev>

Description: Marks up abbreviations.

HTML 3.0 Attributes:

id="text"	name and id for Web page elements
lang=text	language used by intended audience for a Web page
class=text	indicates types or classes of element in a Web page

Put It In, Take It Out

Both the **<ins>** and **<del>** tags hearken back to proofreader and editing marks. They are for use when a document goes through a series of updates by more than one person, which need to be closely tracked, such as in legal documents and workgroup projects.

<ins> ... </ins>

Description: Indicates that enclosed text is to be displayed as an insertion into latest version of the document.

HTML 3.0 Attributes:

id="text"	name and id for Web page elements
lang=text	language used by intended audience for a Web page
class=text	indicates types or classes of element in a Web page

<del> ... </del>

Description: Indicates that the enclosed text is to be displayed as a deletion from the latest version of the document.

HTML 3.0 Attributes:

id="text"	name and id for Web page elements
lang=text	language used by intended audience for a Web page
class=text	indicates types or classes of element in a Web page

What's Next

We covered a lot of material in this chapter, and you might want to take a break, stretch, and grab another cup of coffee before moving on to Chapter 6, where we get into the nitty-gritty of URLs, hyperlinking, and the anchor tag. We also talk more about the <img> tag.

6

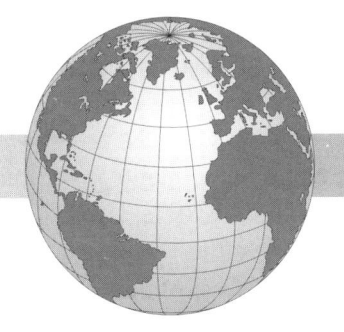

Hitting the Links

We've talked a lot about HTML, the HyperText Transfer Markup Language, but it is important, indeed it is essential, to understand that the World Wide Web would not be able to weave its magic were it not for the HyperText Transfer Protocol (HTTP), the Internet standard that makes it possible to exchange information on the Web. HTTP defines the Uniform Resource Locators that enable us to find and retrieve Web resources (as well as FTP-accessible files, USENET newsgroups, and gopher menus). In fact, it is HTTP that enables Web page designers like you to embed hyperlinks in your documents so that your readers can "click and go."

As happens with all popular phenomena, the terminology that defines this technology is becoming colloquialized through widespread use. No doubt, many Web travelers think of an URL simply as the address of their destinations. And for their purposes, that's probably enough. Indeed, thus far in this book, we've used the term in that casual fashion. But as Web page designers, you should understand these concepts more fully. This understanding will equip you more completely as you develop more complex documents.

URL Makeup

The common metaphor for an URL is a "snail-mail" address, and it's the most common because it's the most apt. Like a home or business address, it's made up of several components that have a defined order, which we all can recite as easily as the alphabet: name of recipient; street number and name; apartment, suite, or room number; city; state; zip code; and sometimes country name. Certainly, there are some variations, and there are more or less complex addresses, but the process of delivery is the same.

To carry the metaphor further, hyperlinks fill the role of the mailperson, actually making the connection to the destination—much more quickly, of course. And, similar to mass mailings, such as catalogs, the same Web page can have many destinations. The difference, and it's a major difference, is that control is with the user; by clicking on links, readers can access as much or as little information as they want, based on individual need or interest. As a Web page designer, you can set up links (provide the address), for example, to the Web page of the elementary school down the block, to a university in London, or to a library in Paris, and your user will be "forwarded" to that location should they so choose. Let's look at Figure 6.1, which shows standard URL construction. Specifically, from the left, here's the breakdown:

- the **service protocol** of the Internet tool used to access the resource, in this case, HTTP
- the **domain name** (address) of the computer (the host) or a group of computers that identifies the Web server serving your Web pages

Figure 6.1
An URL, broken down into its components.

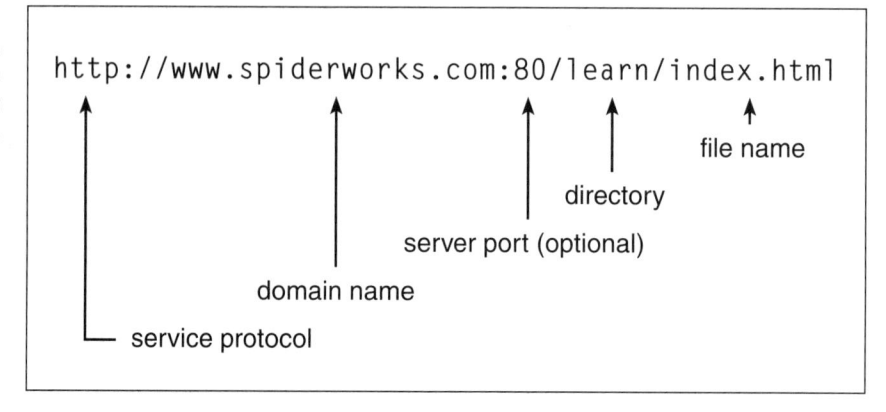

```
http://www.spiderworks.com:80/learn/index.html
```

- service protocol
- domain name
- server port (optional)
- directory
- file name

- the **port** of the computer to which you are attempting to link (this is optional)
- the **path** (directory hierarchy) to locate the file you want
- the **file name** you want, in this case, our trusty `index.html`

Let's examine each of these more closely.

Service Protocols

A number of different standards (protocols) are used for exchanging information on the Internet. The protocols you'll use the most include HTTP, file, FTP, news, and mailto. Most Web browsers, such as Netscape, work with most Internet protocols, which means you can request resources on the Internet using these protocols.

HTTP As you know, you access pages on the Web using the **HTTP** protocol. In turn, the HTTP protocol requires an HTTP or Web server, a program that accepts and acts on these requests. Every server on the World Wide Web is an HTTP server. Most HTTP servers include or work with other protocol servers, such as FTP servers. You've seen the typical URL structure for HTTP throughout this book; we won't recreate it here.

File When you begin to design your Web pages on your Mac, you'll find the **file** protocol useful. It directs your browser to open an HTML file on the hard drive of your Mac, rather than one on a Web site somewhere else. The Web pages we're modeling on our Macs in this book will be accessed via the file protocol. An URL invoking the file protocol is similar in construction to that for HTTP:

`file:///Macintosh%20HD/info/support/help.html`

where file is the protocol name, followed by a colon and triple slashes; "Macintosh HD" is what Navigator sees as the name of your machine, if you haven't changed the name of your hard drive since you installed your Mac. If you have renamed your hard drive it is that new name that will be used as the domain name. Notice the '%20'…that's because a blank space cannot be used as a character in an URL—so it is automatically replaced by its ASCII equivalent '%20'. To complete things, /info/support/ is the path or directory hierarchy; and help.html is the file name.

Once you've got your pages shaped up and looking great and everything works the way you want it to, you can place the pages in your Web site on your ISP's server (or on your own server, if that's the route you want to go) using FTP. You can use Fetch, a terrific FTP package on the CD-ROM, to do this.

FTP Speaking of **FTP,** it's one of the oldest protocols on the Internet. As the name implies, FTP is generally used to transfer software and whole documents, such as text, PostScript, or word processing files, from one computer to another. If you've downloaded a copy of the Netscape browser from Netscape's home page, you did it via FTP. This is what a typical URL for an FTP resource looks like:

```
ftp://ftp.netscape.com/201/mac/201NetscapeInstaller.hqx
```

where the service protocol is FTP followed by a colon and double slashes; the domain name is ftp.netscape.com; the path (directory hierarchy) is /201/mac/, and the file name is 201NetscapeInstaller.hqx.

News If you travel around USENET, a worldwide public-access network on the Internet that has thousands of special interest groups (SIGs), you'll be happy to know that **news** is another service protocol that you can use with a Web browser. In fact, Netscape is a dandy alternative to dedicated newsreaders. The URL for accessing resources with this protocol appears in a somewhat simpler format than the FTP protocol:

```
news:rec.radio.broadcasting
```

where news followed by a colon is the protocol and rec.radio.broadcasting can be any valid USENET (or internal) newsgroup. Netscape's handling of newsgroup articles, replies, and threading is first-rate; when you design your Web page, think about including a link to the USENET newsgroups that pertain to the subject matter of your Web site.

mailto Another service protocol you'll see at the beginning of an URL is the **mailto** protocol. It's used for creating a link that brings up the mail features of your browser. Like an URL invoking the news protocol, the typical mailto URL differs from classic URL structure in that it requires no slashes after the colon following the service protocol.

```
mailto:david@spiderworks.com
```

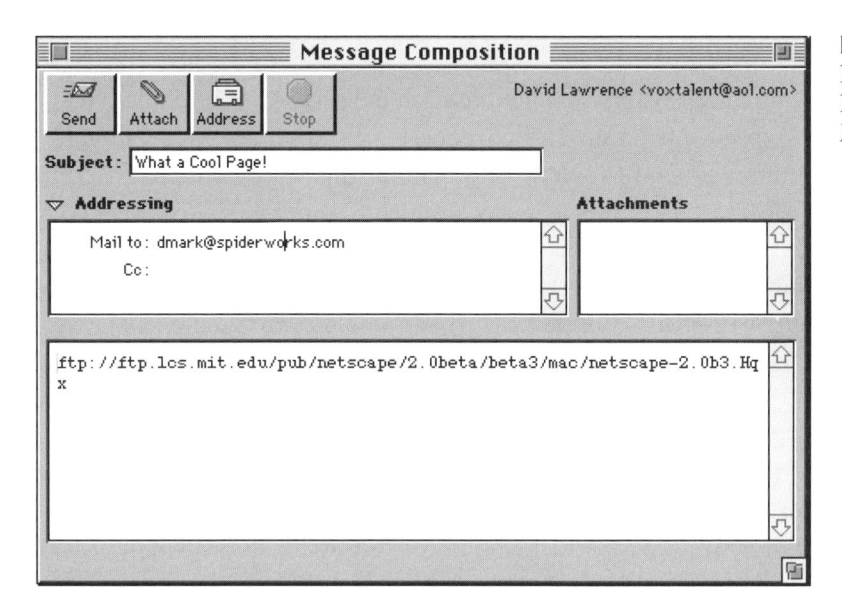

Figure 6.2
Netscape 2.0's Integrated Mail.

Here mailto followed by a colon is the protocol and david@spiderworks.com can be any valid Internet e-mail address. When Netscape is asked to act on this protocol, it pops up a blank mail message with the intended recipient's mail address already filled in the To: box, as shown in Figure 6.2. All you have to do is fill in a subject and the body of the message and click the Send button.

Other Protocols From time to time you will encounter other protocols when you use your Web browser. For example, **gopher** searches, retrieves, and displays documents available on the Internet using a uniquely designed menu-based search engine. While the protocol is nonproprietary, the search engine was written at the University of Minnesota.

WAIS (Wide Area Information Server) locates and retrieves information available in Internet databases by keyword search. The WAIS program is proprietary and was bought in 1995 by America Online. There is also a freeware WAIS program called freeWAIS.

Telnet accesses remote computers on the Internet and allows you to run programs that are on these computers. To invoke this protocol with Netscape, you need a dedicated Telnet application. The most popular Telnet helper application is NCSA Telnet, which is included on the CD-ROM for your convenience.

Domain Name

Following the colon and the double slash in an URL is the domain name of the computer from which the requested Internet resource will come, often prefaced by a host name (more about this below). In our case, the domain name (also called a parent domain name) is spiderworks.com. Our domain name includes the name of our company—spiderworks—and a suffix (also known as the top-level domain)—com. The com suffix is the abbreviation for commercial, which indicates that our firm, spiderworks, is a commercial venture. The total number of characters permitted in a domain name, including the suffix, is 24; valid characters are letters, numbers, the dash, and the underscore.

You can substitute your own name or some other meaningful phrase for a company name in a domain name. However, the suffix is based on the type of organization for which you're requesting the domain name.

Here is a list of possible domain suffixes:

com	commercial ventures
edu	educational institutions
gov	state, local, and federal government agencies
mil	military installations
net	Internet service providers and infrastructure machines
org	organizations that do not fit any of the preceding designations, particularly nonprofit organizations

In addition, there are two-letter country domain designations. Here are a few of these country codes:

us	United States
uk	United Kingdom
ca	Canada

> **By the Way...** The domain name is an abstraction for the unique IP (Internet Protocol) address of a machine serving Internet resources. Generally, an IP address is seen as four 8-bit numbers separated by dots, such as 123.4.56.200. You can use the IP address to connect to a Web site instead of the domain name, if you know the IP address.

Okay. Now you're probably asking yourself what the "www" attached to our domain name (as in www.spiderworks.com) means. It indicates the host name or the name of the machine that contains the Internet resources we wish to offer. "www" is often used to indicate that the address in an URL connects to a Web server. Other host names that are commonly attached to domain names are "ftp" and "gopher." Host names are generally added to domain names when there is more than one host or server for a given domain name, such as a Web server and an ftp server that reside on the same site.

You'll probably want to add the "www" host name to your domain name, and, in fact, your ISP may require it.

> In your forays on the Web, you may encounter domain names that have more parts than a host name, followed by a company name and a suffix. This is because the domain name includes one or more subdomains. For instance, one of the domain names for Apple's site is
>
> `dev.info.apple.com`
>
> The parent domain name here is "apple.com," and "dev" and "info" are each subdomains. Subdomains can be used when your Web site has more than one HTTP server or when you want to "departmentalize" the resources on your site, such as adding the subdomain "info" to your domain name to indicate that the URL will provide the user with information.

Picking Your Domain Name A person or organization can request a name from Network Solutions, Inc., which is one of the two organizations that comprise InterNIC, the Internet Information Clearinghouse. This organization provides registration services for new domain names and IP addresses. In the case of spiderworks.com, we shelled out $10 for the 1-year period following our request (the money is used to help administer the huge workload involved in maintaining the records on all this stuff).

You should check with your ISP before requesting a domain name. The ISP hosting your site may not permit unique domain names on its server and instead may offer you use of its domain name for your Web site address (usually individual Web sites are indicated in the path or directory hierarchy in an URL). Or the ISP may offer you an alias to its domain name.

> **By the Way...**
>
> If you want to register your domain name, the first step is to obtain the correct form from the InterNIC. Just send e-mail to:
>
> `help@internic.net`
>
> A Domain Name Registration form will automatically be sent back to you. I suggest copying the contents of your e-mail message and saving it to a text file on your hard drive. Then sit back, let your ISP answer the tough questions about your DNS (domain name server) and the like; you can answer the easy ones (your name, address, and why you want this domain name), and then e-mail the information back to the InterNIC. If the name you've requested isn't in use, and there are no outstanding warrants for your capture, the InterNIC will grant your request.

Location and Name of the Resource

The remainder of the URL is simple: it's a path (directory hierarchy) to the file you're looking for in your original HTML request. Each directory is separated by a slash (/). The final slash precedes the name of the file that resides at the URL, whether it's an HTML document or a graphics, sound, or movie file.

Absolute vs. Relative URLs

To this point, we've been talking about **absolute URLs** that include all of the information necessary to find the specified item from anywhere on the Web. Every time an URL is invoked, a rather lengthy process occurs in which the host (the machine you've asked for information) is contacted and asked for the item at the URL; the host responds (or doesn't), and the URL's contents are then accessed. If you were traveling on the Internet to another site, all of that information is required; but if you are looking, instead, for a piece of information on *your* site, then you can use a **relative URL**. A relative URL gives a resource file name, but specifies its location relative to the location of the file in which the relative URL exists. It's a lot like addressing an envelope to a next-door neighbor without the city, state, or zip, since you know that stuff (it's the same as yours) and you can simply walk the envelope over without using the Postal System to deliver it.

Figure 6.3
The folder we created in Chapter 4.

In fact, we've already used a relative URL. Recall that we created a folder called `spiderworks web site` and placed it on your desktop. (For easy reference, we've displayed it again in Figure 6.3.

The document we've been working on, `index.html`, is sitting there, along with the `resources` folder, which contains the image we inserted in the document using the <img> tag, as you can see in Figure 6.4.

Figure 6.4
Our fledgling site.

Open `index.html` in BBEdit Lite, and let's examine the <img> tag we used again. Here's the line in our code that inserts the spiderworks logo:

```
<img src="resources/images/spiderworks.gif">
```

Remember, everything within the quotes is an URL that tells us the location of the target image. Note that there is no service protocol, and no colon or slashes or domain name. But it works nonetheless, because in the absence of those elements, the browser assumes that the path leading to the location of the file is at your site, beginning in the same directory as the HTML document making the call; a perfect example of a relative URL.

Creating Links

Let's put all of this new-found URL knowledge to use and create a link to a second document:

1. In the **Finder**, click on the `index.html` document.

2. Go to the **File** menu and select **Duplicate**. Do this twice. Your site will look like Figure 6.5.
3. Rename the first copy staff.html and the second toc.html. Check that your screen looks like Figure 6.6.

Figure 6.5
Creating more pages.

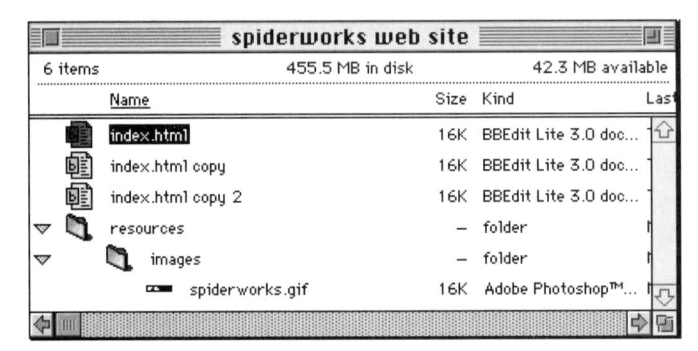

Figure 6.6
Done!

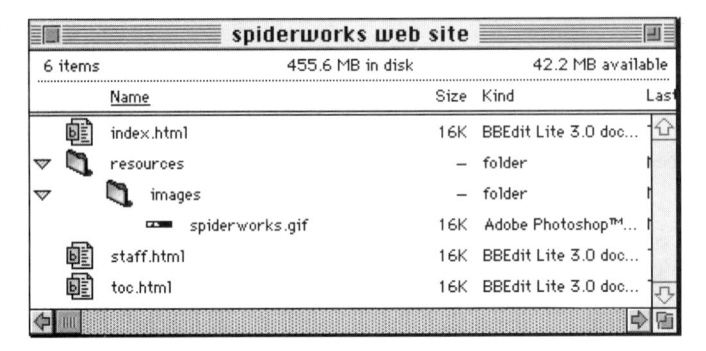

For now, because we know that these two documents contain exactly the same information as index.html, let's hold off editing them. Let's simply create links to these documents, and we'll deal with what they contain later. We want to familiarize you with another tag at this point, the **anchor** tag.

Anchors Aweigh

The anchor tag, **<a>...</a>,** is used in two ways. First, using the href= attribute, it's used (much like the <img> tag) to designate a destination for a link to another item. In this case, we'll be linking to our two just-created pages. Second, using the name= attribute, it gives a name to a particular section within a document.

`<a>...</a>`

Description: Creates an anchor that describes a link between two resources on the World Wide Web.

HTML 2.0 Attributes:

href="URL"	URL of target outside the document
"URL#name"	a specific fragment within the document named by the URL
"#name"	a specific fragment within the same document
"name"	anchor within the same document
name="text"	text string denoting a particular point in the document

HTML 3.0 Attributes:

title="text"	title of target URL
rel="text"	relationship described by the link
rev="text"	reverse relationship described by the link
shape="text"	specifies area within an images links to an URL
methods="text"	meta information concerning HTTP access method
id="text"	name and id for Web page elements
lang=text	language used by intended audience for a Web page
class=text	indicates types or classes of element in a Web page

---

Let's create a link. Remember that whatever text is within the opening and closing tags is affected by the tag. We have created a list that will come in handy for illustrating links. In the `Authoring` folder, look for a file called `anchor list.txt`. Open that file in BBEdit Lite, copy all of the text in that file, and then paste it between the <body>...</body> tags in `index.html`. We're going to link to the document we named `toc.html`.

1. You'll see in the newly pasted HTML source a series of lines that begin with <L1>. This is actually a list. On the second line of the list, position your cursor just prior to the words Table of Contents, as shown in Figure 6.7.
2. Type:

```
<a href="toc.html">
```

Figure 6.7
Code snippet.

```
<LI>our home page (which
<LI>a Table of Contents f
<LI>personal information
<LI>and lots of examples
```

   3. Position your cursor directly after the word Contents and type:

   `</a>`

   to close the tag.

   Here's what your line of code should look like now:

   `<LI>a <a href="toc.html">Table of Contents</a> for Learn HTML on the Macintosh<br>`

   Congratulations. You have just created your first link! By placing the anchor tag on either side of the words Table of Contents, in effect, you've told your browser that whenever anyone clicks in this area, go to the document called `toc.html`. You've also used a relative URL, so the browser will look for the document in the same directory as the current document. The Netscape rendition of this is shown in Figure 6.8.

   Isn't that terrific? Now, what do you think will happen when you click anywhere in the blue underlined area? (Recall that earlier, when we were defining colors, we used blue for hyperlinks, as shown in this example.)

Figure 6.8
Our first link!

You will load the document called `toc.html`. Try it. It should look like our very first version of `index.html`, since, you recall, it's a duplicate.

In-Document Anchors   You can also reference a location within a document. Let's use the anchor tag to tell the browser the name of a section.

1. At the bottom of the `index.html` document, you'll find the HTML source for our address and phone information. Place your cursor to the left of the words "To contact us."

```
<address>
To contact us via mail or phone:<br>
spiderworks<br>
2816 Saddlebred Court<br>
Suite 200<br>
Glenwood, MD 21739-9740<br>
Phone: 301/854-5459<br>
</address>
```

2. Type:

```
<a name="contact">
```

3. Place your cursor to the right of the word "us" and type:

```
</a>
```

to close the anchor tag. Your final line of code should look like this:

```
<a name="contact">To contact us</a> via mail or phone:<br>
```

Notice that this time we used the name= attribute rather than the href= attribute. If you were to browse this in Netscape, you wouldn't see any difference, because we're not actually creating the clickable area to go to a link; we're naming this line in the document to be a target for other anchor tags *to link to*. Let's create just such a link; this time we'll use an HTML extension to speed things up.

1. At the top of the document, in the line that reads "We'll be here, 24 hours a day…," highlight the word "here."
2. Go to the **Extensions** menu and pull down to **HTML Link**. You'll see a dialog box as shown in Figure 6.9.
3. Type in the string #contact. The pound sign (Shift-3) designates this as an in-document anchor point, not an URL somewhere else to be deciphered.
4. Click on OK.

Figure 6.9
The HTML Link extension dialog box.

Here's how the code looks:

```
We'll be <A HREF="#contact">here</A>, 24 hours a day, to serve
you, the reader of Learn HTML on the Macintosh.<br>
```

And the Netscape version is in Figure 6.10.

The link between these two points has been created. If you click on the link, you'll be taken down to that portion of the page. It's just that easy. By the way, you can implement both these methods of using the anchor tag at the same time. For example, let's assume you wanted to create a link in another page to the exact location of the contact information on this page. To do so, you'd combine the two to form this opening anchor tag:

```
<a href="index.html#contact">
```

This tells the browser to take you to the `index.html` page in this directory, and in particular, to the section called `contact`.

Figure 6.10
An in-document link.

> It's a good idea to keep the names of the anchors short and sweet. There's no need to name an anchor "Contact Information for Spiderworks" when "contact" or even "c" would suffice. And this is a context-sensitive situation: in some browsers, "Contact" is not the same as "contact."

By the Way...

Now let's use our new linking power to add some links with pictures. But first, more about the image tag.

Improving Our Image

As we already know, the <img> tag is used to place an image on a page by referencing a graphic via its address on the Web. The image may be a logo, like our spiderworks banner in our `index.html` page, or a picture, graphic, or map used for illustrative purposes.

Let's add a map to our page following these steps:

1. In the `Authoring` folder, find the file `location.gif`.
2. Drag `location.gif` to the `images` folder in our Website where the `spiderworks.gif` file is. The `images` folder is in the `resources` folder.
3. Add this line of code to your `index.html` document at the bottom, just after the </address> tag:

   ```
   <img src="resources/images/location.gif">
   ```

4. Now save the changes in BBEdit Lite and view your document in Netscape. It's shown in Figure 6.11.

Next let's use our linking knowledge to make a connection from text to a graphic. To do so, we'll turn the map we just added into a button (we talk about butttons more in the next chapter) that links users to detailed directions on how to get to spiderworks.

1. In the `Authoring` folder, locate the file `directions.html`.
2. Drag that document to the `spiderworks web site` folder where the `index.html` file is.
3. Open the `directions.html` file to examine the code. As you can see, it's directions to the spiderworks offices:

Figure 6.11
Cool! A map!

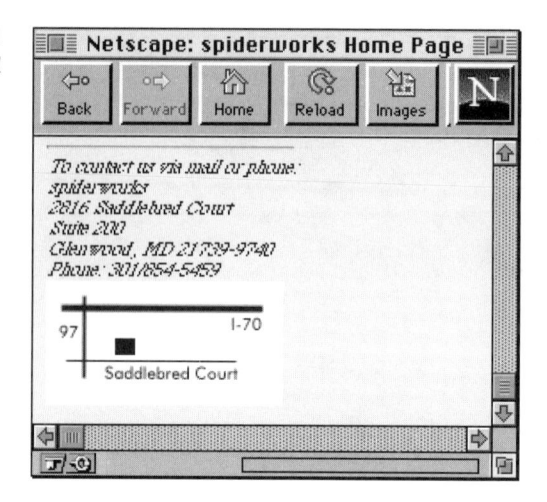

[Screenshot: Netscape: spiderworks Home Page showing contact info and a simple map with Saddlebred Court, 97, and I-70]

```
<HTML>
<HEAD>

<TITLE>Directions to spiderworks</TITLE>
<!-- <base href=http://www.spiderworks.com/directions.html> -->
</HEAD>
<BODY bgcolor="#FFF6C4">
<H1>Directions to spiderworks:</H1>
<OL>
<LI>Go west on Interstate 70 to the Route 97 South Exit
<LI>Proceed 12 miles south on 97
<LI>Turn left onto Saddlebred Court. spiderworks is 6 miles up on
the left hand side.
</OL>
You can print these out and take them with you!
<p><A HREF="index.html">Back to the home page</A></p>
</BODY>
</HTML>
```

Figure 6.12 shows what you see when you view this document in Netscape.

Now let's link these directions to the map we added to our `index.html` document in BBEdit Lite.

1. In the `index.html` file, find the line of code at the bottom that references the `map.gif` image and highlight it.
2. Go to the **Extensions** menu and choose **HTML Link**.
3. Instead of typing in the name of the file, click on the **Choose file** button.

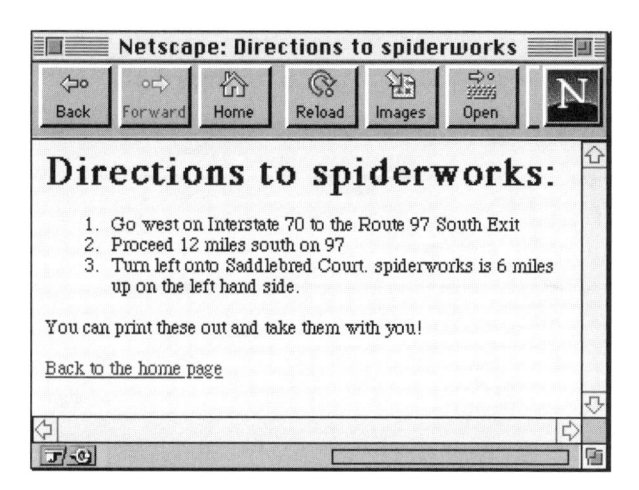

Figure 6.12
Convenient, isn't it?

4. Select the `directions.html` file in the dialog box that pops up. Now, let's look at the code:

```
<A HREF="directions.html"><img src="resources/images/location.gif"></A>
```

Here's what we now have: an image of the map, which is a link to another document that gives us written directions for using the map. Look at your `index.html` document in Netscape (see Figure 6.13). Note: You may have to hit the **Reload** button to see the difference.

The border around the map indicates that it is a link. The border in this case is purple, indicating that we've already visited this document. Go

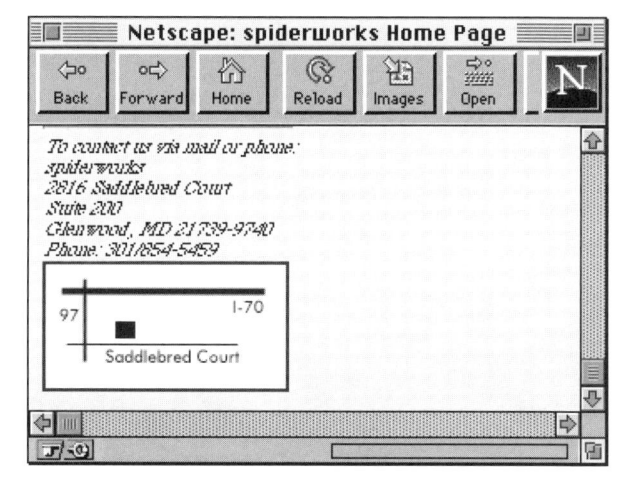

Figure 6.13
A linked image.

ahead and click on the map: It takes you to the `directions.html` document. Then click on the text that takes you back to the `index.html` page. You're traveling the Web!

> **Important!** When creating graphics, don't use blue or purple borders that are similar in appearance to link borders. You can see how that might confuse the viewer.

What's Next

In Chapter 7, we examine linked graphics in greater depth and create navigation buttons and clickable image maps. But first, get up, stretch, grab a beverage. Come back when you're ready.

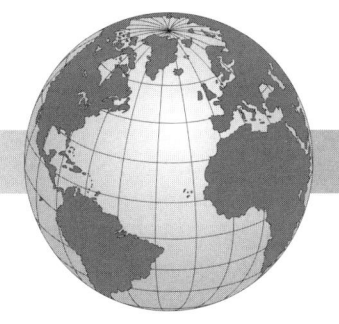

Icons, Buttons, and Image Maps

We live in a world filled with icons, although most of the time we're not aware of them. In fact, many of our actions are directed by them. While navigating in our cars, for instance, we slow down for children, merge from two lanes to one, see that we can't make a U-turn at the next intersection, and know to be on the lookout for deer crossing the road—all without reading a word. Instead, we mentally process simple graphics or images—icons—on signage. And of course, you surely are aware that the Macintosh you work with made its reputation by designing clearly defined, intuitive icons.

Similarly, your Web site can be navigated using icons on buttons and image maps. In many cases, they will be similar to the icons used in other computer programs; others will resemble the icons used to operate stereo equipment or VCRs since Web sites can contain both sound and movies.

The most important thing to remember when using icons as navigational tools in a Web site is to make sure that they clearly represent the words they are meant to replace.

Sizing Icons

Usually, icons used in Web sites are small: 64 × 64 pixels, or about a half-inch square, is probably as large as you want to go, although 32 × 32 is even better since that is the size of the icons in the **Large Icon** view in your **Finder**. Remember: the text used in the majority of Web sites is only 12 pixels tall, so implementing icons any larger would overshadow any adjacent text. And note that a square is not the only shape that can be used for an icon; it's just used here to provide a guide for dimensions.

And certainly, there are exceptions to the size rule—for example, a designer might want to create a graphic impact with an icon, as opposed to using it only as a navigation tool. We are going to stop short of imparting any design advice here, however; that's best left up to people such as Robin Williams, whose books on Macintosh design are essential, and Kai Krause, whose Power Tools and Photoshop know-how is legendary. We're going to concentrate on the utility of Web site navigation, and how icons can enhance that experience.

Some Human Interface Guidelines

Web sites are designed in many different and interesting ways. Some are designed like storybooks, to be read a page at a time, in order, from the beginning to the end. Some are designed like trees or outlines, in that the top of the Web site contains a few general categories, the categories contain subcategories, and so on. Other Web sites, due to space restrictions, are all on one page, and have a sort of top-to-bottom navigation requirement.

Most likely, you'll eventually design Web sites that are a combination of these, but however you choose to set up your pages, it is essential that you have an understanding of what your viewer will see and how they will interpret it as they navigate your site. To that end, we offer a few general guidelines:

- *Keep it simple*. Make sure that the icons you use are clear and concise. Children and adults, foreign and domestic, should be able to look at your icons and understand instantly what you're trying to convey.
- *Don't be too clever*. In your Web travels, you'll come across sites that are way too hip. No doubt they're interesting to look at, initially at least, but the sites that last and flourish are those that, while creative, are also easy to understand.

- *Create navigation pathways that mirror your own trails.* When adding content to a page, take note of how *you* are reading it. If you are using up-and-down construction, add the appropriate icons for that behavior. If you are going more often from left to right, consider that alternative. You are your best guinea pig—pay attention to how you travel your pages while creating them, and if you make it easy on yourself, it will be easy for your readers, too.

> Bruce Tognazzini, Apple's keeper-of-the-GUI-flame, wrote a great book on human interface guidelines. It's not specifically aimed at Web editors, but it offers great insights as to why some interface designs work and some don't. We can't recommend it highly enough. It's called *Tog on Interface*. It's probably available where you bought this book, but if not, call Addison-Wesley at 1-800-358-4566 to order it directly.
>
> The Edward R. Tufte books: *The Visual Display of Quantitative Information* and *Envisioning Information* are great to help you get a grip on how symbols and icons can tell a story. Both are available from Graphics Press in Cheshire, Connecticut at 1-800-822-2454.

- *Use alt attributes in image tags.* Again, we remind you that not everyone uses a graphical browser or has a high-speed link. And a lot of dial-up users, even those with 28.8 Kbps modems, leave their **Auto-Load Images** preference turned off to speed up downloading time (see Figures 7.1 and 7.2). They only click on graphics intermittently. To accommodate these users, always use the alt= attribute in the <img> tag, which allows you to place a text string in the <img> tag that is displayed instead of the image if the image itself is not loaded. Take note of the HTML code for the `index.html` document, and you'll see the judicious use of the alt= attribute: The map contains an explanation of what the viewer would see if they don't see the map.
- *Give people text alternatives.* There are people who prefer speed when browsing over grace and beauty. For those people, a **text-only navigational track** is in order. Navigation may not be as pretty, but it will fly. Text links are almost instantly acted upon by the server, because the time spent generating a response to the user is next to nothing compared to the inversion and flashing of a graphic link.

Figure 7.1
This site took less than three seconds to load with graphics turned off.

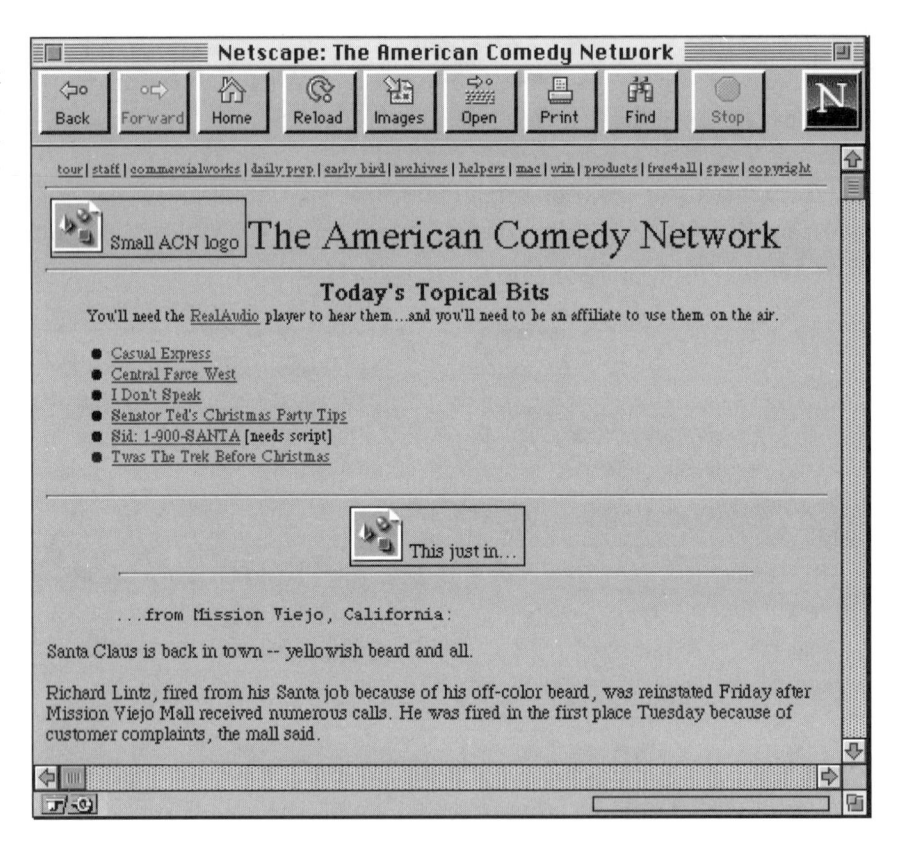

> Text tracks are a good alternative for any site that you build, since there will be times when your audience has precious little time to get where they want to go. Always make sure that you include some way of navigating so that if your intended audience is temporarily bandwidth-impaired they can still get around without a hitch.

Graphical Navigation Techniques

A successful graphical navigation design is one in which the icons do not interfere with the content, and we'll demonstrate how you can add a graphical image to your Web pages without overpowering your message. First, though, let's look at the tool that we recommend you use to create stunning graphics.

Figure 7.2
The same site took over 20 seconds to load at 14.4, with graphics turned on.

Adobe Photoshop: Tool of Choice

Put bluntly, in our opinion, if you don't have Photoshop, you can't consider yourself a serious Web designer. The Web experience is almost totally on-screen; rarely do people print from a browser, and because Photoshop works very well with screen images at 72 dots per inch (as well as print images at much higher resolutions), has incredible text-handling capabilities, and allows you to create subtle effects with graphics at the click of a button, it is ideally suited for creating screen-oriented graphics.

In addition, Photoshop easily translates between PICT, JPEG, and GIF files. Its plug-in technology means that as certain graphic techniques become popular, the features required to perform the technique can be distilled into a plug-in module.

The bad news is (you knew there had to be bad news, right?), Photoshop is expensive: Street price at the time of this writing was around $500. The best deals we've seen are from several mail-order houses that bundle

Photoshop with various scanners. Of course, we're talking about the full version on CD-ROM, not the Limited Edition, which does not have much of the functionality of the full version.

At spiderworks, we use a Microtek ScanMaker IIsp scanner, which we chose over similar products from HP and Apple simply because the deal included the full version of Photoshop, the scanner and all attendant cables, drivers, scanning software, optical character recognition software, and more for the princely sum of $670, which is essentially tantamount to getting the scanner and most of the goodies for free.

Creating and Enhancing Graphics Using Photoshop

Most of the raw graphics you encounter in the Mac world are of two formats: PICT or EPS. But since the Web's primary language is GIF, you'll have to convert any graphic files from other sources to this format. Furthermore, any graphics you create in Photoshop's native format will have to be saved as GIFs as well. If you have Photoshop, go ahead and launch it. (If you don't have Photoshop, you'll need a product like Graphic-Converter, which is provided on the CD-ROM, to make the conversions.)

The Web now also speaks JPEG, and many Web browsers will load JPEG images inline. For photographs, JPEG has better resolution and compression than GIF, so it's worthwhile to make use of this format, too.

In this section, we assume that we convinced you to buy Photoshop. The techniques you're about to learn are simple, and they comprise 90 percent of what you're going to need to add graphics to your Web site. First, we need a GIF file.

How deep is your bit depth?

On Macintosh, one way to determine the quality of a graphic is by its **bit depth**—the number of bits used to describe the color of each individual pixel. When you hear this term, it refers to:

1-bit color = black and white (no gray; the bit is either a 1 or a 0, on or off, black or white)
8-bit color = for all GIF pages
24-bit color = photographic quality

Figure 7.3
Indexed color mode.

Recall from our earlier discussion that the GIF format enables a graphic to contain up to 256 different 8-bit colors, meaning that you can have a palette of 256 of any of the spectrum of colors available to you on your machine. Often, however, the colors in a graphic (the icons on buttons and image maps, for example) are much simpler: a black arrow on a white square or a red pushpin on a wheat-colored background.

1. To convert your opened graphic to 256 colors, click on the **Mode** menu and choose **Indexed Color** (see Figure 7.3). This will bring up the **Indexed Color** dialog box displayed in Figure 7.4.

Figure 7.4
The Indexed Color dialog box.

2. Choose **8 bits/pixel** for the Resolution, **Adaptive** for the Palette, and **Diffusion** for the Dither. This tells Photoshop to create a color palette for this graphic that is as close to the colors it sees in 24-bit mode as possible.
3. Select **Custom** as your palette to see the table of 256 different colors used to create your graphic (see Figure 7.5).

Figure 7.5
The Custom color table.

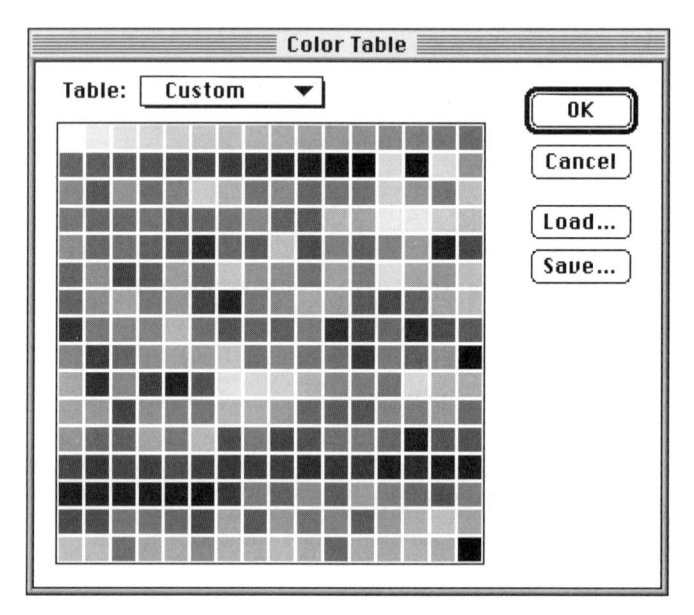

Some GIFty Tricks

There are two maneuvers you can make with GIF files that are unique to their use in Web predesign. First, you can make one of the 256 colors on the palette act as an invisible color, thereby rendering that color "transparent." Then, when viewed in your browser, readers would be able to "see through" the GIF file to the background color or image on the Web page behind the graphic. Here's an example, using a simple graphic of a sun, shown in Photoshop in Figure 7.6 and in Netscape in Figure 7.7.

Let's make it transparent, and then see how it looks in Figure 7.8. As you can see, the gray Netscape background is now visible in the middle of the sun, as well as in between the sun's rays; wherever there was white in the original graphic is now "transparent."

Chapter 7 Icons, Buttons, and Image Maps 141

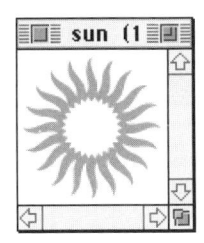

Figure 7.6
Mr. Sun in Photoshop.

Figure 7.7
The sun.html file with a non-transparent graphic.

Figure 7.8
The sun.html file as a transparent graphic.

The second GIF trick is that you can specify how a GIF file is displayed when opened. When you open a GIF file from the hard drive on your computer, even the largest files simply "appear"; you don't see the lines being drawn because it happens so quickly. However, when you're connected to a Web server and the GIF file is being transmitted via a modem, drawing time is noticeably slow and the picture fills in from top to bottom. But through a process called **interlacing,** this drawing time can be reduced. Interlacing works by using the monitor's electron gun to paint only certain

Figure 7.9
The first pass during interlacing.

lines on the first pass (Figure 7.9), alternating lines on the second pass and the third pass until the graphic is clearly presented (Figure 7.10).

Another benefit of interlacing is that, generally by the second pass, the viewer will have a pretty good idea of the makeup of the graphic, and if it is also a navigation button, the viewer can click on it as soon as it is visible. The server does not have to wait until the entire graphic has been loaded to respond to the request to link.

The point at which you choose how you want a GIF file to display is when you save your graphic image: If you choose noninterlaced, the image will be saved to your hard drive in a linear, step-by-step fashion; if you choose interlaced, the data is saved in that fashion, and is displayed accordingly every time it's opened.

> **By the Way...**
> There are two main GIF formats: GIF87a and GIF89a. The older GIF87a format doesn't normally support either transparency or interlacing options. If the graphics program you're using doesn't allow you to save with interlacing or set a color as transparent, then you can be sure that it's saving the file as a GIF87a. Otherwise, you'll be given a choice as to which format you want.

Figure 7.10
The completely loaded graphic.

Plug in PhotoGIF

There's a great shareware plug-in to Photoshop—PhotoGIF by Box Top Software (also included on the CD-ROM—it's shareware, and the dialog boxes *do* get annoying, so pay up!)—that makes it easy to edit any graphic, change it to an indexed color palette, choose whether it's interlaced and which of the colors in the graphic is going to be transparent—all on the fly, during the Save process. Its welcome screen is shown in Figure 7.11.

Figure 7.11
By all means, plug this in to Photoshop.

Figure 7.12 shows what the dialog box looked like when we made Mr. Sun transparent. As you can see, all of the controls are at your fingertips: a check box for interlacing, an 8 × 32 mini-color palette that shows you the colors used in your graphic (much like Photoshop's palette that we saw

Figure 7.12
The PhotoGIF dialog box.

earlier), and the computer's choice for which color to use as your "transparent" color. It selects the color of the pixel in the upper left hand corner of the graphic, but you are free to choose any other color to be "transparent" simply by clicking on it in the palette.

Remember: *Save all your graphics as GIF files!* If you inadvertently save a graphic in PICT or as a Photoshop format file, it won't work on your Web page. Photos are the exception; for them, JPEG is the format to go with. Make sure that GIF files have an extension of .gif, and JPEG files have an extension of .jpeg or .jpg.

Icon Navigation

To demonstrate using icons for navigation, we're going to develop an example that takes a linear, ordered approach to a site, where each step in the process requires having completed the previous step. We're going to create an eight-page series that will guide the user through the procedure of recording an audio cassette. Here are the three icons we'll use:

▶ Go to the next step

◀ Go back to the previous step

▲ Start at the beginning

Here is text content of the steps:

1. Start with a blank cassette. Make sure you're not taping over something you really would rather save.
2. Determine the type of cassette you're using: normal, chrome, or metal.
3. Set the recording controls on your tape recorder to match your cassette type.
4. Put the cassette on which you're going to record in the recorder, and press the Pause and Record buttons.
5. Set the level on the meter so that the LEDs only occasionally glow in the red zone.
6. Reset the CD-ROM player to the beginning.
7. Release the Pause button and wait about 10 seconds.

8. Start the CD-ROM. Monitor the LEDs to make sure that the levels are consistent.

To begin developing these pages, open the `cassette` folder in the `Authoring` folder. You'll see 11 files: the eight steps and the three graphic files that we'll use. Here's the code from the first document, `cassette1.html`:

```
<HTML>
<HEAD>
<TITLE>Recording A Cassette</TITLE>
</HEAD>
<BODY>
<H2>Recording A Cassette</H2>
1. Start with a blank cassette. Make sure you're not taping over
something you really would rather save.
<p>
<A HREF="cassette2.html"><IMG ALIGN=bottom SRC="right.gif"
ALT="Let's go to the next step"></A>
</BODY>
</HTML>
```

Notice that we've made a reference to the next page, `cassette2.html`, and we've included the right-arrow GIF file within the anchor tag. Figure 7.13 shows the Netscape rendering. The graphic invites viewers to learn more by clicking on the icon. Figure 7.14 shows what they see if they do.

The step 2 screen offers two additional options, one of which may be initially confusing: the up arrow. But clicking on it will quickly "explain" its function—to take readers back to the beginning of the process.

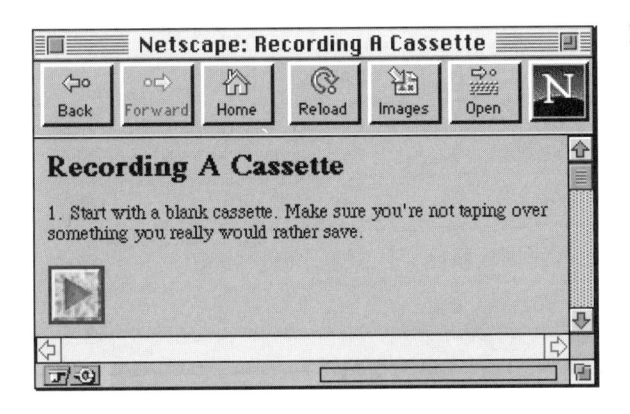

Figure 7.13
Step 1.

Figure 7.14
New options.

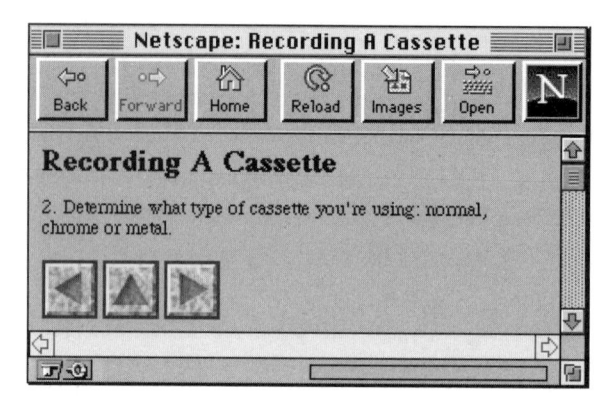

By the Way...

We put together these pages all at once, not one at a time, using BBEdit Lite's **Save As** command. Here's the text we started with:

```
1. Start with a blank cassette. Make sure you're not taping
over something you really would rather save.
2. Determine the type of cassette you're using: normal, chrome,
or metal.
3. Set the recording controls on your tape recorder to match
your cassette type.
4. Put the cassette on which you're going to record in the
recorder, and press the Pause and Record buttons.
5. Set the level on the meter so that the LEDs only
occasionally glow in the red zone.
6. Reset the CD-ROM player to the beginning of the CD-ROM.
7. Release the Pause button and wait about 10 seconds.
8. Start the CD-ROM. Monitor the LEDs to make sure that the
levels are consistent.
<p>
<A HREF="cassette5.html"><IMG ALIGN=bottom SRC="left.gif"
ALT="Let's go back to the previous step."></A>
<A HREF="cassette1.html"><IMG ALIGN=bottom SRC="up.gif"
ALT="Let's start over"></A>
<A HREF="cassette7.html"><IMG ALIGN=bottom SRC="right.gif"
ALT="Let's go to the next step"></A>
```

Next, we created eight documents, all with the same <body> tag text. It was then a simple matter to go to each and change the number of the previous and next steps' HTML file name, and delete the steps before and after the one contained in the document. Neat, huh? Of course, in the first and last document, we eliminated icons that were unnecessary at those stages.

Button Bar Navigation

Another easy way to provide navigation icons is to put them in faux toolbars that mimic the familiar Macintosh (and Windows) bars—icons presented in a horizontal strip, each of which, when clicked, sends the viewer to various parts of a Web site. Figure 7.15 gives an example of a page that provides users with several alternatives.

Let's see if we can create a button bar for our cassette recording example. Open the folder called `cassbars` in the `Authoring` folder, then open the `cassette2.html` file in Netscape so that your screen looks like Figure 7.16.

To create this, we used the border= attribute in the <img> tag. Here's the code:

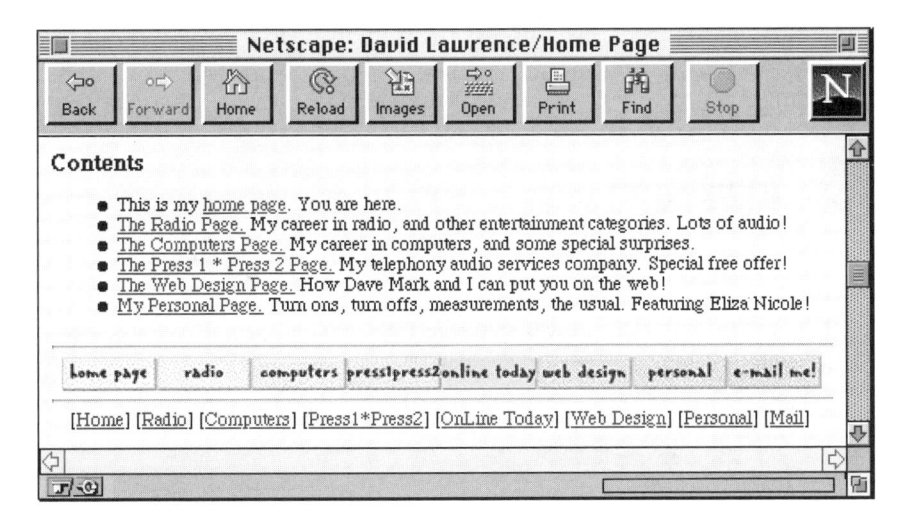

Figure 7.15 Navigation icons presented in a toolbar.

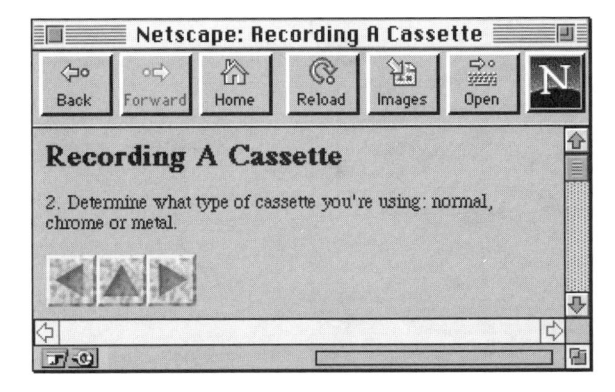

Figure 7.16 Our sample button bar.

```
<A HREF="cassette1.html"><IMG ALIGN=bottom border=0 SRC="left.gif"
ALT="Let's go back to the previous step."></A><A HREF=
"cassette1.html"><IMG ALIGN=bottom border=0 SRC="up.gif"
ALT="Let's start over"></A><A HREF="cassette3.html"><IMG
ALIGN=bottom border=0 SRC="right.gif" ALT="Let's go to the next
step"></A>
```

Note that the code will be all on one line in BBEdit Lite (and if you have wrapping turned off, you'll have to scroll to the right to see the whole line). This was deliberate, because, remember, a return in HTML text is treated as a space in Netscape, and to achieve the effect of the icons butting one another, we removed all spaces and returns.

You can make your button bars of any shape that lends itself to continuity: a long rectangle, a series of spheres, and others. If you're clever, you can make your button bar look just like an image map (which you'll understand more clearly when we discuss them in an upcoming section in this chapter). Button bars are much faster than image maps, since they don't require any processing from the server over and above creating the link.

Text Navigation

For the purposes of this example, let's assume there's a nagging thought in the back of your mind that the up arrow is not all that intuitive on our page. Let's remedy that, and provide a text track at the same time. Open the folder called `casstext` in the `Authoring` folder, then open `cassette1.html` in Netscape using the Open File command. Your screen should look like Figure 7.17.

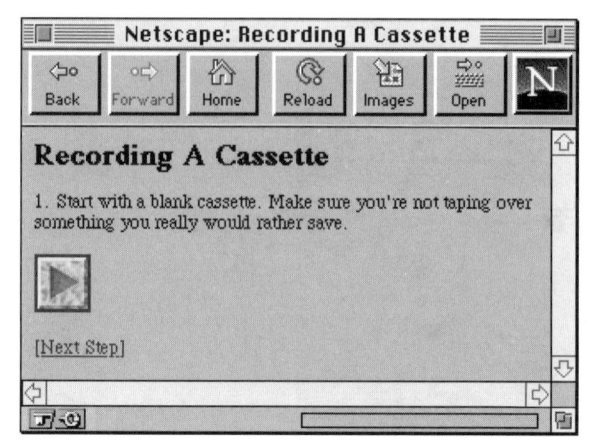

Figure 7.17
Adding a text track.

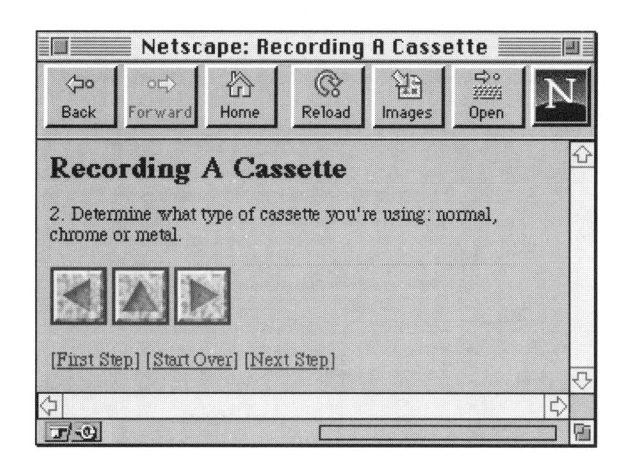

Figure 7.18
The text links work, too.

Let's look at the next step, shown in Figure 7.18. Keep clicking on the buttons, using the text links, to get the next step.

If you look at any of these documents in BBEdit Lite, you'll see the same anchor tags at work for the text links as were used for the arrow buttons.

Image Maps

Image maps go icons and buttons one better: They are graphics that respond in different ways depending on where in them you click your mouse. There are two types of image maps: **server-side** and **client-side.** Server-side image maps are processed by the server. They have been around the longest, and are more difficult to use, since they require a special program on the server to handle the map's processing.

In contrast, client-side image maps are available via a Netscape 2.0 extension, and all of the information necessary for them to work is in your HTML document. All the viewer needs in order to use them is Netscape 2.0—or any other browser that understands the tags necessary to achieve this effect.

Server-Side Image Maps

Let's first examine how to create the venerable server-side image maps, so that we can more clearly contrast the process using Netscape's client-side options. To do so, we'll use the American Comedy Network's (ACN) home page, displayed in Figure 7.19.

Figure 7.19
American Comedy Network's image map.

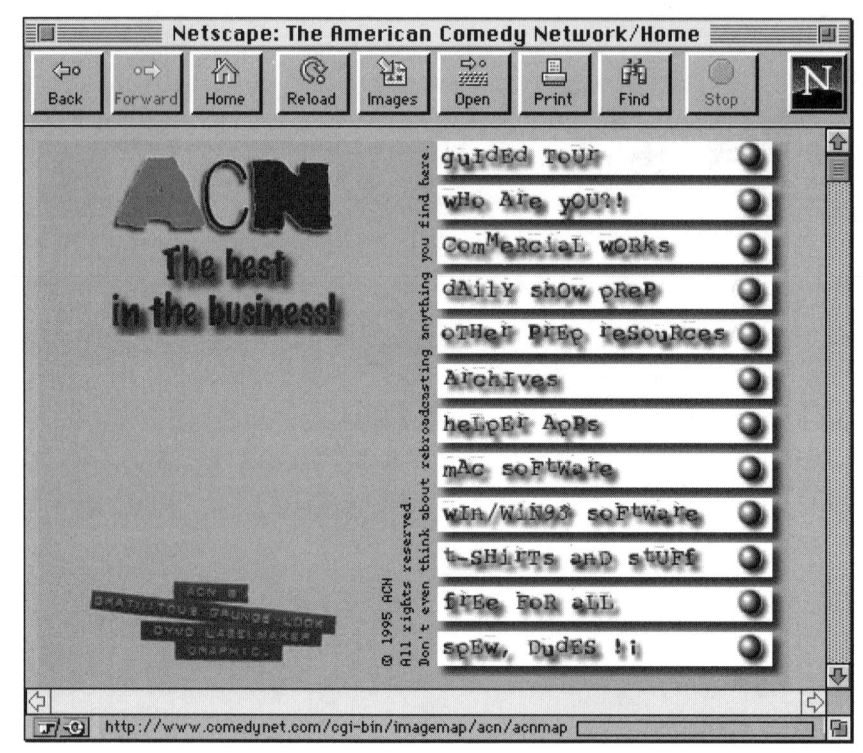

When clicked, each of the long rectangular raised buttons on the right-hand side of the graphic in Figure 7.19 takes you to a different part of the ACN Web site. In fact, even the copyright notice, running vertically alongside the buttons, takes you to a page with a lot of legal copyright mumbo-jumbo they didn't want to include on the main screen. The Dymo label maker graphic at the bottom takes you to a larger version of itself when you click on it.

Preparing the Graphic

Creating an image map is not difficult. You'll need to create the original graphic by drawing original art, using clip art, or scanning in a logo and then saving it as a GIF file. Take the time to plan where you want to go from the page in which the graphic will appear, and list the relative URLs for those different locations either on a separate piece of paper or in a scratch text file on your Macintosh.

Two other elements are necessary to make an image map do what you want it to once you get it loaded on the server: the **image map reference file** and a **cgi script** on the server that can process image map requests. We'll assume that you have access to the `cgi-bin` directory on your Web server and that your ISP will have a script loaded that will handle image maps (we'll also give you some alternatives shortly in case you don't).

Creating the Map

To create the image map reference file, which is nothing but a specially formatted text file, you need a tool that will let you designate areas of your graphic that are "live" and what will result when someone clicks on those areas. The tool is called WebMap (its welcome screen is presented in Figure 7.20), and you can download it by pointing your browser to <http://www.city.net/cnx/software/>. After you've successfully unstuffed the WebMap archive and placed the resulting WebMap folder in a convenient place on your hard drive, go ahead and launch it. Under the **File** menu, open the file called `acnmap.gif` to display the screen shown in Figure 7.21.

You'll also see a floating palette called the **Tools palette** (see Figure 7.22). This contains the shapes that you can draw over your graphic to designate your live areas: rectangles, circles, ovals, and polygons. Each shape is described by the pixels X and Y (starting with 1,1 in the upper left-hand corner of the graphic) and the points that define the shape itself.

- Rectangles are defined by their upper left and lower right coordinates.
- Circles are defined by their center point and any point along the edge of the circle.
- Ovals are defined like rectangles, by the upper left and lower right points of the oval's shape.

Figure 7.20
WebMap, the tool that will help you create an image map reference file.

Figure 7.21
The ACN graphic in WebMap.

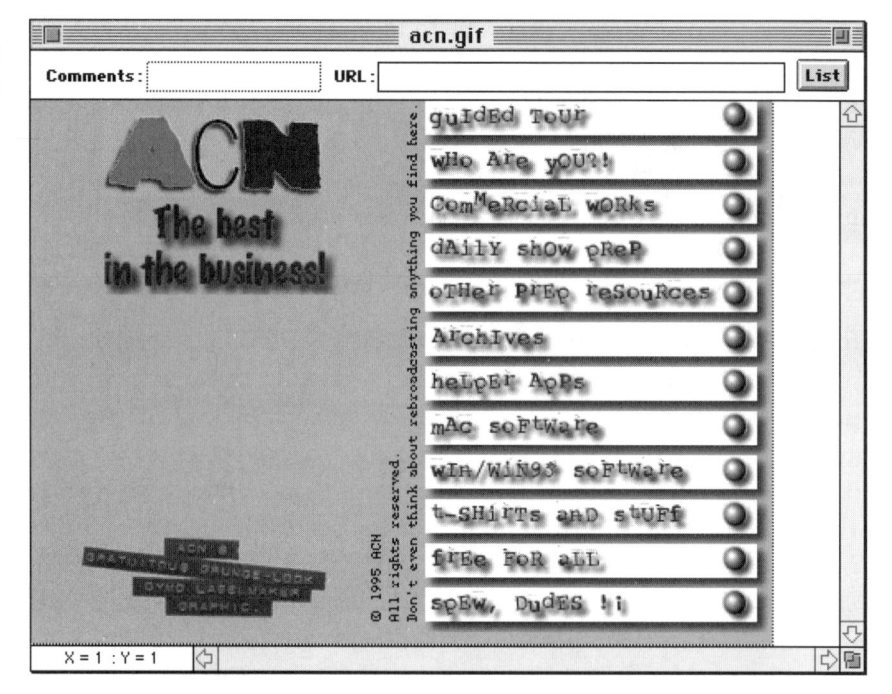

- Polygons are defined by the list of vertices that are created as you click on different points to create them. There may be many more than three vertices that define the polygon, but the last point and the first point are the same. The polygon is used to make irregular shapes live areas.

Each live area defined in an image map is then assigned to an URL. When the viewer clicks on the area, the URL associated with that area is loaded. One URL defined is called the default. This is the URL that you

Figure 7.22
The Tools palette with the Rectangle tool selected.

want to be loaded when the viewer clicks on any area that is *not* live, and usually results in a rebound to the image; the assumption is made that the viewer just missed a live area, not that the viewer wants to go to another site.

1. Using the **Tools** palette, draw a rectangle by clicking and dragging from upper left to lower right of the uppermost button (**guided tour**) on the right-hand side of the ACN graphic. Be careful to include only the white area that forms the body of the button, as shown in Figure 7.23.

Figure 7.23
Defining a live area in WebMap.

2. Once you've done this—selected your live area—type the name of the document to which you want to link in the URL box at the top of the window. In this case, we'll type `acntour.html`, as shown in Figure 7.24, since that's the wave of the file that starts ACN's guided tour.

Figure 7.24
Defining the URL.

3. Click on the **List** button to the right of the URL entry box. You'll see that the URL has been added. It is displayed in Figure 7.25.

Before we re-create the entire ACN image map, let's take a look at the code for the map document:

```
#
# Created by WebMap
# Monday, September 18, 1995 at 12:28 AM
# Format: NCSA
#

default /acn/acnhome.html

poly /acn/acndymo.html 79,254 128,256 183,277 181,290 145,305
78,304 25,270 32,259 79,254

rect /acn/acntour.html 239,0 440,20
rect /acn/acnstaff.html 239,25 441,47
```

```
rect /acn/acncomwks.html 239,51 441,73
rect /acn/acnprep.html 239,77 441,99
rect /acn/acnpaper.html 240,104 440,124
rect /acn/acnpast95.html 239,130 440,151
rect /acn/acnhelper.html 239,155 441,177
rect /acn/acnmacsw.html 240,182 441,203
rect /acn/acnwinsw.html 240,208 440,229
rect /acn/acnmall.html 240,234 440,255
rect /acn/acnfree4all.html 240,260 440,281
rect /acn/acncomments.html 240,286 439,307
rect /acn/acncright.html 205,3 236,307
```

Figure 7.25
Our list of live areas so far.

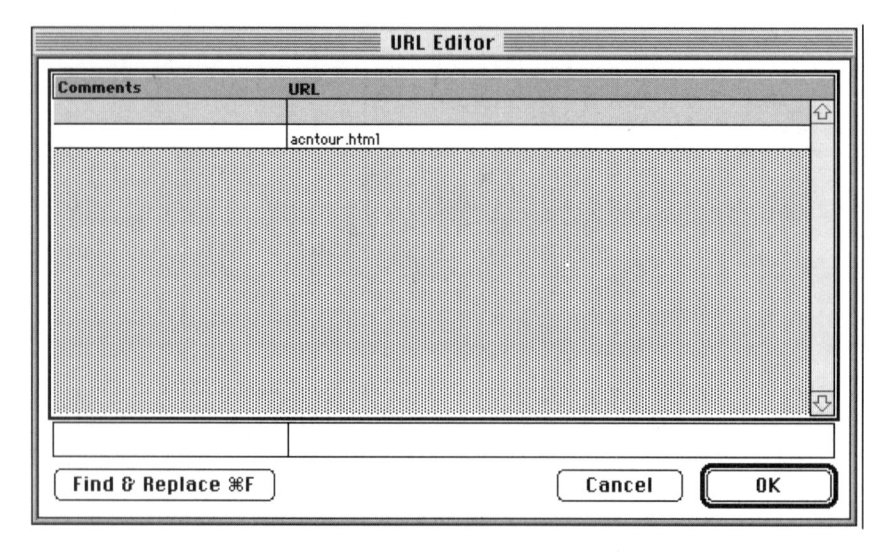

As you can see, there are live areas for each of the buttons on the right of the main ACN graphic, a live area for the label maker graphic, and one for the default URL, which brings the viewer right back to the ACN itself to try again.

Once you've defined all of your live areas, it's time to export the list into a text file choosing the NCSA or CERN format (the two main map format standards). If you don't know how to do this, contact your ISP for your server's format (almost all of them use NCSA). Then open it in BBEdit Lite. This is where you'll specify the correct path for the URLs, which depends entirely on your server. In ACN's case, the URL path is of the form:

```
/acn/[filename].html
```

because the cgi script that we used, `imagemap`, expects to see the URL of its targets begin with the home directory of the site. We placed all of our documents at the "root" level of that directory, so we started our path with /acn. Your server will most likely be different, so don't be frustrated if your map doesn't work properly the first time. You must be precise about the structure of the URLs in the Map file: the image map CGI requires specific information. Once you determine the path image map expects to see, creating new image maps is a lot easier.

Testing the Map

Unlike regular HTML code, which, for the most part, you can open on your local hard drive and test with your browser, you can't determine whether your image map will work until you load it on your server and start testing it. Believe it or not, most problems are caused by such minor mistakes as misspelling an URL or not specifying your path correctly. But through trial and error, and maybe a few calls to your ISP's tech support line, you'll nail it. Here are a few pointers:

- Remember that the map itself is a text file, and most image map CGIs require that you save the text file with UNIX line breaks. Fortunately, BBEdit Lite allows you to save your text files in just such a manner (it's an option in the Save dialog box), so make sure you do so. In fact, all of your HTML files should be saved with UNIX line breaks.
- Remember that the full path name must be specified for any external URLs to which you may be linking.
- Make sure that you choose the correct server type when you export your text file; NCSA-style coordinates differ slightly from the CERN-style coordinates, but, again, most ISPs use NCSA-style maps.

What to Do When You Can't Access CGI-BIN

If your ISP doesn't give you access to the `cgi-bin` directory (due to security issues or for other reasons), our recommendation is to try to be creative with button bars and make something similar to image maps, as we've discussed earlier. You can also take a graphic and, using Photoshop, divide it into pieces that load as individual graphics, each with its own associated anchor tag. For example, you could easily represent a tic-tac-toe board not as a 3-inch × 3-inch graphic image map, but as 9 distinct squares, 3 each in 3 successive rows, each with its own URL, to get the same effect.

Or, you can use client-side image maps.

Client-Side Image Maps

Everything about client-side image maps is the same as for server-side image maps, except that the code for the map coordinates is not kept in a separate document to be interpreted by a CGI script. Rather, it is code that exists in the Netscape 2.0 HTML document itself.

Remember, if a browser can't interpret a tag, it will usually ignore it. Therefore, you can create client-side image maps without much fear that your pages will "break" if someone browses them using something other than Netscape Navigator 2.0.

The tags that are implemented for client-side mapping for Netscape 2.0 are **<map>...</map>**, the empty tag **<area>**, and the new **usemap=** attribute for the <img> tag. Simply put, the <map>...</map> tag is the container for the list of <area> tags that define your live areas; the usemap= attribute specifies an URL that contains the <map> container for the image.

<map>...</map>

Description: Defines a list of regions that are live within a graphic for client-side image mapping.

HTML 2.0 Attributes:

name="text"   label for map

The only thing you have to worry about here is using the <map> tag to name your map. Any <area> tags that fall within the start and end <map> tags will be considered part of the same map. The name= attribute is the same as the name= attribute in the anchor tag in that if you want to place a <map> container within the same document as the <img> tag that calls it, you would define your usemap= attribute with a pound sign (#) preceding

Chapter 7 Icons, Buttons, and Image Maps   157

the map's name. For instance, `<img acnmap.gif usemap="#acnmap">`, which we'll decipher in a moment.

`<area>`

Description: Defines a live area and the URL associated with that live area within a client-side image map.

HTML 2.0 Attributes:

shape=RECT	shape is defined as a rectangle
coords=integer, integer, integer, integer	upper-left and lower-right pixel coordinates for shape, where 0,0 is the upper-left corner of the graphic
href=string	URL
nohref	defines area as having no action

The <area> tags take the place of the lines in the server-side image map file that define the live regions. The **coords=** attribute allows you to specify the shape's boundaries, and the **href=** attribute acts as the reference to the URL that is loaded when the live area is clicked. Luckily, the coordinates appear in the same order as in the NCSA server-side coordinates list. All you have to do is insert a comma between the two sets of numbers for each area you define in the <area> tag.

If you want a particular area to be "dead," say an area within an area you've already defined as live, you can use the **nohref** attribute. Don't, obviously, use both the nohref and href= attributes at the same time.

Here's how the ACN server-side image map file translates to client-side:

```
<img acnmap.gif usemap="#acnmap">
    .
    .
    .
<map name="acnmap">
<area shape="rect" href="acndymo.html" coords="79,254,145,305">
<area shape="rect" href="acntour.html" coords="239,0,440,20">
<area shape="rect" href="acnstaff.html" coords="239,25,441,47">
<area shape="rect" href="acncomwks.html" coords="239,51,441,73">
<area shape="rect" href="acnprep.html" coords="239,77 441,99">
```

```
<area shape="rect" href="acnpaper.html" coords="240,104 440,124">
<area shape="rect" href="acnpast95.html" coords="239,130 440,151">
<area shape="rect" href="acnhelper.html" coords="239,155 441,177">
<area shape="rect" href="acnmacsw.html" coords="240,182 441,203">
<area shape="rect" href="acnwinsw.html" coords="240,208 440,229">
<area shape="rect" href="acnmall.html" coords="240,234 440,255">
<area shape="rect" href="acnfree4all.html" coords="240,260 440,281">
<area shape="rect" href="acncomments.html" coords="240,286 439,307">
<area shape="rect" href="acncright.html" coords="205,3 236,307">
</map>
```

The difference between the image maps you see in Netscape 2.0 and the server-side image maps is that the URL displayed at the bottom of the screen changes as you pass over different regions of the image. With server-side image mapping, only the coordinates change as the cursor moves.

You've probably noticed that there are only "rect" shapes in our client-side example. It's not because we're lazy, it's because that's all the current client-side image map spec allows. Hopefully, the HTML 3.0 standard will include all of the shapes currently allowed by server-side image map standards.

What's Next

In the final two chapters, we learn how to create forms and tables, and how to create and serve up multimedia files such as sound and movies to your viewers. Finally, we'll tell you how to properly manage your Web site, from population (posting Internet resources on a Web site) through Web site maintenance. You're just a few short lessons away from making your Web site a reality.

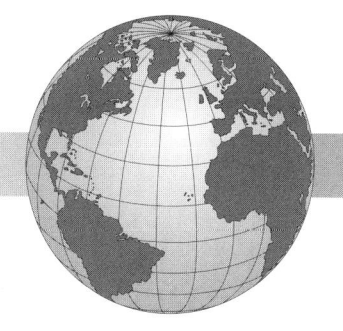

Forms and Tables

One of the many reasons the Web has captured the attention of so many—business and recreational "travelers" alike—is its remarkable flexibility. In this chapter, we're going to talk about two important ways you can stretch the capabilities of your Web pages, using forms and tables. Two-way interaction—that is, communication—is made possible through the use of forms: as an example, after viewing your Web pages, users can be presented with a form to fill out requesting more information about your product or service, which is then forwarded to you immediately. Talk about instant gratification! And happily for you, the designer, creating these forms in HTML is not difficult—the browser handles most of the tough layout work. Tables, of course, are the great organizers. Nothing is more effective for displaying a lot of important information with disparate components than tables.

Forms: The Back End

No form can be of any use unless a **forms-processing CGI script** has been placed in the `cgi-bin` directory of the computer your Web server resides on and, subsequently, unless access to that script has been given to the Web site's pages. If your ISP is using an NCSA httpd server on a Unix platform (as many are), **mailto,** a CGI script, is automatically loaded in the cgi-bin directory when the server is installed. We'll focus our attention on it in this section.

> **Important!**
> Although the name is the same, don't confuse the mailto CGI with the mailto: service prefix or protocol, which we discussed in the last chapter. The two do similar, but altogether different things. The mailto CGI takes the raw data entered on forms (which is simply hideous to look at in its raw form) and reformats this convoluted stream of characters into a clearly readable e-mail message that is sent to the e-mail address you choose. With the mailto CGI, you can ask the user to fill in specific information on a form you've developed. The user clicks on a link to activate the form.
> The mailto: protocol works with the e-mail features that are built into your browser. (Not all browsers support this protocol, but Netscape does.) You can't create a form for users to fill out using this feature; all the user can do here is to send a form-free e-mail message to the e-mail address you've designated. The mailto: protocol is also activated when the user clicks on a link. That's why it's sometimes called a mailto: link.

Querying the Server

There are two different ways you can send data to, or query, the server: the **get** method and the **post** method. Briefly, post is the preferred method because it can handle a much larger amount of data at one time, whereas queries using the get method tend to become truncated arbitrarily when they are too long.

Thus, for the purpose of this discussion, we assume that you are working on a standard NCSA httpd server on a UNIX platform, and you are going to use the post method of querying when creating forms. Hence, we'll be sending our forms data to the mailto CGI script.

The Front End: The Form Itself

Forms enable you to accomplish a variety of tasks: passively gather data on people who visit your Web site, allow people to search your Web site (or others) for information, even provide the means to sell products and services.

We'll build a sample comment form that incorporates all of the formatting options you have at your disposal. (We've included the code in the

Authoring folder as the file called form.html in case you want to use it on your site later.)

A form can appear anywhere on a Web page, and you can include more than one form on a page. Before you create a form, though, you should determine exactly the kind of information you want to gather, then categorize that information as one of these three basic forms: **free-form text, one-option,** or **multiple-option choices**. If you've ever built a File-Maker Pro database and worked with the Field Formatting menu item, you've got a jump on what we're going to learn here. HTML forms support all of the typical Mac-like interface designs for creating an information-gathering interface: popup menus, scrolling pick lists, checkboxes, radio buttons, and text input.

We'll also be adding a button to our script that enables users to send the data they've entered (this is where the mailto CGI script takes over and relays the data entered to your e-mail box). We'll also show you how to add another button that gives users the opportunity to back out, should they decide not to send any data at all. One important point here: All of the tags we'll be using must be contained within a single set of **<form> …</form>** tags. The form tags and all of the tags they contain are called the form element.

<form>…</form>

Description: Generates a form and processes data entered.

HTML 2.0 Attributes:

method=post	method of submitting data to the server via a separate stream (preferred)
get	method of submitting data to the server by appending it to an URL
action="URL"	URL for data submission and processing

Building the Form

Let's create our form. We want to give our visitors an opportunity to say hello to us, let us know what they think of the site, and make suggestions

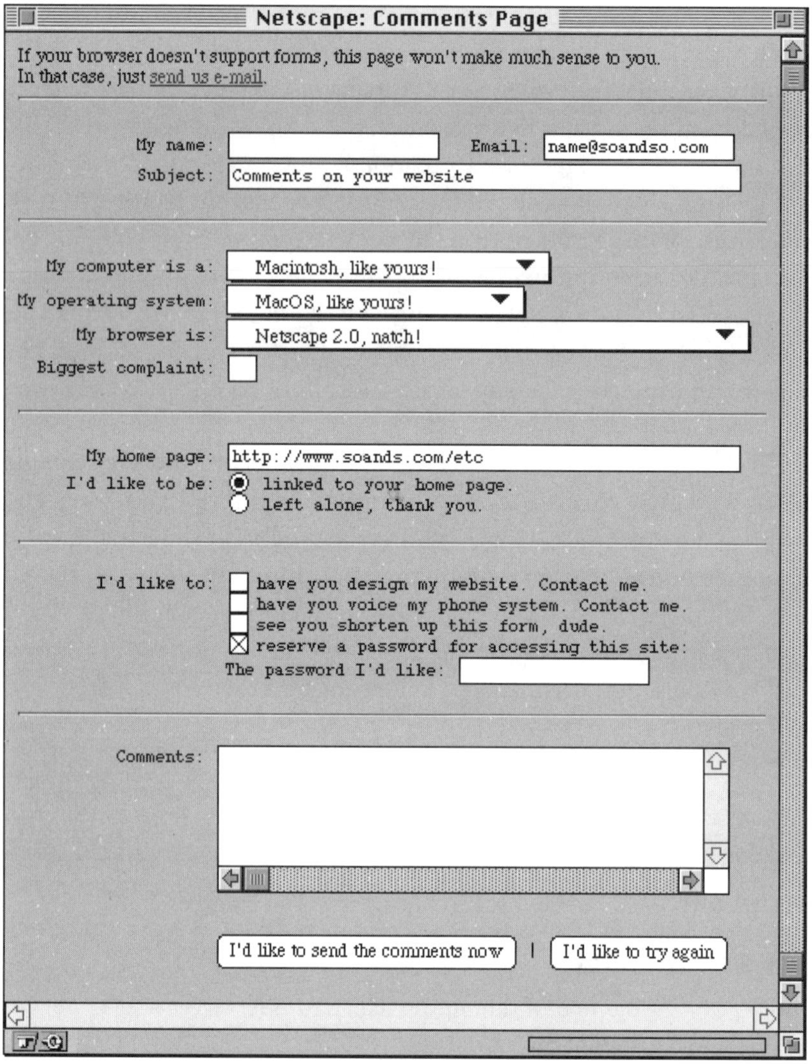

Figure 8.1
The Comments form.

for improvements. We also want to know what type of computer system they're using, along with some other info. Figure 8.1 shows you what the finished form will look like in Netscape.

Notice that we immediately take into account those viewers whose browsers don't support HTML forms. The "courtesy" line at the top of the form in Figure 8.1 ("send us e-mail") gives those viewers a link using the mailto: link so that they can send a free-form mail message to the

Webmaster. We've added a horizontal rule to separate it from the actual form.

Again, note that the mailto: protocol is in no way related to the mailto CGI script, so don't get them confused.

> A frequently asked question is whether it's possible to put a preselected string in the Subject: line on the empty e-mail screen that your browser puts up when a mailto: link is clicked. The short answer is no. However, this is such a popular request that the HTML 3.0 committee may address it by adding both subject= and body= attributes to the <anchor> tag so that you can put a string in both those fields. This would preclude the frustrating experience of receiving e-mail from someone who was perusing a specialized page in your site, and that message simply saying "Yes, send me info" when you have no clue as to what info the viewer wants.

The next set of lines in Figure 8.1 begins the actual form. Here's the HTML source:

```
<form method=POST action="http://www.your.com/cgi-bin/mailto">
```

The <form> opening tag sets two important options:

- The **method=** attribute specifies the method by which the data from the filled-out form will be submitted to the server. (Remember, we recommend always using post instead of get).
- The **action=** attribute identifies the URL of the CGI script that will process this data. You must use a fully formed—absolute—URL (no relative links here), and specify the exact path to the mailto CGI script in the `cgi-bin` directory. If you don't specify a value for the action= attribute, the server will assume you want the data sent to the document itself. You don't want that; you want to send it to the CGI script.

Just Your Name, Rank, and Serial Number, Please   The next lines of HTML introduce the heart of the form, which is made up mostly of a series of **<input>** tags. Here are the first lines of the source for the form in Figure 8.1.

```
<input type="hidden" name="followup-page"
value="http://www.your.com/~Webmaster/thanks.html">
<input type="hidden" name="recip" value="Webmaster@your.com">
<pre>          My name: <input name="name" size=20
value="">    Email: <input name="email" size=18
value="name@soandso.com">
```

<input>

Description: Displays an input field of various types in the browser window. Used only inside of the form element.

HTML 2.0 Attributes:

type=	checkbox	field that appears as single-toggle checkbox (on/off); users can select multiple checkboxes from the same list
	password	data entered by user in this field appears on screen as bullets or asterisks to hide value
	radio	field that appears as single-toggle radio button (on/off); users can select only one radio button from same list
	reset	specifies the field as a reset button; clears all entered data in form when clicked on
	submit	specifies field as button that submits form when clicked on
	text	specifies field as text entry
checked		preselects a checkbox or radio button
name=text		user-assigned variable name for a field, passed to URL specified in <form>
size=integer		width in characters of text entry field
value="text"		specifies preassigned value to contents of item, or label for reset/submit buttons; used only for text, password, and range types

HTML 3.0 Attributes:

type=	file	permits user to attach files to a form and submit it to the server
	hidden	field that hides data from the user and is not accessible by him/her; however, data in this field is passed to the URL specified in <form>

<input> (continued)

image	field that shows an image, which, when clicked on, submits the form; requires src= attribute
range	field that permits users to enter an integer in range specified by min and max attributes
scribble	field that diplays an image that a user can draw upon by clicking the mouse
accept="text"	a list of types of files that the file attribute will permit to be sent
align=	specifies alignment characteristics for images used by image, reset, scribble and submit values for type=; values for align= are left, right, top, middle, and bottom
disabled	indicates that a field is not accessible by user
error="text"	error message that indicates that the wrong data was entered into a field by user
max=integer	maximum value for the range value for type= attribute
maxlength=integer	maximum number of characters in text field
min=integer	minimum value for the range value for type= attribute
src="url"	URL of image for type=image attribute
id="text"	name and id for Web page elements
lang=text	language used by intended audience for a Web page
class=text	indicates types or classes of element in a Web page
md="text"	verification checksum string

Wow! Just to get some information into a form?

Let's take this tag one bit at a time. The <input> tag is a workhorse and its versatility requires the huge number of attributes you see above. Taken slowly and carefully, <input>'s different options will begin to make much more sense.

The <input> tags in a form act as the information entry points. We can create all kinds of options for the user by selecting the appropriate type of <input> tag to use for each question on the form. If we want text input, like the viewer's name or e-mail address, we can specify that a text box be displayed. If we want the viewer to make a choice from a list that we've created, we can specify radio buttons, checkboxes, and more. We can even specify a special text box that will hide what the user is typing in on a form by displaying bullets rather than the actual text (if you've ever entered a password on your Mac you have a good idea of what that looks like).

A closer look at the <input> tag's attributes and their possible values will allow you to make sense of <input>'s power.

First the **name=** attribute. For every <input> tag you use to get information from the user, the name= attribute allows you to assign a short, descriptive variable name to the information itself. As an obvious example, you will want to assign a name like "email" to what someone would enter as their e-mail address, or "homepage" to the URL of their Web site. The name= attribute is then used to organize the information so that the mailto CGI program can send you a neat, readable version of what the viewer entered in your form.

You can pick just about any value you want for your different name= attributes, except for two reversed values that the mailto CGI needs: "follow-up page," which is the page that is displayed in the browser to let users know that their information has been successfully sent, and "recip," which is the e-mail address to which you want mailto to send the finished product. We've included, as the first two lines of our form, these two prerequisite <input> tags.

We'll look at the size= attribute in a moment.

The **type=** attribute of the <input> tag is used to specify what kind of input field the browser will display (text box, checkbox, radio button, etc.) for that particular <input> tag.

In the first two lines of the form in our example, we've set the type= attribute to the special value of "hidden," because although the mailto CGI script expects those two pieces of information (i.e., the name and the value) you don't need to show them to the viewer, nor do you want the viewer to change them. (Don't assume, however, that this means that people can't find out those values, should they so desire. All they would have to do is view the HTML source in any browser and they'll see the values you put there.)

The next line of the HTML for our form (Figure 8.1), beginning with the <pre> tag, invokes preformatted text and displays it in a monospaced font, which will help us to line everything up. Since any text within the

<pre>...</pre> element is displayed literally in the browser, and we want the form to start directly after the horizontal rule, we'll keep the HTML for our first <input> tag on the same line and enter the first input field, whose name= attribute's value is "name." Don't get confused; this <input> tag is the text field where the user enters his or her name.

The **size=** attribute's value tells the browser how many characters wide to make the input field; in this case, we've indicated a 20-character wide field. And finally, the **value=** attribute is left empty. When there is a text string within the quotes (as there will be in some of our other fields), it is displayed when the form is viewed in Netscape as a default. If it's not altered, it's sent along with the rest of the data as the value of the input field. If we wanted to be more specific for the user, we could have specified a value for the value= attribute of "Please type your full name here" or words to that effect. (The next <input> tag, the e-mail field, has a default that gives viewers a clue as to how to format the text they type into this field. More on that in a moment.)

If we were to stop right here, close this with a </form> tag and have only one input field, we could submit the one piece of data by hitting the Return or Enter key in the text field. No submission button would be necessary since the server assumes you're done when you hit one of those keys. But we have a lot more to do and a lot more information we want to present.

We've already talked about the e-mail text field, and other than having a value for the value= attribute, its <input> tag has pretty much the same form as the name field. Figure 8.2 shows what our form looks like so far.

Let's add a Subject line to give the user a place to type a topic in the form. Adding this line of code:

```
Subject: <input name="subj" size=50 value="Comments on your
Website"><p>
<hr>
```

Figure 8.2
The beginning of our form.

Figure 8.3
The form's top segment.

[Screenshot: Netscape: Comments Page window showing "If your browser doesn't support forms, this page won't make much sense to you. In that case, just send us e-mail." with fields for My name, Email (name@soandso.com), and Subject (Comments on your website).]

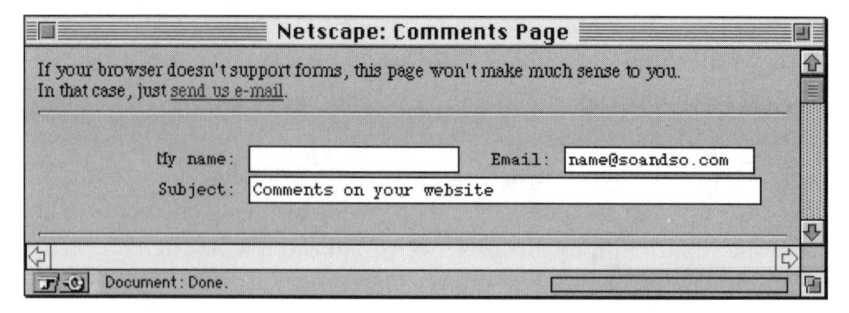

with the appropriate number of blank spaces preceding the text to line up this text entry field with the first two puts the finishing touch on the first segment of the form. In Figure 8.3, you can see that the subject's value= text string appears when browsed, just like the e-mail text field's does. Notice the value of the value= attribute. Guess what: It's been our experience that although viewers always change their e-mail address, most users never change that text. To wrap up this section of the form we can add an <hr> tag (<pre> handles this nicely, displaying the horizontal rule, then going back to the monospaced Courier as its display font).

What's Your System? The next section of the table is where we want to ask our users about their computer equipment. Rather than making this an open-ended inquiry that would probably result in inconsistent responses, we'll offer them choices in each category, all easily accessible from a familiar format: drop-down menus. To achieve this, we'll need two more tags: the **<select>...</select>** element and the **<option>** tags within it.

<select>...</select>

Description: Presents the user with a list (either drop-down menu or a scrollable list) from which to choose an <option>.

HTML 2.0 Attributes:

name="text"   user-assigned variable name, passed to URL specified in <form>

size=integer   displays the selections as a list; the value specifies the number of selections displayed in the list window. In most browsers, if the size is given, the list is scrollable. Otherwise, the list is a drop-down menu.

<select> (continued)

multiple	enables the user to select more than one item from a list

HTML 3.0 Attributes:

disabled	indicates that menu is not accessible by user
error="text"	error message that indicates the user selected an incorrect menu selection
src="url"	URL of image to be displayed instead of a menu or list; users click on areas of image (hot zones, defined by defined by shape attribute of option element) to make selections
align=	specifies left, right, top, middle, or bottom alignment of image specified by src= attribute
height=integer	height of image specified by src= attribute
width=integer	width of image specified by src= attribute
units=text	specifies the units (possible values are pixel and en) of height and width attributes; pixels is default
id="text"	name and id for Web page elements
lang=text	language used by intended audience for a Web page
class=text	indicates types or classes of element in a Web page
md="text"	verification checksum string

<option>

Description: Represents choices for the user on menus specified in the <select> element. Only found within the <select> element.

HTML 2.0 Attributes:

selected	denotes this choice is to be displayed by default when the menu is rendered by the browser
value="text"	actual words associated with selection
shape="text"	specifies an area (hot zone) within the image specified by the src= attribute in the <select> element that is to be used in place of a menu; may have the following values:

<option> (continued)

"default"	default menu selection
"circle x, y, radius"	specifies a circle hot zone; center is x, y (in pixels or as scale of 0.0 to 0.1 across and down the image) and the radius is in pixels
"rect x, y, width, height"	specifies a rectangular hot zone; upper left corner is x, y (in pixels or as scale of 0.0 to 0.1 across and down the image) and width and height indicates size in pixels
"polygon: x1, y1..., xn, yn"	specifies a polygon-shaped hot-zone, with n sides; each x, y pair is a point connected to the next x, y pair, with xn, yn connecting back to x1, y1 y (x, y are given in pixels or as scale of 0.0 to 0.1 across and down the image)

HTML 3.0 Attributes:

disabled	indicates that menu is not accessible by user
error="text"	error message that indicates user selected an incorrect menu selection
id="text"	name and id for Web page elements
lang=text	language used by intended audience for a Web page
class=text	indicates types or classes of element in a Web page
md="text"	verification checksum string

The <select> tag is mainly for drop-down menus, although there is an alternative we will show you in a moment. Every <select> tag includes one or more <options> from which the user may choose and any one of those set options may be preselected for the user.

```
My computer is a: <select name="computer">
<option selected>Macintosh, like yours!
<option>Intel PC
<option>UNIX Box
<option>piece of garbage
```

```
       </select>
My operating system: <select name="operating_system">
   <option selected>MacOS, like yours!
<option>Windows
<option>DOS
<option>some flavor of UNIX
<option>bites, big time.
</select>
    My browser is: <select name="browser">
  <option selected>Netscape 2.0, natch!
<option>AOL
<option>Compuserve
<option>Prodigy
<option>Mosaic
<option>TCP Connect II
<option>Arena
<option>Lynx
<option>prone to bombing when I least expect it
</select>
  Biggest complaint: <input name="complaint" size=2 value="">

<hr>
```

In the HTML above, users are presented with three drop-down menus, from which they may choose one and only one of a number of different computer types, operating systems, and browsers. We've also designed a very tiny text entry box in which the user can complain (two characters is enough for anyone's complaint, don't you think?).

All three of the computer system questions have preselected options (using <option selected>) whose text will immediately be displayed to the user. If you don't assign a selected attribute to any of your options, the browser will display the first option you list within your <select> ...</select> element. The user is free to change this pre-school option, but whatever the user chooses after perusing those menus, just before submitting the data, will be the final values sent to the server. You can see the result in Figure 8.4.

If you assign a value to the size= attribute of the <select> tag, Netscape renders the field as a scrollable list rather than a drop-down menu, as shown in Figure 8.5. The number or value for the size= attribute will determine how many lines of data the browser will display in the list.

When the **multiple** attribute is present in the <select> tag, then the user can select more than one item in the list by using the Shift key when clicking on selections. Be warned, though: while the multiple attribute is supported in Netscape, not all browsers support it.

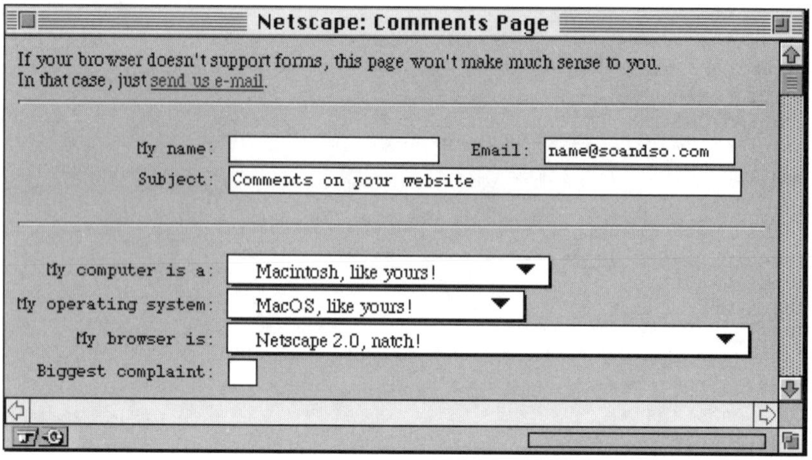

Figure 8.4
Using drop-down menus in forms.

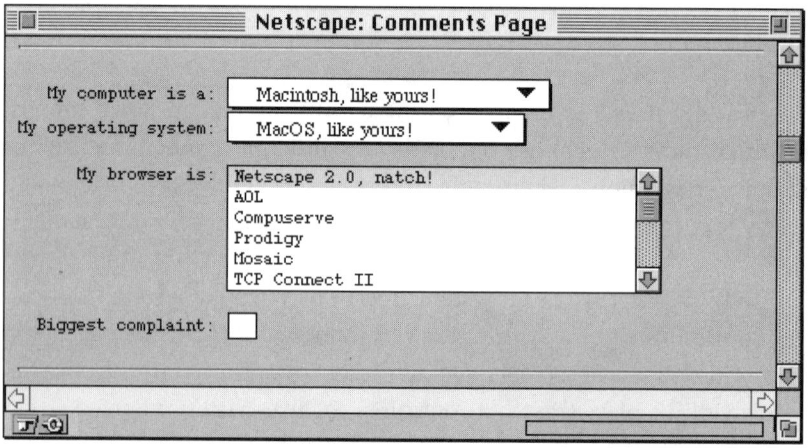

Figure 8.5
A form picklist.

Let's Link Up The next section of the HTML for our form introduces two more attributes for the <input> tag: **radio buttons,** which are used to limit the user to one choice from a given set of options; and **checkboxes,** which allow users to choose more than one option at a time from a given set of options. The following HTML shows how we've used them in our example:

```
My home page: <input name="home_page_url" size=50
value="http://www.soands.com/etc">
     I'd like to be: <input name="link" type=radio
value="link the URL" checked> linked to your home page.
               <input name="link" type=radio
```

```
value="don't link the URL"> left alone, thank you.

<hr>
        I'd like to: <input name="design_my_website" type=checkbox>
have you design my website. Contact me.
                   <input name="voice_my_phone_system"
type=checkbox>have you voice my phone system. Contact me.
                   <input name="shorten_this_form" type=checkbox>
see you shorten up this form, dude.
                   <input name="get_a_password"
type=checkbox checked>reserve a password for accessing this
site:
                   The password I'd like: <input
name="password_requested" type=password size=18 value="">

<hr>
```

Figure 8.6 provides the Netscape rendering.

As you can see in the first section, we've given users the opportunity to link their home page to ours. All they have to do is click on the radio button indicating their choice and enter the URL of their home page. We've prechecked (set as the default) the positive response ("I'd like to be: linked to your home page.") using the valueless checked attribute, but of course, users are free to change that when they fill out the form. The important thing to note with radio buttons is that they can only choose one or the other…not both.

In contrast, in the next section, by using checkboxes, users can request information on one *or more* services that we offer. In this case, we've prechecked the option to reserve a password. This is followed by a box in which users can type their passwords. In our case, we want users to enter

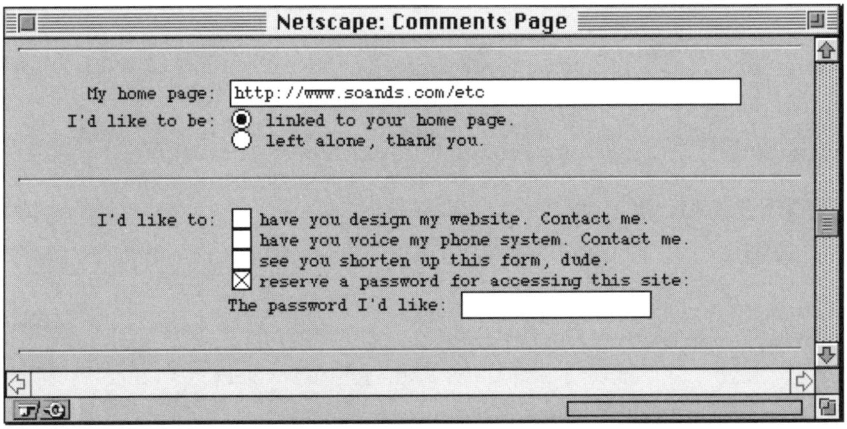

Figure 8.6
Radio buttons and checkboxes used in a form.

a password that they'd prefer to use should this page ever become password-protected. The line of code that produces this introduces a new type= value: **password**. This <input> tag presents the user with a typical text entry box, but whose display is not typical; instead of displaying exactly what has been typed by the user, the user sees either bullets (••••••••) or asterisks (********) depending on the browser they are using. This is, of course, to protect password confidentiality. (The type=password value has other uses than for passwords—imagine the fun children might have at a Web site that lets them pass secret messages back and forth with their friends.)

> **By the Way…** In the proposed HTML 3.0 standard, you'll be able to specify the character you want echoed back in the password text box using the new **dingbat=** attribute.

Tell Us What You Really Think The final section of the form, shown in Figure 8.7, gives users the opportunity to type a lengthy comment. We accomplish this with the **<textarea>…</textarea>** tag pair.

<textarea>…</textarea>

Description: Allows the user to enter a multiline text block.

HTML 2.0 Attributes:

name="text"	user-assigned variable name, passed to the URL specified in <form>
value="text"	specifies this preassigned value to contents of text box
rows=integer	number rows in the text box
cols=integer	number of columns (characters) of the text box

HTML 3.0 Attributes:

align=text	specifies left, right, top, middle, or bottom alignment of text box
disabled	indicates that menu is not accessible by user
error="text"	error message that indicates user selected an incorrect menu selection

<textarea> (continued)	
id="text"	name and id for Web page elements
lang=text	language used by intended audience for a Web page
class=text	indicates types or classes of element in a Web page

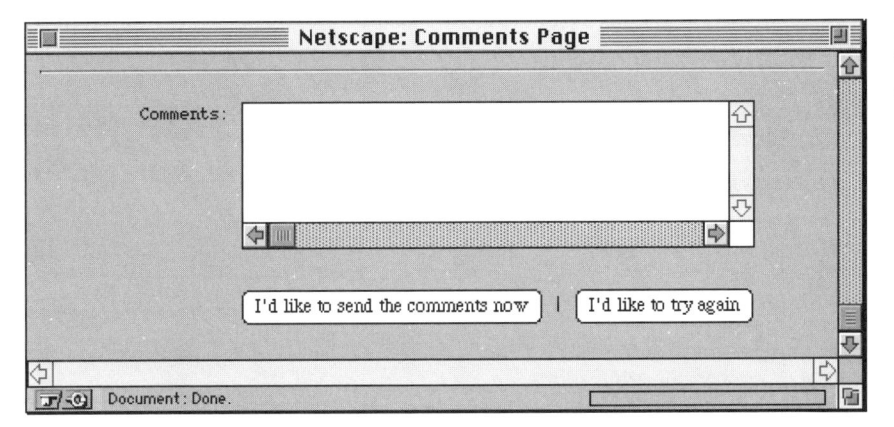

Figure 8.7
Giving the user room to "talk."

By specifying the height in number of rows or lines, and the width in columns or characters, we have provided ample space in which the user can add any final thoughts before sending the completed form to us. We also could have placed our own default commentary in this text box using the value= attribute.

The comment buttons underneath the Comments: box were created using <input> tags and two special type= values listed in the <input> tag table: **submit** and **reset**. And by incorporating a string of text as the value of the value= attribute, we can attach any label we want to the buttons. Submit and Reset are the default labels... if you want to use those, then you don't need any value= attributes at all.

> You can also use images as submit and reset buttons. For example:
> `<INPUT TYPE="image" SRC="/submit.gif" NAME="submit">`
> `<INPUT TYPE="image" SRC="/reset.gif" NAME="reset">`

By the Way...

If the user clicks on the Reset button, all data entered will be cleared from the form, and the user can then start over. Place this button on the form with care and clearly label it as a reset feature. Especially in long forms, a well-crafted set of data can be erased by a careless click of the mouse on the reset button by the user.

If the user clicks on the Submit button, the data in all the input fields, along with the name of the variable assigned to each field, is sent to the URL specified in the action= attribute in the opening <form> tag. Here's a typical e-mail message generated by the mailto CGI script and sent to the Webmaster's mailbox:

```
Date: Tue, 05 Mar 1996 18:13:40 -0500
From: jdoe@her.com (Jane Doe)
To: Webmaster@your.com
Subject: Comments on your Website

----------------------------------------
followup-page: http://www.your.com/~Webmaster/thanks.html
recip: Webmaster@your.com
name: Jane Doe
email: user@her.com
subj: Comments on your Website
computer: Macintosh, like yours!
os: MacOS, like yours!
browser: Netscape, natch!
complaint: :: laughing ::
home: http://www.her.com/~jdoe/
link: link the URL
design_my_website: on
shorten_this_form: on
get_a_password: on
password_requested: madison4eliza1
----------------------------------------

I think this is a great example of
foresight and planning. Please contact
me at your earliest convenience, either
by e-mail or at (301) 555-1212 x1234 to
discuss your Web design services.
```

As you can see, the mailto CGI script took all of the data fields and paired up the name of the field with any value the user typed in or selected (you don't want to see how it looked before mailto got hold of it—it's frightening). Now the data is yours to do what you will with it.

Notice that the user in the "I'd like to be:" list has clicked on the "linked to your home page" radio button (this is indicated by "link: link the URL" line in the e-mail message). By clicking on the radio button, the user has toggled it to "on." The other radio button, "left alone, thank you," was not selected by the user and does not appear in the e-mail message. The radio button remains in the "off" position.

The user has also clicked on three checkboxes for the "I'd like to:" list:

1. "have you design my website. Contact me." (design_my_website)
2. "see you shorten up this form, dude" (shorten_this_form)
3. "reserve a password for accessing this site" (get_a_password)

This selection is indicated by the word "on" after each checkbox selection in this e-mail. The user has toggled these checkboxes to "on" by clicking on them. The checkboxes not selected remain "off" and do not appear in this e-mail.

One final page we need to create before our forms work is complete is the follow-up page specified in the first hidden <input> line of HTML in our forms page. (Remember this line: <input type="hidden" name="followup-page" value="http://www.your.com/~Webmaster/thanks.html">?) This follow-up page will be simply a line of text that thanks users for filling out our form and assuring them that we received it. We'll provide links to return users to the rest of our Web site. Here is the HTML:

```
<html>
<head>
<title>thanks!</title>
</head>
<body>
<h3>Thank you!</h3>
<p>Your information has been sent to us.</p>
<a href="index.html"> spiderworks home page </a>
</body>
</html>
```

Tables

When you need to present columnar information or information that is best presented in a spreadsheet manner, tables are for you. Most browsers, including Netscape, support tables, although some do not. You may want to consider also providing a text-only page with the data you wish to put in your table. As in a spreadsheet, each compartment of a table is called a **cell**, and anything can appear in a cell: text, pictures, links, even a form like the one we just created. Perhaps there is no more famous table than the Periodic Table of the Elements, and you can see a version of it rendered in

Figure 8.8
The Periodic Table.

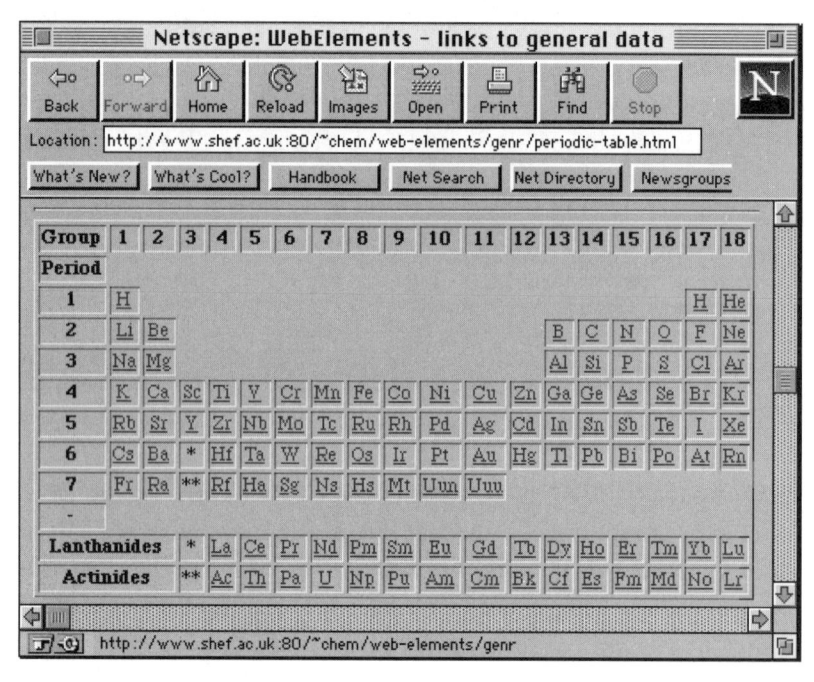

[Screenshot of Netscape browser showing "WebElements - links to general data" page at http://www.shef.ac.uk:80/~chem/web-elements/genr/periodic-table.html, displaying the periodic table of elements arranged by Group (1-18) and Period (1-7), with Lanthanides and Actinides rows at the bottom.]

Netscape in Figure 8.8. Rest easy, though, we're not going to explain how to construct tables for use in your Web pages with that monstrosity as our starting point; we'll start with something much less complex.

Tagging Tables

Before we actually begin crafting a table, we'll introduce you to the tags that we have to incorporate into our code when working with tables. The first is called—surprise!—**<table>…</table>**. This tag was introduced by Netscape and made part of the proposed HTML 3.0 standard.

<table>…</table>

Description: Creates a table with rows and columns; data appears in individual cells

Netscape 2.0 Attributes:

border=integer   width of border around cells in pixels; if no value is specified for border, a default border is drawn.

\<table\> (continued)

cellpadding=integer	the space in pixels around the contents of the cell
cellspacing=integer	the space in pixels between cells
width=integer	width of table in pixels or as percentage of displayed page within which the table will be rendered

HTML 3.0 Attributes:

align=	specifies alignment characteristics for table; values for align= are bleedleft, bleedright, left, right, and center
colspec="text"	specifies how columns in table will be aligned; values for text are a space-separated list of alignment types (l for left; r for right; c for center; j for justified; d for alignment of by decimal characters, as specified by dp=attribute) followed by width in units for each column
dp="text"	specifies the decimal point character when the "d" value is used in the colspec= attribute; the default is a period
noflow	specifies that text following table will be displayed below table, rather than to right or left of the table
width=integer	width of table in units (differs from Netscape attribute in use of units attribute)
units="text"	the type of units that colspec and HTML 3.0 width will be given in; values include en (one-half of current point size of current font); relative (fractions of display table for width and of the table width for colspec; and pixels
id="text"	name and id for Web page elements
lang=text	language used by intended audience for a Web page
class=text	indicates types or classes of element in a Web page
clear=text	specifies at what point in the margin that text will flow around an image or figure
nowrap	prevents browser from automatically wrapping text

The <table> tag pair can be regarded as a sort of wrapper that encloses all of the HTML that defines a table. You can, as with forms, have as many tables within a page as you want. Unlike forms, though, you can even place a table within another table.

The **<th>** tag pair is where we enclose table headers and column and row titles. Table headers can appear over a single column, alongside a single row, or across several of either.

<th>...</th>

Description: Displays table headers.

Netscape 2.0 Attributes:

align=text	aligns table headers horizontally for row; values are left, right, and center
valign=text	aligns contents in cell horizontally for row; values are top, bottom (default), and middle of current cell, and baseline for first line of text
width=integer	width of cell in pixels or as percentage of table width within which the cell will be displayed

HTML 3.0 Attributes:

align=text	aligns table headers horizontally in cell for row; values are left, right, center, justify, and decimal (this requires the dp= attribute)
dp="text"	specifies the decimal point character when the "d" value is used in the align= attribute; the default is a period
colspan=integer	number of columns the header will span; default is one
rowspan=integer	number of rows the header will span
id="text"	name and id for Web page elements
lang=text	language used by intended audience for a Web page
class=text	indicates types or classes of element in a Web page
nowrap	prevents browser from automatically wrapping text

You may have noticed that the align= attribute appears under both Netscape 2.0 and the proposed standard for HTML 3.0. While many browsers support the Netscape version of the <table> elements, only Arena, unavailable for the Macintosh at the time of this book was written, supports the proposed HTML 3.0 standard fully. Thus, some of the values specifed for align= in HTML 3.0 won't work in most browsers.

Table rows are defined using the **<tr>** tag pair, which is the essential building block of tables.

<tr>...</tr>

Description: Creates rows in a table.

Netscape 2.0 Attributes:

align=text	aligns data in cells horizontally for row; values are left, right, and center
valign=text	aligns data in cells vertically for row; values are top, bottom (default), and middle of current cell, and baseline for first line of text in each cell
width=integer	width of cell in pixels or percentage of table width within which the cell will be displayed

HTML 3.0 Attributes:

align=text	aligns table rows; values are left, right, center, justify, and decimal (this requires the dp= attribute)
dp="text"	specifies the decimal point character when the "d" value is used in the align= attribute; the default is a period
id="text"	name and id for Web page elements
lang=text	language used by intended audience for a Web page
class=text	indicates types or classes of element in a Web page
nowrap	prevents browser from automatically wrapping text

The **<td>** (for **table data**) tag pair is very important in the construction of tables, because between its opening and closing tags is the cell content.

Within a table, the <td> tags can have different attributes; think of cells of tables as being independent HTML entities, plain here, bold there, centered over there, an image here. You define the number of columns in a table by the number of <td> tags you use in a row. For instance, if you use seven <td> pairs of tags within each <tr>...</tr> element, you will have seven columns.

<td>...</td>

Description: Delimits the content of each cell in a table.

Netscape 2.0 Attributes:

align=text	aligns data in cell horizontally; values are left; right, and center. Left is default.
valign=text	aligns data in cell vertically; values are top, bottom (default), and middle of current cell, and baseline for first line of text in each cell

HTML 3.0 Attributes:

align=text	aligns data in cell horizontally; values are left, right, center, justify, and decimal (this requires the dp= attribute); default is center
dp="text"	specifies the decimal point character when the "d" value is used in the align= attribute; the default is a period
colspan=integer	number of columns the cell will span; default is one
rowspan=integer	number of rows cell will span
id="text"	name and id for Web page elements
lang=text	language used by intended audience for a Web page
class=text	indicates types or classes of element in a Web page
nowrap	prevents browser from automatically wrapping text

Finally, there's the **<caption>** tag pair, which should be self-explanatory. The caption acts as the title, description, or identifier for the table.

`<caption>...</caption>`

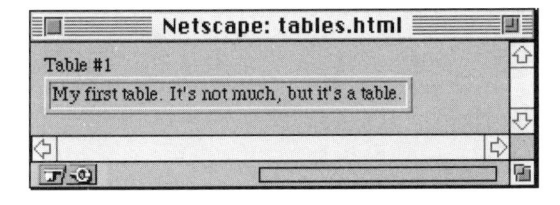

Description: Displays contained text as a legend for the table or figure. Appears only in <table> and <fig> elements.

Netscape 2.0 Attributes:

align=text   aligns caption; values are top and bottom

Building Tables

We're going to build our first table gradually, but eventually, we'll "decorate" it with a border and a caption; we'll pad the space around the contents of a cell to make it easier to read, and we'll add other cells that span multiple rows and columns for a more interesting look. But let's not run before we can walk. Here's the HTML for our first table:

```
Table #1
<table border>
<tr>
<td>My first table. It's not much, but it's a table.</td>
</tr>
</table>
```

Figure 8.9 shows how it looks in Netscape. It's a simple one-cell table. As you can see, Netscape rendered the cell just large enough to encompass the text we included in our HTML. Notice the border attribute in the <table> tag: It tells Netscape we want a border around our cells.

Figure 8.9
A basic single-cell table.

Let's try something a little tougher: a simple 2 × 2 matrix. Here's the HTML, followed by the Netscape view in Figure 8.10.

```
Table #2
<table border>
   <tr>
     <td>Upper left</td> <td>Upper right</td>
   </tr>
   <tr>
     <td>Lower left</td> <td>Lower Right</td>
   </tr>
</table>
```

Figure 8.10 Adding rows and columns.

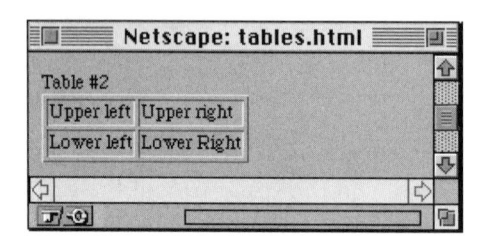

Now we have two rows and two cells in each row, as defined by the <td> tags within each <tr> element. At least it's starting to look more like a table. Let's add some headers. In the first row of this table, we'll specify horizontal headers; they get a table row (<tr>...</tr>) all to themselves. The HTML follows, and the Netscape view is in Figure 8.11.

```
Table #3
<table border>
   <tr>
     <th>Computer</th> <th>OS</th>
   </tr>
   <tr>
     <td>Macintosh</td> <td>MacOS</td>
   </tr>
   <tr>
     <td>Intel-based PC</td> <td>Windows</td>
   </tr>
</table>
```

Figure 8.11 Using horizontal headers.

In Netscape, table headers are automatically rendered as bold, centered type, delineating them from the actual data contained in the table.

Now let's show these headers vertically. Rather than giving the headers their own table row, tuck them before the first cell in each row. Figure 8.12 shows the results.

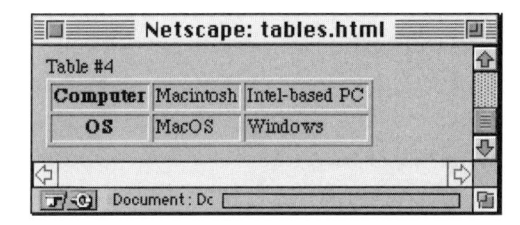

```
Table #4
<table border>
        <tr><th>Computer</th>
            <td>Macintosh</td> <td>Intel-based PC</td></tr>
        <tr><th>OS</th>
            <td>MacOS</td> <td>Windows</td></tr>
</table>
```

Figure 8.12
Using vertical headers.

Headers can also span ranges of cells. Adding the **colspan=** attribute accomplishes this, as shown in this HTML and in Netscape in Figure 8.13.

```
Table #5
<table border>
   <tr>
     <th colspan=2>Macintosh</th>
       <th colspan=2>Power Macintosh</th>
   </tr>
   <tr>
     <td>Quadra 660</td> <td>Quadra 660</td> <td>Power
Macintosh 7500</td> <td>Power Macintosh 7500</td>
   </tr>
   <tr>
     <td>Performa 450</td> <td>PowerBook 540c</td>
<td>Performa 6200CD</td> <td>PowerBook 5300cs</td>
   </tr>
</table>
```

In this figure, you can see that two columns are included under each of the headers, and, again, the browser renders the table beautifully to just the size we need to display all of the text we have in each cell.

Figure 8.13
Headers spanning more than one column.

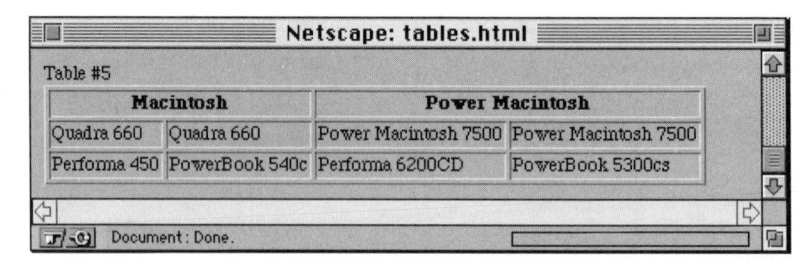

Let's create a more useful table incorporating all the tags we've learned so far. Let's say we wanted to compare chocolates on two different criteria: texture and creaminess. In chocolate manufacturing, the butterfat content of the chocolate is described on a scale called "creaminess"—the more butterfat, the better. Texture is described as being between dense and brittle, with commercial chocolate manufacturers often adding a waxy thickener to a cheaper, brittle product to provide a modicum of protection against breakage during shipment. What does this have to do with HTML, you may ask. Only that it'll help you understand the table we've concocted in Figure 8.14. And it may help to explain why we (and maybe you also) prefer Godiva chocolate over Hershey's (although Hershey's chocolate is better than nothing).

Here's the code for our first example with this new content. The Netscape rendering follows in Figure 8.14.

```
Table #6
<table border>
	<tr>
	<td>
	<th rowspan=2></th>
	<th colspan=2>Taster's Criteria</th>
	</td>
	</tr>

	<tr>
	<td><th>Texture</th><th>Creaminess</th></td>
	</tr>

	<tr>
	<th rowspan=2>Brands Tasted</th>
	<th>Hershey's</th>
	<td>slightly waxy</td><td>milky</td>
	</tr>

	<tr>
	<th>Godiva</th>
	<td>dense</td><td>buttery</td>
	</tr>
</table>
```

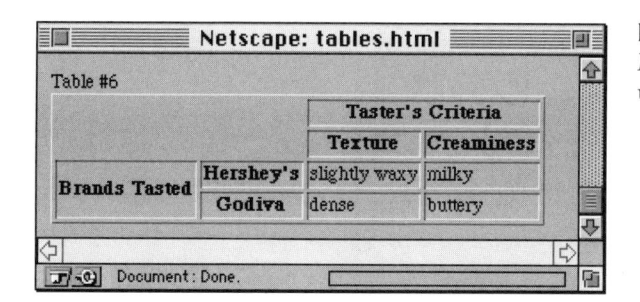

Figure 8.14
More complex use of headers.

Notice in the code that the "empty" table header tag (<th rowspan=2></th>) resulted in unfilled space in the table. Also notice that the headers are automatically centered, and that data cells are automatically left-aligned because these are the defaults in Netscape.

Borders and Cell Enhancements

Before we demonstrate how to implement borders and cell enhancements, first refer back to Table #2 (Figure 8.10), where we had just added two rows and two columns. Here we're going to use the same data, but incorporate the **cellspacing=, border=,** and **cellpadding=** attributes.

First change the border to 8 pixels as shown in the HTML for Table 7. Because Netscape adds shadowing to cell borders, it has three-dimensionality, like a picture frame, as you can see in Figure 8.15. Notice that only the border surrounding the outside of the table is affected, not the inner borders of the cells themselves.

```
Table #7
<table border=8>
   <tr>
      <td>Upper left</td> <td>Upper right</td>
   </tr>
   <tr>
      <td>Lower left</td> <td>Lower Right</td>
   </tr>
</table>
```

Figure 8.15
Altering the table's border attributes.

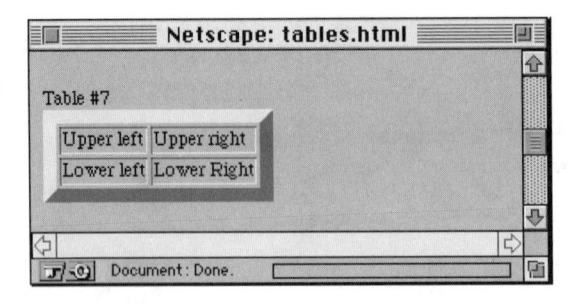

Next let's see the effect of setting the border back to the default, but altering the space between cells. We'll use the cellspacing= attribute for that. The following HTML shows how it should be typed.

```
Table #8
<table border cellspacing=8>
   <tr>
     <td>Upper left</td> <td>Upper right</td>
   </tr>
   <tr>
     <td>Lower left</td> <td>Lower Right</td>
   </tr>
</table>
```

Figure 8.16
The effects of cellspacing.

In the Netscape rendering in Figure 8.16, you can see the difference caused by using the cellspacing attribute. We can also change the spacing within the cell *around* the contents of the cell with the cellpadding= attribute. Here's the HTML, followed by the Netscape view in Figure 8.17.

```
Table #9
<table border cellpadding=8>
   <tr>
     <td>Upper left</td> <td>Upper right</td>
```

```
    </tr>
    <tr>
      <td>Lower left</td> <td>Lower Right</td>
    </tr>
</table>
```

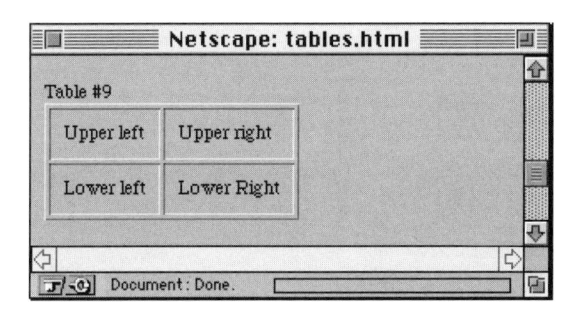

Figure 8.17
Using the cellpadding attribute.

Or we can use both cellspacing and cellpadding. Here's the HTML, followed by the result in Figure 8.18.

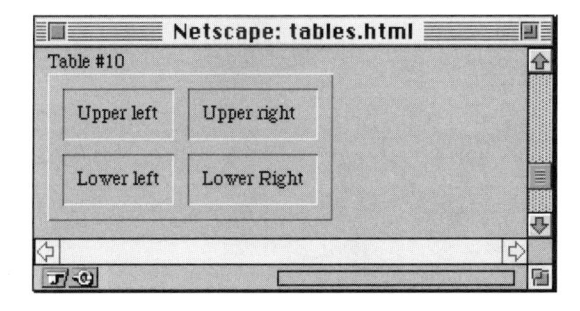

```
Table #10
<table border cellpadding=8 cellspacing=8>
    <tr>
      <td>Upper left</td> <td>Upper right</td>
    </tr>
    <tr>
      <td>Lower left</td> <td>Lower Right</td>
    </tr>
</table>
```

Figure 8.18
Cellspacing and cellpadding used simultaneously.

We can also incorporate all three: borders, cellspacing, and cellpadding. Here's how we type the HTML to get the result in Figure 8.19.

```
Table #11
<table border=8 cellpadding=8 cellspacing=8>
```

```
    <tr>
        <td>Upper left</td> <td>Upper right</td>
    </tr>
    <tr>
        <td>Lower left</td> <td>Lower Right</td>
    </tr>
</table>
```

Figure 8.19 Using borders, cellspacing, and cellpadding at the same time.

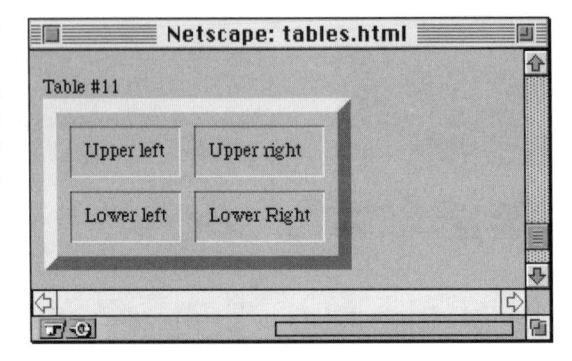

Of course, we could go minimalist and include no borders at all, the result of which is in Figure 8.20. Obviously, however, in this case, we could have rendered this result without using Netscape's table capabilities at all.

```
Table #12
<table>
    <tr>
        <td>Upper left</td> <td>Upper right</td>
    </tr>
    <tr>
        <td>Lower left</td> <td>Lower Right</td>
    </tr>
</table>
```

Figure 8.20 Disbanding all borders.

There may be a situation, however, when you want to present columns of information without using preformatted (monospaced) text, like when you need proportional text or an image in a cell. In that case you could set the HTML up as shown here (see Figure 8.21 for the result):

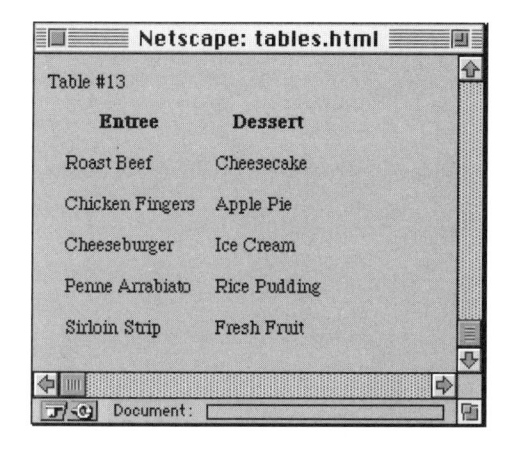

```
Table #13
<table cellspacing=8>
   <tr>
     <th>Entree</th> <th>Dessert</th>
   </tr>
   <tr>
     <td>Roast Beef</td> <td>Cheesecake</td>
   </tr>
   <tr>
     <td>Chicken Fingers</td> <td>Apple Pie</td>
   </tr>
   <tr>
     <td>Cheeseburger</td> <td>Ice Cream</td>
   </tr>
   <tr>
     <td>Penne Arrabiato</td> <td>Rice Pudding</td>
   </tr>
   <tr>
     <td>Sirloin Strip</td> <td>Fresh Fruit</td>
   </tr>
</table>
```

Figure 8.21
Using table tags to design a two-column list with heads.

Depending on the content of your Web pages, tables can be valuable tools for displaying information. Remember, they can also contain images and links, since anything you can put in the body of an HTML document, you can put in the cell of a table.

Incidentally, all of the preceding table code is in the document called `tables.html`, in the `Authoring` folder.

> **Important!** You can't anchor a link to an individual cell of a table in Netscape, although you can in other browsers. Netscape takes you to the top of the table, no matter what cell your <a name=> is placed within in the table itself. We hope this will be corrected in future versions of Netscape.

What's Next

We'll be diving headlong into multimedia next, so get out your cassette decks, CD players, VCRs, and the like. We'll show you how to put sound and movies into your Macintosh, save them in formats everyone can read, then integrate them into your Web site. And get your headphones out so you don't wake up the family.

9

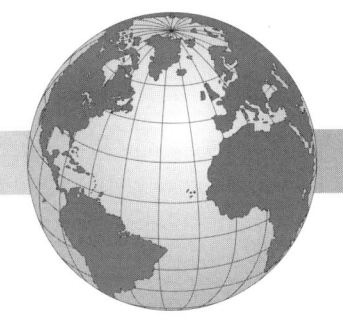

Multimedia: Sound and Movies

Integrating sound and movies into your Web site is the next step to achieving the full sensory multimedia experience that you've found on other Web sites—and the Macintosh makes it easy. In this chapter, we'll show you how to integrate them seamlessly into your site.

Let There Be Sound

It's always frustrating to watch the owner of a new PC try to figure out sound, because as Macintosh users, we're spoiled—it's already there. PC users often have to fool with a sound card, software, and speakers, although Windows 95 is changing this situation somewhat. Don't get me wrong, not everything is plug and play for Mac users on the Web, but with a little foresight, we can adapt both our files and our expectations and create terrific *sounding* pages.

On the Macintosh, we can double-click on sound files in the **Finder**, and they simply play, using routines embedded in the MacOS itself; we do not need a special application to play back audio. Those sound files, whose file name suffixes, when found on the Web, are usually of the form **.snd**, are Mac-specific.

Unfortunately, on the Web, .snd files are not the standard; **au** or **µ-law** files (sometimes called the Sun or NeXT format or the Unix format; the suffix is **.au**) are, with **aiff** files (for Audio Interchange File Format, suffix **.aif** or **aiff**) a close second. You may also come across **MPEG** audio (suffix **.mp2**). You're probably more familiar with MPEG as a video standard, but the standard also contains an audio portion of the standard. While the quality of MPEG audio files is pretty good, many sound helper apps don't support it. And let's not forget **.wav** files for the Windows platform. Again, not all helper apps support this file type, so you won't be reaching your widest potential audience by using it.

All this is not to say we *can't* place Macintosh sounds in our Web sites, but to make our sound files as user friendly as we can for our audience, we'll concentrate on .au-suffixed files, and demonstrate how to convert sound files you may already have to this common Web format.

For playback, we'll rely heavily on the concept of helper applications, those apps that are launched by Netscape (or any other graphical browser) to perform a specific function that the browser itself does not. Playing sounds is among those functions, and there are several sound-related helper applications included on the CD-ROM for you to use.

> **Important!** No matter which sound file format you use, it's a good idea to provide a link to the tools necessary to hear them. Tools are available all over the Internet, and you can point to their locations with a link (you may even want to consider placing copies of them in your Web site if the traffic to your site warrants it). Then, users who visit your sound-laden Web site can, if necessary, download the appropriate helper application, install it on their hard drive, then return to your page and hear your site as well as view it.

Basics of Mac Sound Reproduction

We'll cover the basics of Mac-based sound reproduction so that you can intelligently maneuver the common dialog boxes in the sound recording and editing applications we'll be using. If you are already familiar with this information, skip ahead to the next section.

We must be cognizant of the limited bandwidth of most of our users. In general, 28.8 is the highest speed most users will be able to achieve when dialing up your site. So the larger the sound file, the longer it takes to download. Bear this in mind as we explore how sound is represented digitally by your Macintosh and by other machines, including your ISP's server.

Sound on your machine (Mac or not) is described by three different properties in the files that contain them:

- **Sampling frequency:** This is the number of times per second the sound is described to and by your computer. The higher this number, the better; the typical options are, in rounded figures: 11,000, 22,000, and 44,000. These numbers are often shown as 11K or 11kHz, 22K or 22kHz, and 44K or 44kHz. There are other rates, but these are by far the most common. To give you an idea of the relative clarity of these different sampling frequencies (and not counting any differences in the bit rate and number of channels—the other two main sound properties), 44K is the standard for audio CDs and is considered the best available; 22K is much better quality than you might assume (the quality of 22K is better than half as good as 44K), but certainly there is a discernible drop in quality. Think of 22K as a really good metal-biased cassette sound. 11K is passable, and certainly understandable, but approaching AM radio quality as opposed to good clean FM quality sound. The trade-off? Size. If a file is 1 megabyte when sampled, or recorded, at 44K, it will be 500K sampled at 22K and 250K sampled at 11K, all other factors being equal.
- **Bit rate:** Sound files are also described in terms of how many bits of data describe each sample: 8 or 16. Again, 16 is better than 8, this time by a clear doubling in fidelity; but again, 16-bit files are twice the size of 8-bit files.
- **Number of channels:** This refers to good old stereo versus mono. However, on the Web, stereo does not necessarily sound better than mono, and because stereo sound files are twice the size of mono sound files, mono is more prevalent on the Web. Of course, if your sound files have critical stereo information in them (like that left-to-right jet whooshing and sonic boom on the Blue Angel tribute Web page), you need to take that into consideration when deciding which format to use.

Thus, a 44K, 16-bit stereo sound file that is 4 Mb in size (Figure 9.1) is twice the size of a 44K, 16-bit mono sound file at 2 Mb (Figure 9.2), four

Figure 9.1
44K, 16-bit stereo.

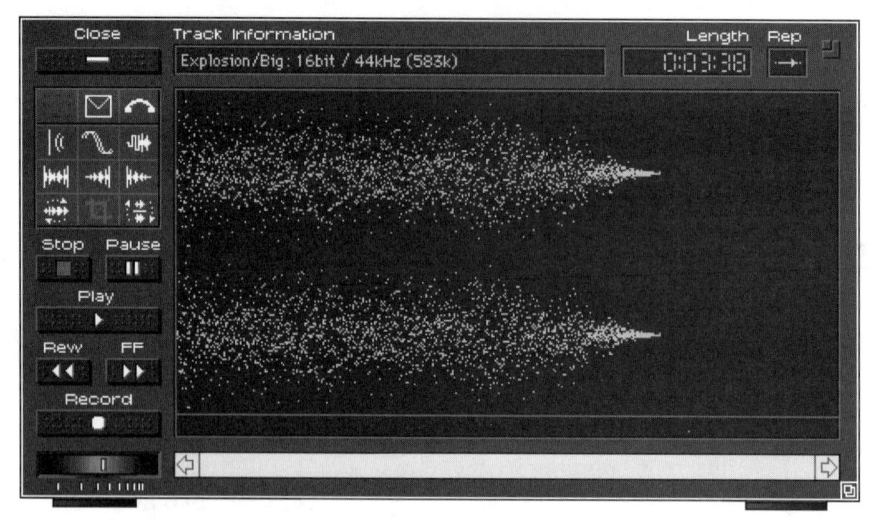

Figure 9.2
44K, 16-bit mono.

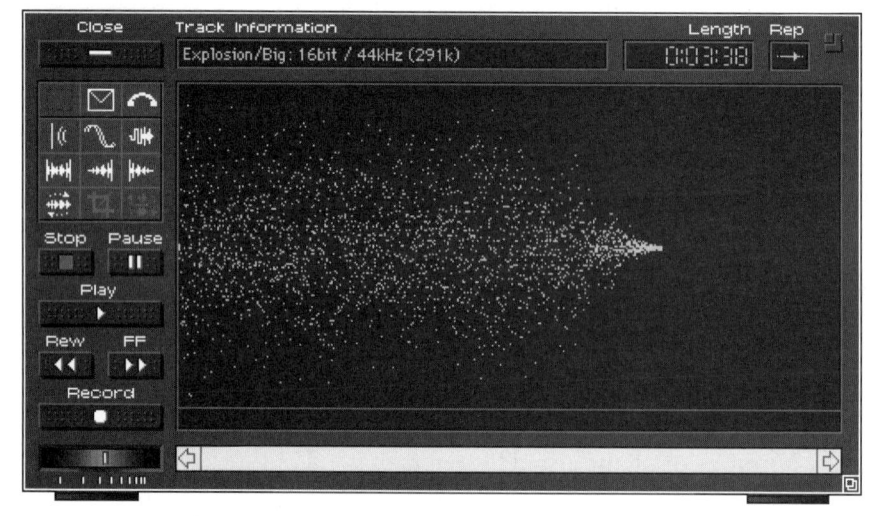

times the size of a 22K, 16-bit mono sound at 1 Mb, eight times the size of a 22K, 8-bit mono at 500K (Figure 9.3), and 16 times the size of an 11K, 8-bit mono sound at 250K (Figure 9.4). That format, 11K, 8-bit mono, is perhaps the most common sound format on the Web—mono, again because stereo isn't usually necessary, and because most computers don't have major sound systems hooked up to their audio outputs. In addition, and perhaps more important, the download time is one-sixteenth that of a true CD-quality high-fidelity sound.

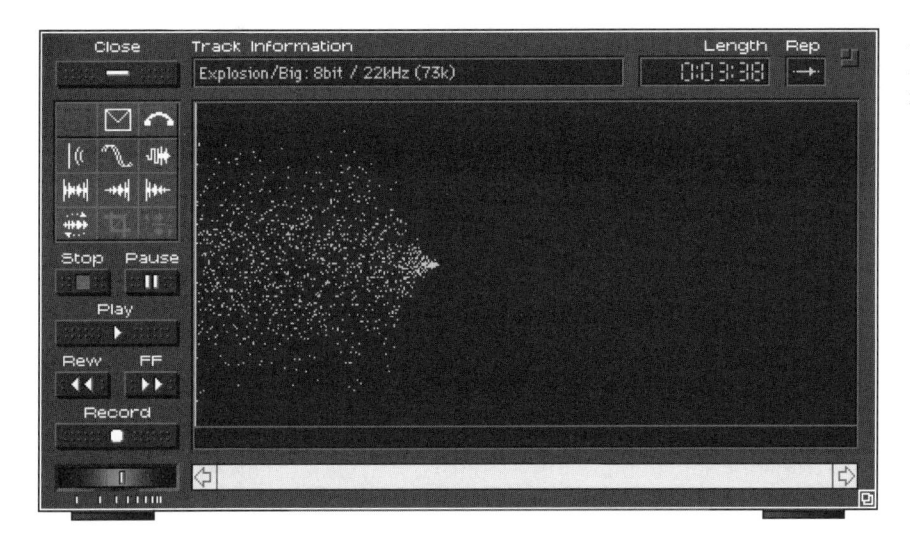

Figure 9.3
22K, 8-bit mono.

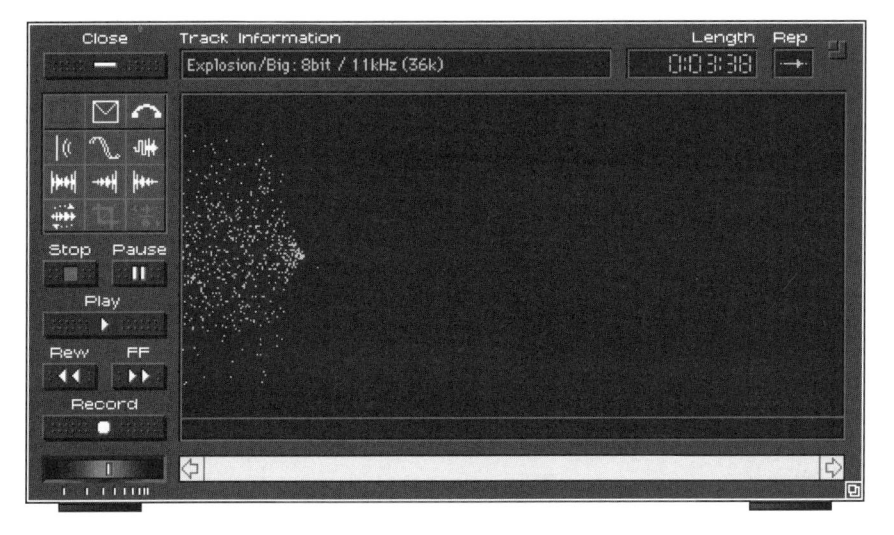

Figure 9.4
11K, 8-bit mono. Notice the vast decrease in file size…from 583K down to just 36K.

There is, of course, much more to sound reproduction, including the length of the sound and format based-compression, but these topics are beyond the scope of this book. For our purposes, we'll be including 11K, 8-bit mono sound files on our Web site, and 99 percent of the people who visit our Web site will think they sound just fine—and they'll download quickly as well.

Integration

Integrating sounds into your HTML pages is exactly like integrating GIFs: you use the anchor tag and the href= attribute to point to the location of the sound file. For here is a sample anchor tag for a sound file:

`<a href="resources/sounds/au/jingle.au">`

When the link to a sound file is clicked, the sound file is downloaded to the user's hard drive. At this point, the helper application that the user has selected in the **Preferences** menu of Netscape to play that particular sound file's format is launched through Apple Events; then the sound is played by that helper application.

We're not only going to play sounds but make and convert them as well, so we've provided a terrific helper application on the CD-ROM that does both. It's called SoundApp, and it's by Norman Franke. Netscape is already configured to have SoundApp launch whenever you download a sound, but in case something happens to your preferences (for instance, it get corrupted, as happens from time to time) and you need to reset that choice, here are the steps to follow:

1. Go to the **Options** Menu and choose **General Preferences** (it's the first menu item, as you can see in Figure 9.5).
2. Under **General Preferences**, click on the **Helpers** tab to bring up the helper application scrolling list.
3. Scroll down until you find mime type **audio/basic**.
4. Browse your hard drive until you find **SoundApp**, then click **OK**.

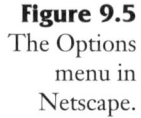

Figure 9.5
The Options menu in Netscape.

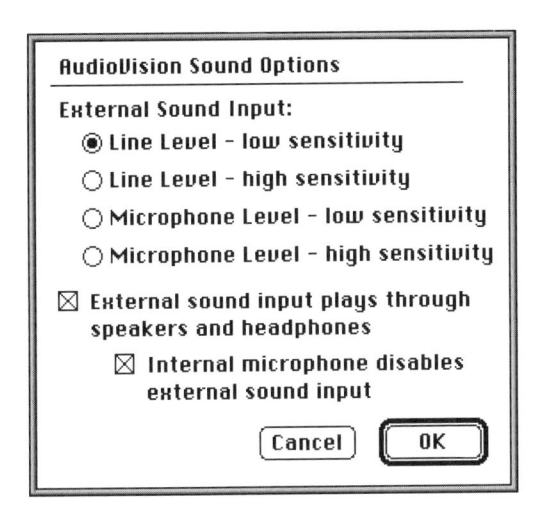

Figure 9.6
Setting the correct line level.

You'll find that SoundApp is very versatile: it can convert sounds between any formats it understands, including Mac .snd files, Windows .wav files, and .aiff and .au files. It can also take sounds from audio CDs and convert them to .au files. It can also record directly from the audio input of your Macintosh, which means that any source you can plug into your Mac is fair game: microphones, preamps, and other low-level inputs, as well as cassette recorders, tuners, VCRs, and other line-level inputs. Just be sure to set your Sound control panel to the appropriate level (see Figure 9.6) to avoid overdriving or underdriving the Macintosh's audio inputs.

At some point, you might want to upgrade to AudioShop from Opcode Systems as your helper application for sound. It offers some recording and effects controls that SoundApp does not. It's also terrific for editing sounds, as it enables drag-and-drop movement of audio pieces, trimming, ramping up and down for fading volumes, normalizing (which makes the sound the loudest it can be without digital clipping), and it has extensive playback features. But for the most straightforward sound production for inclusion in a Web page, SoundApp is your best bet.

Listen Up!

With SoundApp configured as our all-around sound playback helper application, the ability to hear sounds on the Web is a snap. Whenever you encounter a link on the Web to an audio file, whether it's a System 7 sound file, an .aiff file, a Windows .wav file, or an .au file, you'll hear it as soon as it's downloaded. If it's a Macintosh-based sound and it's been compressed using Stuffit, you'll hear it right after Stuffit Expander decompresses it. (You have configured Stuffit as your decompression helper app, correct? If not, we suggest you do so right away.)

Netscape handles all the details. Once you click on the link—assuming that the server that houses the file you want isn't overloaded with requests—you'll start to receive the download into the folder you've specified as your temporary folder. If you haven't already done so, it's a good idea to take the time to configure where the temporary folder is placed. For some strange reason, Netscape's default temporary folder is the System Folder, and you don't want any downloads going there.

> **By the Way...** Netscape places the URL of each sound file, picture, movie, or whatever is downloaded into the **Comments** box of the **Get Info** window. That way, if you want to travel back to a Web site where you downloaded a particular file, but you can't remember where the site is, you can simply perform a **Get Info** on the file you downloaded. Voilá! You're on your way!

Converting Sounds

To demonstrate what goes into preparing sound to include in a Web site, we'll look at two different examples: a cut from a CD and a bit of audio from a source that needs to be digitized first.

Here's a quick disclaimer: most music CDs contain copyrighted material, and you'll need to get the permission of the artist or recording company to actually post this music on your Web site. There are CDs that contain cuts that are in the public domain, though. And we think it's kind of cool to know how to excerpt something from a CD.

Converting the CD cut is straightforward, but you will need a CD-ROM drive on your Mac. If you don't have one, skip to the section on recording sounds, and come back here when you get a CD-ROM drive.

The process is a two-step process: the cut needs to be converted first to QuickTime audio, then to an .au file. Let's do it.

1. Using SoundApp, select **Import to QuickTime** in the **File** menu to open the file of your choice on any audio CD, as shown in Figure 9.7.
2. You'll be presented with a dialog box (Figure 9.8) with sections on channels, sampling, and bit depth. Choose **11.025 kHz, 8-bit,**

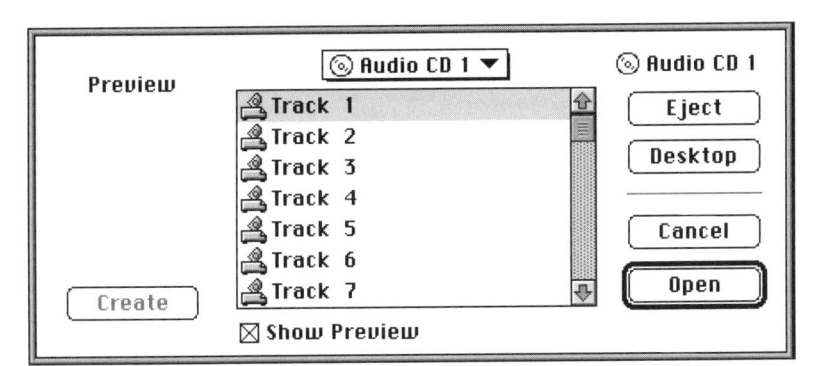

Figure 9.7
Importing the cut to convert to QuickTime.

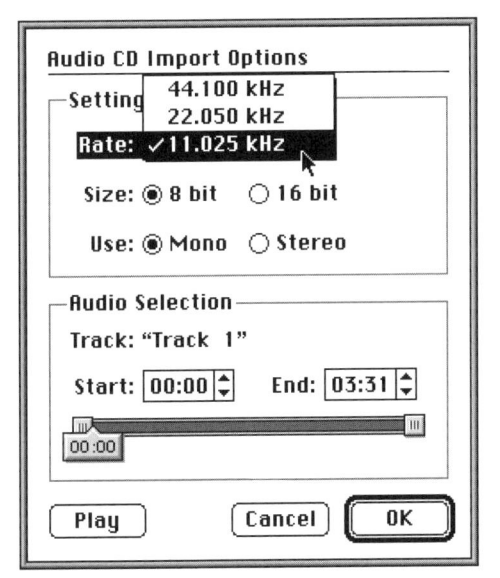

Figure 9.8
Import Options dialog box.

mono. Save this imported QuickTime audio file on your desktop. Call the file whatever you like.

3. Under the **Options** menu, choose **Convert To** and the **NeXT** option. (This option saves the file as an .au file.) SoundApp will indicate that it is processing the conversion (see Figure 9.9).

Figure 9.9
SoundApp imports the file, then converts it.

4. SoundApp will prompt you for additional information, including file name and where you want to save the converted sound. Use a file name that ends with a suffix of .au, such as, in this case, testsnd.au. Remember, your audience is worldwide and cross-platform, so make it easy for them to identify the sound they're about to download.

> **By the Way...** You can also configure SoundApp to do all of this automatically via drag and drop: simply hold the Shift key down as you drag a cut from a CD onto the SoundApp icon, and the entire process will take place automatically.

Recording Sounds

You can just as easily record a sound using a different piece of software: SoundMachine by Rod Kennedy. Here's how:

1. Go to the SoundMachine **Recording** menu (Figure 9.10). As we've mentioned before, you can record sounds from any source that can be connected to your Macintosh, including cassette players, tuners, VCRs, or microphones.
2. Choose **Set Format (µ-law)** and the **Custom** sample rate as 11.025 kHz (Figure 9.11). (Remember, µ-law is another term for an .au file. Don't you just love Unix?)
3. SoundMachine will prompt you for a location in which to save your .au file. It provides a default file name with the .au suffix, as you can see in Figure 9.12.

Figure 9.10
The Recording menu in SoundMachine.

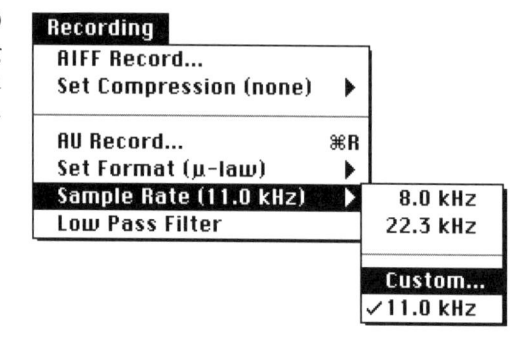

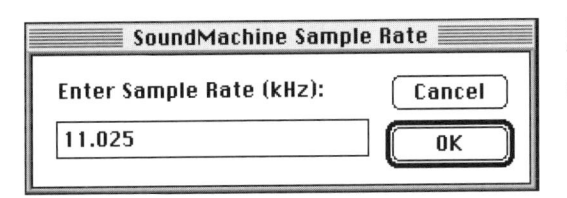

Figure 9.11
The sample rate dialog box.

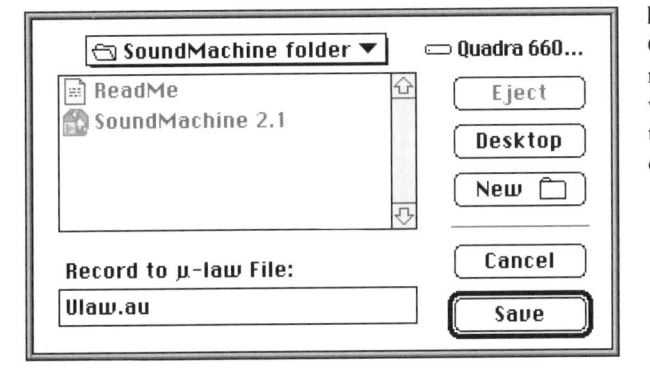

Figure 9.12
Change the file name if you want, but keep the .au extension.

4. You'll be presented with the **Record** dialog box (Figure 9.13). Click on **Record** and **Pause** and set your output levels on your input source (CD-ROM drive, VCR, what have you). To record, click on **Pause** again. SoundMachine will record from whatever input source you have set in your **Sound Control Panel** (CD-ROM drive, VCR, etc.). You can see here the amount of time you can record is based entirely upon how much free hard drive space you have left, and in this example, we have almost 11 minutes available.

Once you've recorded your sound, SoundMachine will automatically play it back, and show you a playback progress dialog box (Figure 9.14).

You can rename the resulting file to anything you like, but make sure to use lowercase letters (as with all of your files) so that any browser can read it. Place the .au file in the resources folder in our Web site, `spiderworks`

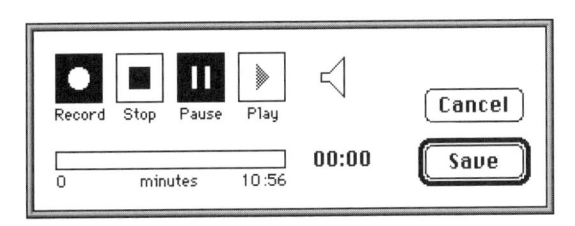

Figure 9.13
Recording sound.

Figure 9.14
Playback dialog box.

web site. You can create an anchor link to it on one of your Web pages. When users click on that link in Netscape, the sound should play through SoundApp.

We've talked briefly about using the anchor tag to link to a multimedia file such as a sound file in this chapter. As you'll recall from Chapter 6, the anchor tag can also be used to link to a Web page. How can you tell the difference between a link to a multimedia file and a link to a Web page when you look at the HTML source? Easy. Look at the last file or directory of the URL. The Web page link will always end in either a directory name (and then default to the index.html document within that directory) or a specific document that usually ends in the suffix .html. The multimedia link's file name will end in .gif or .jpg for graphics, .au for sounds, or .mov for QuickTime movies. When you link to a multimedia file, the file is either displayed or played after downloading if you have the correct helper app.

Working with Lengthy Sound Files

Sound files composed of lengthy content such as speeches, radio programming, audio books, and the like are not well suited to the methods of conversion to the Web that we've been discussing, because, even at high-access speeds, they take too long to download. This is not to say that it is impossible or shouldn't be done; rather, it requires a different approach, called **streaming**.

Streaming is a means of delivering sound content from a source (in this case, your Web server) so that slices of the audio content begin feeding into the user's machine, and playback begins almost immediately. This is in contrast to the entire sound file being downloaded before playback begins. Because the source material is being handled on a "get a bit, play a bit, get a bit, play a bit" basis, the audio can be, and sometimes is, endless.

There are two major players in the audio streaming world: Xing (pronounced Zing) Technologies and Progressive Networks. Xing's product is called Streamworks, and Progressive's is RealAudio. But because Xing has not made as deep an inroad into the Macintosh market, we concentrate here on showing you how to create RealAudio files. The two products are very similar, and if you want to switch to Streamworks at some point, you will be able to apply what you learn here to that product as well.

RealAudio   Unfortunately, RealAudio doesn't sound all that great, but it is important to keep in mind that audio streaming is a revolutionary process, in its infancy. Part of the current problem is that the compression scheme used to minimize the size of RealAudio files also affects the quality of the sound, which has been described variously as "bad FM" and "scratchy vinyl." The RealAudio Encoder (which is included on this book's CD-ROM) uses a 9:1 compression ratio (assuming 11K, 8-bit mono; higher if the source has better sampling or bit depth), which means that RealAudio sounds take up only 1K per second, about three and a half megabytes per hour of material. There is also a new version of RealAudio available called the high-fidelity or 28.8 encoding scheme. Both of these schemes are available within the RealAudio 2.0 Encoder.

Converting Sounds to RealAudio   The simplest way to convert sounds to RealAudio is to drag and drop them on the RealAudio Encoder. This generates a RealAudio .ra file. When we do this, the Encoder presents us with several options, as you can see in Figure 9.15.

1. Choose the appropriate encoder (14.4 for traditional RealAudio files, 28.8 for higher-fidelity files, which are also twice as large).

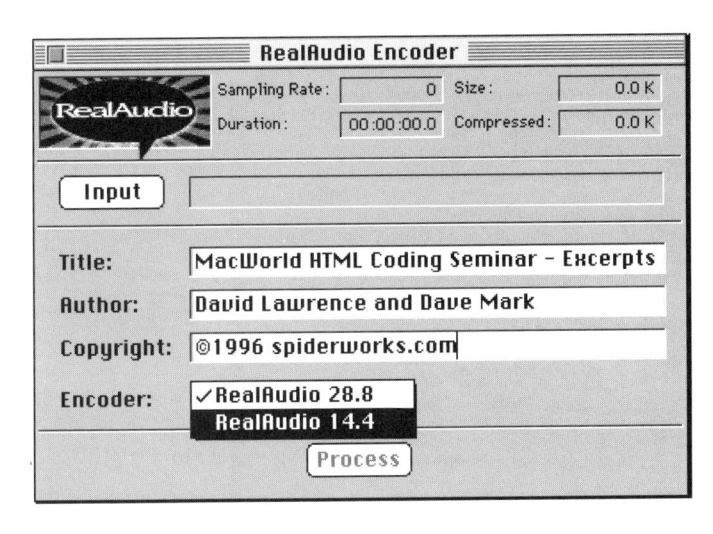

Figure 9.15
RealAudio Encoder information.

2. Enter the title of the file and copyright information.
3. Click the **Process** button.

The resulting .ra file can be played back by the RealAudio Player to confirm its validity. Note that you can also drag and drop a number of files simultaneously onto the Encoder; the encoder will stop and ask for the title and copyright information for each one, and encode each in turn. You can preset this information in the **Preferences** dialog box (Figure 9.16) to save time.

> **Important!** Because the encoding process is so CPU-intensive, if you plan on working with a lot of lengthy sound files, it would behoove you to upgrade to a PowerMac if you haven't done so already. On a speedy PowerMac or Unix server, you can convert an incoming sound to RealAudio more quickly than it takes to play it back. That means you can dish up live audio to your audience! Progressive Networks has a server/software package you can purchase to provide this type of live audio, and it's very popular with radio stations looking to jump on the Web.

Once you've created your .ra file, you have one other file to create, the .ram (for Real Audio Metafile) file. You may notice when sliding your mouse over a RealAudio link on a Web page that the file in the URL has the .ram suffix. This is because the RealAudio server software (which resides on the UNIX server) needs to talk with the user's machine and the

Figure 9.16
Setting preferences to save time.

RealAudio player, and this requires more than the standard HTTP connection that is in place when the user browses a Web page.

The RealAudio metafile accomplishes this bridge. The metafile tells the RealAudio server where to find the RealAudio file (it's actually a one-line text file that contains an URL that points to the actual .ra file). Then it creates a conduit between the server, file, and the user's RealAudio Player, and allows the user to fast forward the file, as well as rewind, stop, and pause it. The metafile is what you point to with your link, not the RealAudio file itself. This is an important distinction: if you create a link to the RealAudio file itself, and the user clicks on on it, like any non-HTML file, it will download, and that's not what you want. By pointing to the metafile, which in turn points to the actual RealAudio file, a download doesn't occur. Rather, the metafile manages the playback of the audio, uses the server as the engine, the .ra file as the source, and the RealAudio player on the user's Macintosh as the helper application that gives the user playback options. When the user clicks on the link to the metafile, the metafile is read by Netscape, which recognizes it as a .ram file, and thus launches the RealAudio player; the data streaming down the line to the user's Macintosh begins playing back almost immediately.

When the RealAudio server software is installed on your ISP's Web server, your ISP's system administrator sets the root path. This is simply the path that is followed from the root level of the machine, right through to the RealAudio directory. To create the metafile, you need to know three things: where the RealAudio Server's root path ends, where the actual .ra file is, and the .ra file's name. The metafile, whose name for convenience sake should probably be something like `sound1.ram`, will look something like this:

`pnm://your.server.com/Website/resources/sounds/ra/sound1.ra`

Notice that the metafile's URL has a new service prefix or protocol: **pnm.** This stands for Progressive Networks Metafile. This becomes a prefix that the Web server recognizes only after the RealAudio server is installed, just like http:, ftp:, mailto:, or any of the other prefixes. The path is simply an arbitrary one: it tells the .ram file where to find the .ra file.

> **Important!** Of course, using RealAudio's streaming functions in your Web site to create real-time audio and to start playing the file before download is complete assumes that your ISP has installed the RealAudio server for your use on the Web site. If this has not been done, you can't take advantage of what Real-Audio does best: streaming very long audio files. However, even if you don't have access to a RealAudio server, you can encode RealAudio files and place them in your Website for downloading, just like any other multimedia file. In that case you *would* link directly to the .ra file, and your sound will simply download completely before playback will occur.

In the .ram file, you can also designate where in the sound you want playback to begin by adding a dollar sign (as a separator) and a time argument to the URL. For example, suppose the metafile file `passages.ram` was an hour-long reading of a book on tape called *Passages*, which contained several chapters. Let's assume that Chapter 1 of the book is at the very beginning of the .ra file, Chapter 2 starts at 5 minutes and 40 seconds into the hour, and Chapter 3 at 15 minutes and 5 seconds into the hour. The HTML to give the user a choice of where in the book to begin listening might look like this:

```
<a href="pnm://your.server.com/books/passages.ra">Chapter 1</a>
<a href="pnm://your.server.com/books/passages.ra$05:40">Chapter 2</a>
<a href="pnm://your.server.com/books/passages.ra$15:05">Chapter 3</a>
```

It's also possible to contain several days' worth of audio content within one file. Each hour's worth of RealAudio sound takes up about 3.6 Mb of space, so a few days' worth of, say, Congressional speechmaking would take less than 100 Mb. The time argument would be of the form:

```
$dd:hh:mm:ss.ss
```

where *dd* is day, *hh* is hour, *mm* is minute, and *ss.ss* is seconds and hundredths of seconds.

> **By the Way...** It's a good idea to include a link on your page to Progressive Network's Web site, so that users who don't have the RealAudio player can access it. A simple line of code like this will do the trick:
>
> `<a href="http://www.realaudio.com">Get the RealAudio Player</a>`
>
> The RealAudio front page has links directly to the download pages.

Movies

Getting movies into your Mac is a snap. All Power Macintoshes and most of the later-model 68040-based Macs have a video-in port. Some have RCA-style jacks, some have S-VHS-style jacks (with which you can actually use an AppleTalk cord to connect your VCR or camcorder to your Mac), and some have both. Although there is no Web standard for video per se, MPEG represents the only video standard that is viewable on any machine. However, QuickTime is viewable on both Mac and Windows, which represents more than 90 percent of the market, so that's what we'll be using here.

The software necessary to import movies comes with any Macintosh that can accept video input. Check the **Apple Extras** folder that came preinstalled on your Mac, or refer to the CD-ROM that came with the Mac for the application called FusionRecorder or Avid's VideoShop (it will vary based on when your machine was made). These are not the only two applications that will accept video input, and, in fact, if you are going to be doing a lot of video work, you probably should consider upgrading to VideoShop or Adobe Premiere.

The overall process for recording video is as easy as recording audio: you need to select a few basic parameters, and then record your movie and save it as a QuickTime document with the .mov suffix. Once saved, you'll need to "flatten" the movie (reduce the number of colors) to accommodate Windows users who have a limited number of colors available to them (more about this later). You then link the .mov file to your HTML documents exactly the way you link any other multimedia file (with an anchor tag) and you're off to the races. The HTML for the link would look something like this:

```
<a href="resources/movies/mov/master.mov">
```

Anyone with a Mac who clicks on the link will download the movie. The user's browser will send an Apple Event to SimplePlayer, MoviePlayer, or whichever playback software is specified in the Netscape helper application preferences to handle QuickTime movies, and the movie will play. If you don't have either of these, you can get the entire QuickTime package at <http://quicktime.apple.com/qt/sw/sw.html> which includes MoviePlayer.

Figure 9.17
Choose Record to memory for the smoothest recording.

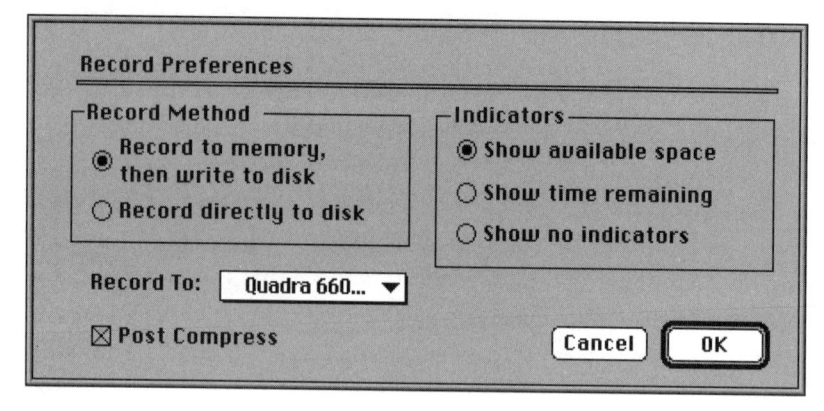

Not surprisingly, size is a major consideration with video; even the smallest of movies consumes an incredible amount of room, and there is no readily accessible alternative for streaming video as there is for audio. Yet.

There are ways, however, to manage the movies you include in your Web page. You can choose to record to memory, by accessing the **Fusion Recorder Preferences** dialog box (see Figure 9.17). Choosing Record to memory results in the smoothest recording, but limits you to the amount of RAM available to the application. And recording directly to disk, another option, may result in choppy recording, depending upon how fast your hard disk can be written to.

You can also control the size of your movies in several ways. In the **Record** menu (Figure 9.18), you can adjust the size of the movie screen itself, the number of frames per second recorded, and the compression used when the video is being recorded.

Figure 9.18
Fusion-Recorder's Record menu.

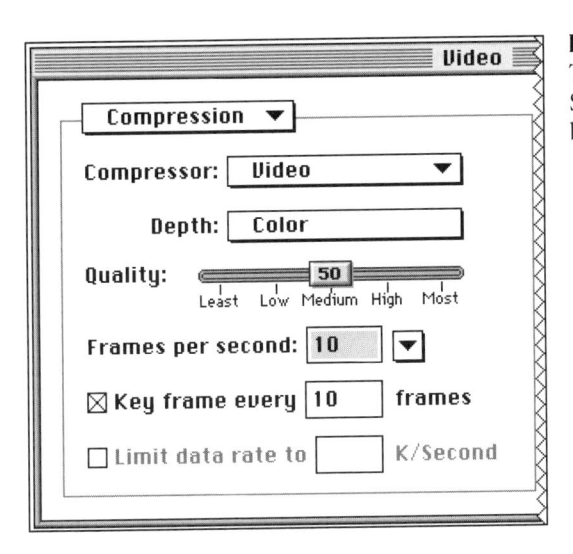

Figure 9.19
The Video Settings dialog box.

The **Record Window Size** item lets you choose among several sizes of finished product. **Quarter Size** is 160 pixels by 120 pixels (every size is a multiple of 4 × 3, the aspect ratio of the standard television screen) and is the most popular size for movies, as it strikes a pretty decent balance between file size and viewability. You could, theoretically, create a movie that was as small as, say, 16 by 12 pixels, but you couldn't easily make out any images.

The **Video Settings** option also helps control the size and quality of your finished product. Video, for simplicity's sake, is usually recorded by a VCR or camera at 30 frames per second. Video uses the same process as film, whereby frames played in succession create the illusion of movement. However, 30 frames per second requires an inordinate amount of hard drive space for even the shortest clips. By reducing the number of frames per second recorded from the source video, you can substantially reduce the size of your QuickTime movies; 15 is okay, and 10 is passable. You can set that in the **Video Settings** dialog box, shown in Figure 9.19. All you really need to worry about here is the **Frames per second** figure. The **Quality** slide bar is effective, but any setting above Medium will do.

To control the audio quality, go to the **Sound Settings** dialog box, shown in Figure 9.20. Look familiar? It should—it's very similar to the controls for SoundApp. Since most movies have a soundtrack associated with them, you can further control the size of the movie file by adjusting the sound along with the video settings.

Figure 9.20
The Sound dialog box.

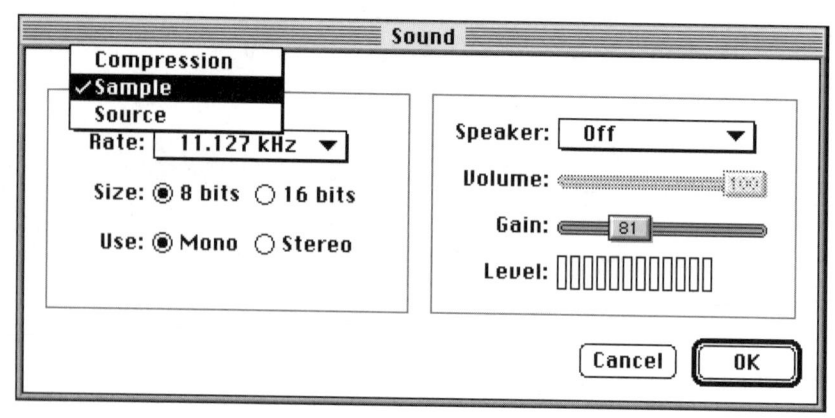

Once you have everything set up, it's only a matter of rolling tape and recording your movie. Be sure to save the file in lowercase letters with the suffix .mov. You can record directly from a VCR, laser disc, video game, TV tuner, cable box, or standard video camera. Connectix makes the QuickCam, which is a great way (for under $100) to get black-and-white video into your Macintosh quickly.

Once you save your movie, you'll want to do one last thing: flatten it. As noted earlier, this is an accommodation for Windows users who have limited color palettes with which to view their movies. By using the drag-and-drop application FlattenMooV in the `Goodies` folder on your CD-ROM, you make it possible not only for a much wider audience to view your movies, but you will significantly decrease the size of your file. Just drag your file onto FlattenMooV, and it will limit the colors and resave the movie in the location of your choice. Be aware that if you have a large movie, you'll need twice the hard drive space (temporarily): one for the original and one for the flattened version. Once you confirm with your movie playback software that the flattened movie is in good shape, you can delete the unflattened version since you won't be using it.

As with audio files, move the movie to the `Resources` folder in `spiderworks web site`, then add an anchor tag to link it to your Web page. Check it through Netscape, and you're finished.

What's Next

In Chapter 10, we introduce another Netscape 2.0 HTML extension: frames. You'll find that a whole new way of looking at your Web pages is waiting for you and the users who peruse your site.

10

Frames

Nothing in the Netscape HTML suite is as visually exciting as frames. With them, we can add a new dimension to our pages, one in which static objects coexist peacefully with dynamically changing content.

> Viewing pages with frames requires Netscape Navigator 2.0 or later.

The downside is that frame pages exponentially increase the time required for coding. As we will soon find out, every major frame element on a page requires a different HTML document. And if we include an image map, we increase our workload again. And (this is a big "and") we have to code differently for those users who don't have access via Netscape 2.0. It's actually a lot easier to just add a few lines that read: "Hey! You need Netscape 2.0 to read this page!" (and many do this once they realize how much they have increased their coding time), but that's being lazy. The coding time frame also probably explains why we've been slow to see many frame-based sites on the Web.

All that said, frames are fun when they come together properly, and including them enables you to bring a new level of sophistication to your pages (not to mention increasing your worth as an HTML programmer). We'll take frame creation one step at a time, to make sense of the process.

To get a handle on the concept of frames, think of several Web pages combined, with each of their designs apparent to the user in an all-in-one document called a **frameset**. And different from typical HTML pages, clicking on a link in one frame can change content in that frame or other frames in the frameset, or, as is familiar to us from traditional non-framed HTML, bring up a whole new page.

As noted, using frames increases the management necessary for each page: we have to manage the frameset, which includes how the individual frames look when placed in the frameset; the content of each frame; and how each interacts with the others. A simple example is shown in Figure 10.1. This two-frame frameset phone book consists of a list of names on the left-hand side and the information associated with each name on the right. When a user clicks on a name in the list, the content changes in the other frame.

Figure 10.1 Content in one frame (left) remains unchanged.

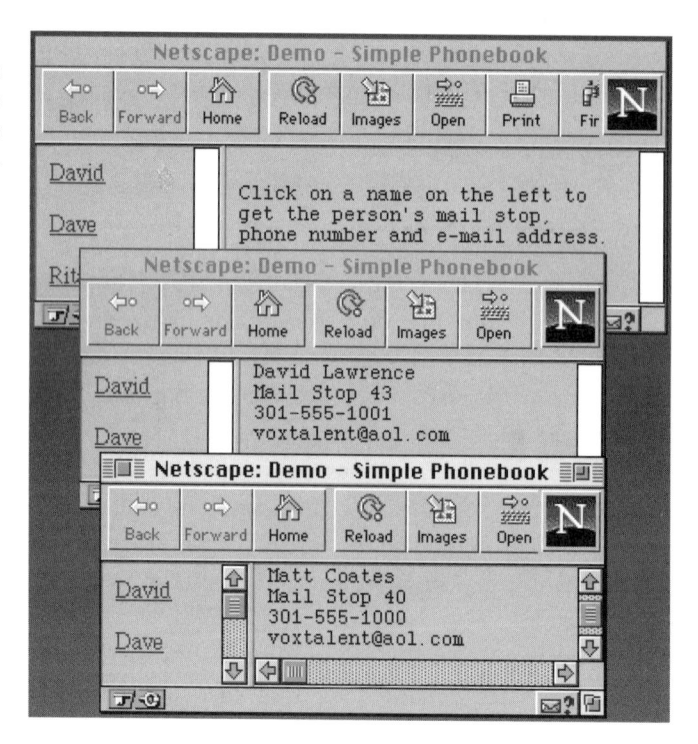

Frame Me!

A frameset is the container, or top level, in which individual frames are placed. The <frameset> tag's primary purpose is to describe to the browser how to arrange the individual frames *within* the frameset in the browser's display window. In essence, in frame-based pages, the <frameset> tag plays the role that the <body> tag plays in regular HTML pages.

> If you include any tags that are usually found within <body> tags before the <frameset> tag in the HTML document, Netscape will interpret those and ignore the <frameset> tag. Make sure you can check that no <body> tag exists in your frame-oriented HTML.

<frameset>...</frameset>

Description: The main container of a frame-oriented document. Contains two or more frames. Replaces <body>...</body> container in frame-oriented HTML documents.

Netscape 2.0 Attributes:

rows = "string"   value list representing percentages of window height, actual pixels, or relative values

cols = "string"   value list representing percentages of window width, actual pixels, or relative values

---

There are three ways you can describe the layout of frames within a <frameset> using the **rows=** or **cols=** attributes, and each of the two attributes works the same with the three methods:

- **By percentage of window width or height:** This means that if the window is resized, your frames stay relatively the same size. The total number of values for the rows= and cols= attributes are exactly the same as the number of frames on the page. If you specify four values in a cols= attribute, you get four columns as described by the values themselves. For example, to get four equal columns, use this code:

```
<frameset rows="25%, 25%, 25%, 25%">...</frameset>
```

- **By absolute pixel size:** Reserve this for frames that house predictably sized elements, such as banners, icon bars, or the like, because if the entire browser window is resized, the other frames will not form the same design.
- **By relative remainders:** This is accomplished with the asterisk (*) as the operator. You can combine the different techniques (you'll have to if you use remaindering and absolute pixel size) in your HTML frames documents. Think of the asterisk as equivalent to the phrase "what's left over."

Using Percentages to Describe Frames

The following examples demonstrate how to use these ways to describe framesets. Let's take a look at percentages first. The code:

```
<frameset rows="30%, 70%">...</frameset>
```

describes two rows, the upper one taking up 30 percent of the available window space and the lower one containing 70 percent. You can see the result in Figure 10.2.

Notice that there is already another document involved: `blank.html`

```
<html>
<head>
<title>blank.html</title>
</head>
<body>
Here's a blank frame...
</body>
</html>
```

Figure 10.2 Frames with 30/70 percent rows.

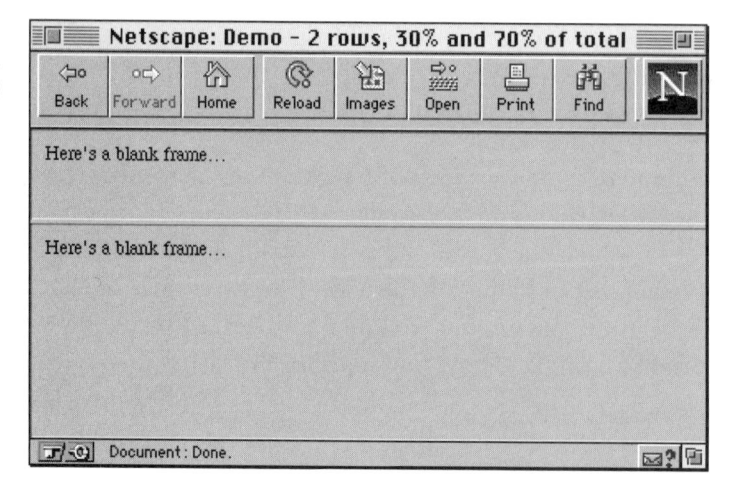

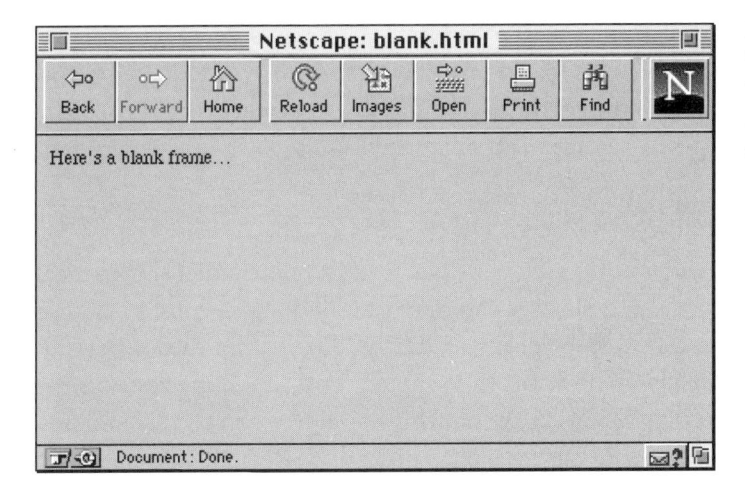

Figure 10.3
The blank.html document by itself.

We're using this as a placeholder so that you can see the frames show up. Figure 10.3 shows what `blank.html` would look like if you browsed it individually.

Columns would look similar. By simply substituting the cols= attribute for the rows= attribute, we'd see Figure 10.4.

Using Exact Pixel Size and Relative Remainders to Describe Frames

Sometimes, individual frames are described in a <frameset> element by absolute pixel sizes. To do this you specify an integer (with no percent

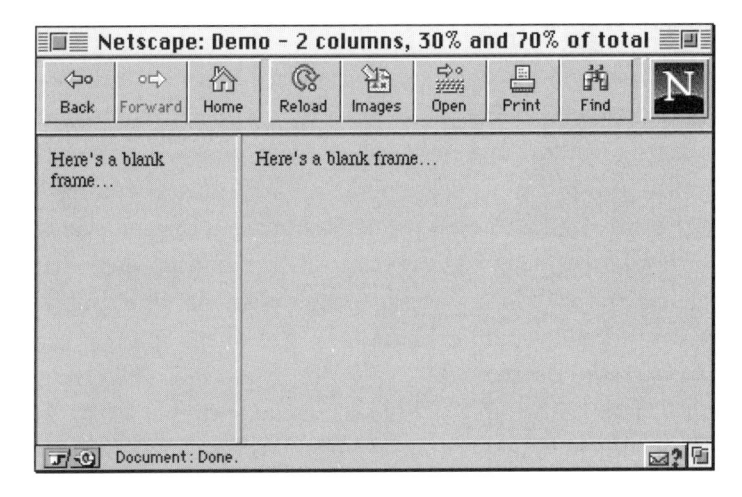

Figure 10.4
Frames as columns.

sign) for the value of the rows= or columns= attributes. Netscape will display the frame in the exact size in pixels. But remember, as soon as the user resizes the Netscape frame, there goes the size in pixels you picked, so be careful when specifying frames of exact pixel size.

Serving up Left Overs

Although you will want to use exact pixel sizes for some dimension-critical frames, such as those that carry carefully sized graphics, icons, or button bars of a fixed width or height, you can see how easily the viewer can destroy your vision of how the page should look simply by resizing the browser window. Judicious use of our third option for row= and column= values in the <frameset> tag can help a great deal. Review time: so far we have defined our frames by percentage of row or column space, which evenly redistributes the area given to each frame when the browser window is resized: as the user shrinks or grows the browser window, the percentage-based frames shrink or grow in the same proportion. Now, we also have the option of specifying an exact pixel size for each frame—but if the browser window gets resized by the user to some size other than the exact total of all of our frames combined, strange results may occur: too small and one of the frames gets truncated; too large and some blank gray window space appears. Our third option, for a value for row= or column= is the asterisk (*). A single asterisk in a list of row= or column= attributes is a "relative-sized" or "what's left over" frame and gives the asterisk frame all remaining space. For example, if we described a <frameset> tag with columns="100,*", then the browser will set up the window with two columns: the left column will be 100 pixels wide, and the right column will get all that's left (about 368 pixels, since the standard Netscape browser window is initially displayed at 468 pixels in width on the Macintosh). If the viewer resizes the window, the right column will adjust, and the left column will remain 100 pixels wide. A couple of variations: if you have more than one relative-sized frame, the remaining space is divided evenly among them. If there is a value in front of the asterisk, that frame gets that much more relative space. Think of it as a multiplier. As an example, <frameset columns ="3*,*"> would give three-fourths of the space to the first frame, and the rest to the second.

Remember, the frame is simply a holder for content that exists in another HTML document. The **<frame>** tag has as its first attribute **src=**

where the value is the URL of the document whose content appears within the frame. That's an important distinction: frames are not containers (there's no closing </frame> tag); they are more like rows or columns in a table, which in turn have <td>...</td> containers with the actual content of each cell.

<frame>

Description: The basic tag for referencing each frame in a frameset.

Attributes:

src = URL	address of the content of the frame
name = "string"	user-defined name of frame, used with <a>'s target= attribute, to direct any links to the target frame rather than the frame itself
"_blank"	loads link into new window
"_self"	loads link over itself
"_parent"	loads link over parent frame
"_top"	loads link into new window
marginwidth = integer	margin width of frame in pixels
marginheight = integer	margin height of frame in pixels
scrolling = "yes"	scroll bars are drawn even if not necessary
"no"	scroll bars are not drawn; some content is hidden if too large for the frame
"auto"	default; scroll bars are drawn only if content is too long or wide (or both) to be viewed in its entirety
noresize	this frame will not be resizable

We're not only introducing the building block of the frames-oriented page, we are also revisiting the anchor tag to add a new, frame-specific attribute called **target=**. More on that in a moment. Using the **name=** attribute, you can assign a name to individual frames so they can be the target of other frames. The phone book example shown at the beginning of the chapter used the **name=** attribute along with the target= attribute to ensure that when a user clicked on a name, the content—not the names frame of the target frame—changed. Here's the code to generate that phonebook.html in the Authoring Folder. First, the frameset:

```
<html>
<head>
<title>Demo - Simple Phonebook</title>
</head>
<frameset cols="30%,70%">
<frame src="names.html">
<frame src="info.html" name="info">
</frameset>
</html>
```

Note that the window is set up with relative percentages, so that no matter how the user resizes the window, the names frame takes up 30 percent of the window, and the information associated with each name takes up the remaining 70 percent. We could have also specified cols="30%,*" and gotten the same results.

Okay. Now we have two frames side by side. Here's the code for the HTML document info.html, which will be displayed in the right-hand frame, the information on the names:

```
<html>
<head>
<title>info.html</title>
</head>
<body>
<font size=+1>
<pre>
Click on a name on the left to
get the person's mail stop,
phone number and e-mail address.

<a name="David">David</a> Lawrence
Mail Stop 43
301-555-1001
voxtalent@aol.com

<a name="Dave">Dave</a> Mark
Mail Stop 50
301-555-1200
dmark@aol.com

<a name="Rita">Rita</a> Daniels
Mail Stop 43
301-555-1001
oltrita@aol.com

<a name="Matt">Matt</a> Coates
Mail Stop 40
301-555-1000
oltmatt@aol.com
```

```
<a name="Pamela">Pamela</a> Munoz
Mail Stop 45
301-555-1019
oltpamela@aol.com

<a name="Stu">Stu</a> Mark
Mail Stop 48
301-555-1013
stumark@aol.com

<a name="Jack">Jack</a> The Engineer
Mail Stop 44
301-555-1017
engineerdude@aol.com

<a name="Suzanne">Suzanne</a> Kibota
Mail Stop 47
301-555-1025
sz@aol.com

</pre>
</font>
</body>
</html>
```

The white space between each name is courtesy of the <pre>...</pre> tags, included so that each name can be accessed separately. (We could have added mailto: links to each e-mail address so that once users found the person they were looking for, they could instantly call them or e-mail them with a simple click, but we didn't. You can though!)

Here's the code for the HTML document names.html, whose content will be displayed in the left-hand frame, the names frame:

```
<html>
<head>
<title>names.html</title>
</head>
<body>
<font size=+1>
<a href="info.html#David" target="info">David</a><p>
<a href="info.html#Dave" target="info">Dave</a><p>
<a href="info.html#Rita" target="info">Rita</a><p>
<a href="info.html#Matt" target="info">Matt</a><p>
<a href="info.html#Pamela" target="info">Pamela</a><p>
<a href="info.html#Stu" target="info">Stu</a><p>
<a href="info.html#Jack" target="info">Jack</a><p>
<a href="info.html#Suzanne" target="info">Suzanne</a><p>
</font>
</body>
</html>
```

Aside from noting the Netscape-specific <font> tag used to increase the size of each name, notice the links: they are simple anchor tags, linking each person's name to his or her information within the info.html document. The **target=** attribute tells the browser to reflect the changes in the target frame, named "info" back in the <frameset> document. If we didn't use the **target=** attribute by default, the information would load over the name list itself and replace the list of names. That isn't what we want; we want the changes reflected in the frame on the right, and by using the target= attribute in the anchor links, it is.

You can also use a set of special reserved names:

- **_blank** loads the content into a new window.
- **_self** loads the content over the calling frame. (That's what we didn't want to have happen in the phone book.)
- **_parent** loads the content over a parent frame, which is a frame that makes changes to the current frame. For example, we could ask the info page to load a .gif of the person whose information we've selected. No parent? It will load the content as if it were a _self call.
- **_top** loads this link at the top level. It, too, reverts to loading over itself if there is no top-level frame.

We can also control the height and width of the margins (the white space around the content, not the lines that divide the frames) with the **marginheight=** and **marginwidth=** attributes. Both expect an integer as a value, and will add that number of pixels of clear space around your content.

Finally, you already know that you can resize the browser window, but you should know that users can change the sizes of frames, too. If they move their cursor over the dividing line between the cells of our phone book document, they'll see the cursor change to a column-sizing icon, shown in Figure 10.5.

Users can then click and drag and change the size of the frames themselves. To prevent this, we can use the **noresize** attribute (it's empty, so there's no need for a value); users then will be unable to resize the frame itself, but will still be able to resize the window.

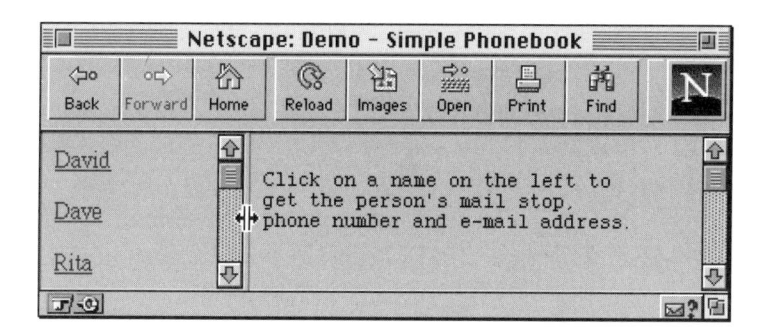

Figure 10.5
The cursor changes when over a frame dividing line.

Coding for the Frame-Impaired

As noted at the beginning of this chapter, we do have to take into consideration those users who are not using Netscape 2.0. The tag pair **<noframes>...</noframes>** is specifically for this purpose.

<noframes>...</noframes>

Description: Content within this tag container is browsable by non-Netscape Navigator 2.0 clients.

Netscape 2.0 Attributes:

None

In older Web browsers that don't support frames, whatever code is within the <noframes> tag pair is displayed instead of the frame design. Conversely, Netscape Navigator 2.0 (and later versions) will ignore anything within the <noframes> tags.

It's always a good idea to build a nonframe-based version of your content than to leave potential viewers in the cold as to what the page contains. To that end, save that page of code you're about to convert to frames and drop it between the <noframes> tags.

What's Next

At this point, you should know enough to create some pretty interesting pages. You're certainly free to start uploading pages to your server if you know how to do that. If you don't, or if you don't have an Internet Service

Provider (ISP), read the next chapter. We'll show you how to log on to our ISP, DigEx, where you already have 5 megabytes of space waiting for you to play with. We'll show you the tools you need to populate and maintain your Web site, as well as how to integrate some of the cgi-bin scripts we learned about earlier.

Take some time now to perfect your pages on your Macintosh, test your links, images, sound, and movies, then go to Chapter 11 to learn how to strut your stuff.

Population and Maintenance of Your Web Site

Unless you are using a server that is under your direct control (and it's doubtful you'd be reading this book if you had that level of responsibility), you'll need to work with your Internet Service Provider, or ISP, to effect some of the changes and settings in this book. Your ISP has on staff (in one form or another) a person or team that is very familiar with your server and how to make it work properly. Get to know this person or the members of this team very well. Learn their first names. Be nice to them. Send them gifts at the holidays. They are your friends and, more important, they are your first line of tech support.

Every ISP is different, with varying rules as to who has what permissions and what services are available to your Web space; therefore, we're going to arbitrarily examine one working relationship: the end user who has been given a particular amount of Web space to sample with his or her account. Often this "practice space" is in the 2 to 10 megabyte range. Usually, you can pay for more space if you need it; the prices vary, but $1 per megabyte per month above the minimum is standard.

In purchasing this book, you already have Web space available to you. Digital Express Group (DIGEX) in Maryland, the home of the spider-works server, has graciously allowed you to log on to its servers for one month at no cost, just to try out the concepts presented in this book. If you like it, you can stay on as a DIGEX subscriber, and choose from a number of plans that best suit your needs.

> **By the Way...**
>
> For information on this plan, call Digital Express at 1-800-99-DIGEX, and mention *Learn HTML on the Macintosh*. Or log in as a new user as outlined later in this section. Keep this book handy when you call, as they'll be verifying some information. Once you're signed up, you have 30 days to play. There's no obligation on your part to continue.

We picked Digital Express because they have some of the finest tech support in the industry, available 24 hours a day. The technical staff includes people who in the past have set the standards for Internet communication and protocols. And if you ever need your own personal server, DIGEX can provide it; it has a separate tech force to meet the needs of those customers.

Digital Express has a plan called Personal IP, where your Macintosh is assigned an IP number that remains constant (rather than drawing from a pool of IP numbers every time you sign on), so that you can access more Internet services, especially those that require a static IP address for verification. DIGEX's Personal IP is a full Internet account, including access to such services as Telnet, whois, e-mail, IRC, and newsgroups. DIGEX supports PPP and SLIP connections, as well as frame relay.

In this chapter, we'll show you how to use your 30 days and 5 megs of Web space, including how to populate your space, how to set permissions so that the world can see your pages, and how to access DIGEX's mailto and forms CGI scripts. You are free to use any ISP you want (you may already be signed up with one), and although the concepts and directions presented here are specific to DIGEX, they are applicable to whatever service provider you use.

Choosing Your Connection Type

Choosing between SLIP and PPP is a matter of personal preference; in fact, we can't think of one reason, for the purposes of Web site development and

Chapter 11 Population and Maintenance of Your Web Site

maintenance, to choose one over the other. SLIP stands for Serial Line Interface Protocol, and PPP stands for Point-to-Point Protocol. Both are ways that your Macintosh MacTCP or Open Transport extensions connect, via standard 33,500 baud or below modem, with a terminal server at the ISP's location. The protocols are nothing more than the way that this occurs.

Pick one. We chose PPP because we like the freeware FreePPP point-to-point protocol interface control panel (and we've included it on the CD-ROM). We could just as easily have chosen SLIP as our protocol and used it with InterSLIP or MacSLIP (which we've also included on the CD-ROM) to make our connections. It's your call. DIGEX prefers PPP (and you will find more service providers doing the same) for several technical reasons. All the examples in this chapter were made with a PPP connection.

To connect to DIGEX:

1. Use any standard modem software set to 8-N-1, at any speed up to 28,800 BPS, and dial in to the DIGEX server closest to you at one of the numbers listed in Appendix A.
2. Enter **lhtml** as the user ID and hit **Return** instead of entering a password (see Figure 11.1).
3. You'll be given dial-up information and asked to enter the type of account you want: a shell account or a Personal IP account. If you have a credit card, you can sign up and be online immediately. Otherwise, DIGEX can mail information to you. Remember, you'll have 30 days from the time you sign, then you'll be charged for your time.
4. Once you get a user ID and a password, set up your login information with FreePPP's **Config PPP** control panel, as shown in Figure 11.2.

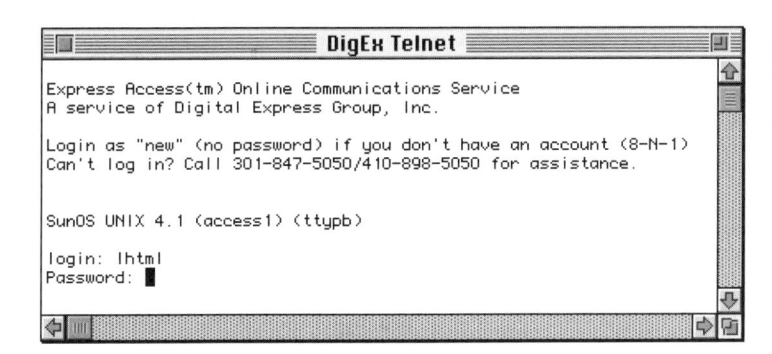

Figure 11.1
Logging in to DIGEX for the first time.

Figure 11.2
Config PPP's main window.

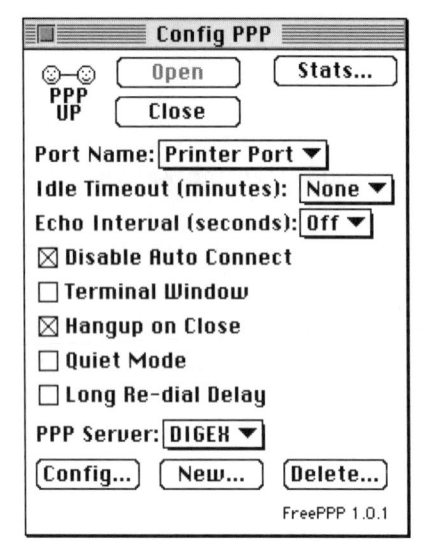

The **Config** button takes you to where the dial-up numbers, PPP passwords, and other details are entered; doing this is as much a science as it is an art, and the folks at DIGEX are there to help you. (And you can always send us e-mail at learnhtml@aol.com or lhtml@spiderworks.com. We can't guarantee instant response, but we'll do our best to respond quickly.)

After you get Config PPP set up properly and you are logging on consistently, you can use the PPPop applet to quickly log on to the server. It's as simple as clicking on the downward pointing arrow shown in Figure 11.3.

Figure 11.3
PPPop's simple user interface.

Once you are connected, test your TCP/IP-based applications: NCSA Telnet, Netscape, and Fetch. They should all work nicely.

Preparing Your Server

Throughout this book, we've espoused the concept of modeling your Web site on your Macintosh so that since your Web site works locally, putting the files out on the server in the same hierarchy is almost an afterthought. Here's where that pays off in spades.

Before you put the HTML files that you've created on the server, you need to understand a few things about the directory path that your server will create. Every Unix machine has a number of users; some have a few, some have thousands. Each user has a directory (called the user's **home directory**). It is common for that home directory to contain the Web space that comes with the account on the server. It is also common to see the following URL format:

```
http://www.ispservername.com/~username
```

The tilde (~) is a Unix convention that describes a shortcut to the browser (or ftp client) between the root directory and the user's home directory. The actual path might be:

```
http://www.[server]/local/etc/home/users/username/public_html/index.html
```

The tilde takes some of that extensive path out of the way, and directs inbound inquiries to the proper directory. When you sign up with DIGEX, your home directory will contain that /public_html directory.

Setting Permissions

In DIGEX's case (and most likely in the case of any ISP that has security concerns), you'll need to set some permissions before you can populate your Web space. Here's where we start doing a little dance with Unix commands.

You'll need to establish your SLIP or PPP connection before you can do any of these things, so go ahead and do that now. Either open the Config PPP control panel and click on Open, or, if you have the PPPop applet configured, click once on it to dial your ISP.

Once connected, launch NCSA Telnet. Connect with the access.digex.net server. Log in with your user ID and password. You will automatically be placed in your home directory.

A Little Unix   We know. You forgot that we told you that you'd have to learn a few Unix commands. Well, it's time. And they're not so bad. Really.

The first two are ls and cd. ls simply means "list the contents of the directory I'm currently in," and cd means "change directories to the one I specify." In this case, if you type ls when you are presented with the first prompt, you'll see four directories (think of them as folders). One of them is /public_html. That's our target.

1. Type:

   `cd public_html`

   to get to the public_html directory. It should be empty.

> **Important!** If the public_html directory does not exist, you will need to create it. To do so, type:
>
> `mkdir /ftp/<username>/public_html`

2. To set permission to create files in the new directory you'll need a third Unix command, `chmod`, or `'change mode'`. This command is for setting the file handling privileges within directories, and is fairly complex. Here, we need to type:

   `chmod 755 /ftp/<username>/public_html`

Once you get your Web space populated (and we're getting close…promise!), your main Web page, index.html, will be visible at the following URL:

`http://www.access.digex.net/~userid`

where *userid* is your login name on the DIGEX server. That's the URL you can put on your business cards.

Populating Your Directories

OK. You're ready to populate your directories.

We're about to add yet another tool to our utility belt—an FTP program from Dartmouth called Fetch. FTP stands for File Transfer Protocol—think of it as uploading and downloading on the Internet. Fetch is the program we'll use to get our files from our Mac's hard drive to the hard drive of our ISP's server. Fetch makes it particularly easy to do this by allowing dragging and dropping between windows on your desktop.

Fetch's installer is in the `Helpers` folder on the CD-ROM. Copy the installer to your Mac and double click on it. Once Fetch is installed, launch

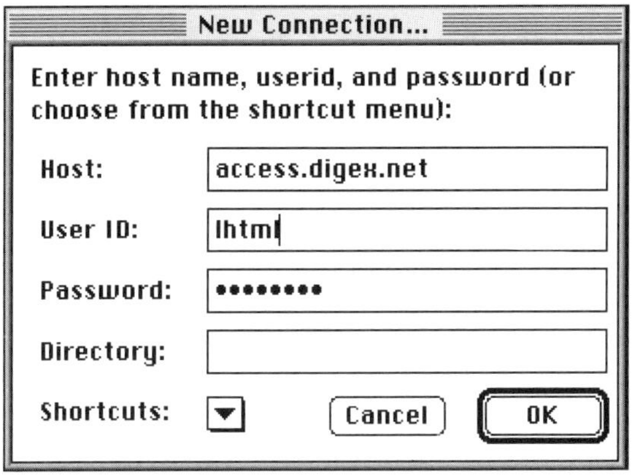

Figure 11.4
Logging on via Fetch.

it and choose **New Connection** from the **File** menu, and enter the data shown in Figure 11.4. Make sure you put in your userid and password.

Once you're connected, you'll see all of the files in your home directory. Ignore them and scroll down to the bottom of the list and look for your public_html directory (see Figure 11.5).

Double-click on it to open it. You'll see a blank screen, an empty directory, just waiting to be filled with the Web site you've designed (Figure 11.6).

Using Bookmarks for Populating Before we start populating the directory, let's discuss the necessity of using bookmarks as part of this process. Bookmarks are documents saved by Fetch that, when opened, take you directly to a particular directory on a particular server. In this case, we want your public_html directory.

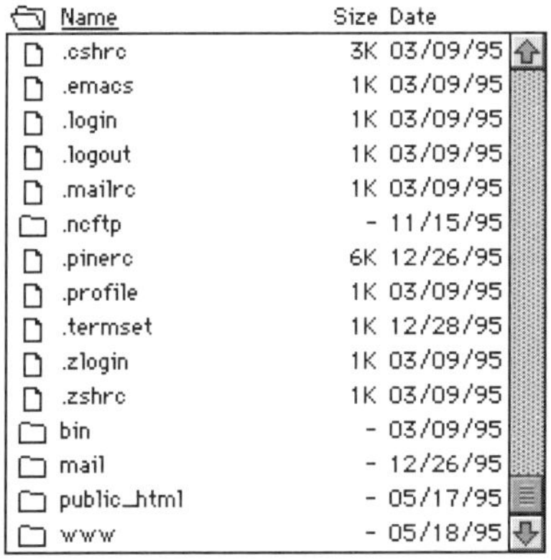

Figure 11.5
Your home directory.

Figure 11.6
A brand new public_html directory.

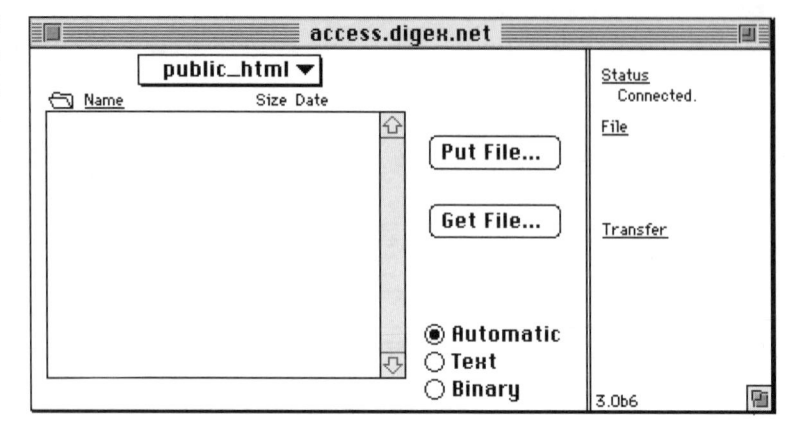

Use the **Save Bookmark** command under the **File** menu, as shown in Figure 11.7. You'll be prompted for a name to call your bookmark; the server name is the default, but you can change it to suit your needs.

From now on, whenever you want to launch Fetch and go directly to your main Web site directory, just double-click on your bookmark. You can create an alias for the bookmark and place it on your desktop or under your Apple Menu. You might find that later on, you'll want to add several bookmarks that point to often-updated directories in addition to the main public_html directory.

Setting the Transfer Mode With Web sites, it's rare that you'll be sending anything to your server in any format other than Raw Image (also known as Binary). This mode transfers files exactly as they appear and without any Macintosh headers or other information—just the raw text

Figure 11.7
Save Bookmark command.

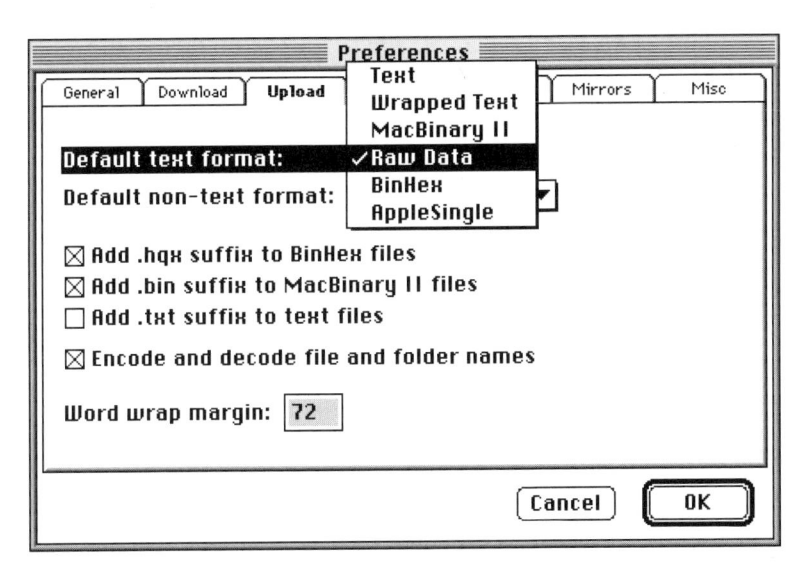

Figure 11.8
Setting default transfer mode in Fetch.

data. Fetch is like any other FTP client in that in transferring files, it attempts to keep their format intact. If we choose another type of transfer, Fetch gets a bit too smart, and starts adding suffixes to files (such as .txt to text files, which almost all of our files are). We don't want this, since we're saving all of our files with the appropriate extensions, like .html and .gif, when we create them.

We can direct Fetch to transfer *all* files in Raw Image mode by choosing the **Preferences** command from the **Customize** menu. Choose **Upload** from the tabs in the dialog box (see Figure 11.8) and select **Raw Data** for both the text and nontext files' pop-up menus.

Loading Files

We're all set to start loading up our files.

1. Open the folder on your hard drive that contains your Web site mirror. If there are any folders that you need to create on the ISP's server (a resources folder? folders within that?), do so now.
2. Choose **Create New Directory** from the **Directories** menu (see Figure 11.9).
3. You'll be prompted for a directory name (see Figure 11.10).
4. Once you create the new directory, you'll need to tell Fetch to refresh the file and directory lists, showing you what you've done.

Choose **Refresh File List** under the **Directories** menu, and your `resources` folder will appear. You can then double-click on the resources folder icon to open it, and then create subdirectories within it if you choose.

Figure 11.9
Creating a new directory with Fetch.

Figure 11.10
Name your new directory.

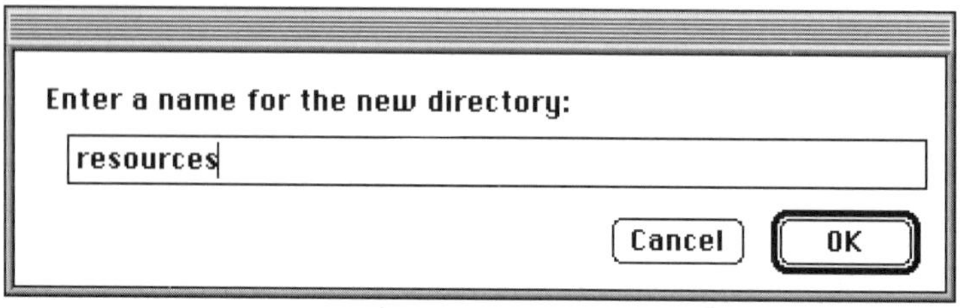

Setting Permissions Once you've created all of the directories you need, you can start dragging files to the Fetch window. Start at the `public_html` folder with the index.html document, and any other documents you want to place in your main Web directory. Then, double-click on the `resources` folder to change to that directory, and start populating the files and folders that go in there.

When you're all through, we have to go back to Telnet and reset permissions on our newly transferred files. Because Unix is such an open system, it has a fairly robust set of security features built in. One of these is file and directory permissions for reading, writing, and executing. You need to give permission to the world at large to read and execute these files in order for the Web server to be able to display them to everybody.

To do so, log on and type the following command at your first system prompt (usually access#):

```
chmod -R a+rx public_html *
```

This command is about the only other Unix command you need to know; in essence it means "change modes of permission on all of the files you find in the public_html directory so that they can be seen by the world. Do this recursively through all nested directories (remember resources and its subdirectories?) as well."

Working Faster

Now that you know how to populate the server after creating individual directories, here's a clue for working more efficiently. In Fetch, you can generate nested directories, directories within other directories, as you work. For example, we could have populated our Web site simply by opening our public_html directory on the ISP's server in the Fetch window, selecting all of the files and directories within our main HTML folder on our Mac, and dragging them into Fetch's window. Fetch would ask in what format we want files transferred (image/binary, naturally), and then go about the task of re-creating, on the server, the hierarchy as it exists on your hard drive.

Working with Your Service Provider

If you have your own server (as we do with spiderworks), and it's housed at the site of an Internet Service Provider, there will be times when you need someone to physically be at your server, either to restart it when it's hung or to load a new application, or to effect some change.

Installing RealAudio's server is a great example. That process requires accessing some directories that are usually off limits to anyone but the system administrators. Learning to work with these experts will go a long way toward getting things done quickly and in turn adding exciting content to your Web site.

In addition, some enlightened service providers (like DIGEX) offer certain Web design options, even to those who don't have their own servers.

Web Forms/E-Mail

DIGEX allows its shell and Personal IP users (that's you!) access to the Mailto-1.5 CGI script. This enables you to create your own custom e-mail forms, as we did in Chapter 8, with more options than the mailto: service prefix. You can request any information you want from users, not just their names and e-mail addresses, and e-mail will automatically be sent to you. Following their e-mail submission to you, the user will be directed to another Web page of your choosing, usually a thank-you page that tells them that their information was sent properly. If you recall, we set up just such a page when we looked at forms in Chapter 8.

Web Page Stats

Statistics are generated for each user who requests them, listing the number of hits to Web pages owned by that user. The stats also indicate the number of hits per page, per hour of the day, and per host name. The stats are sent once per week via e-mail.

Stats are generated using the Getstats package, and the report you receive lists not only the number of accesses your site got, but also which files were most popular, which domains on the Net hit your site most often, which countries accessed your site, and much more.

Clickable Image Maps

All DIGEX Shell and Personal IP customers can add clickable images to their Web pages, as we learned how to do in Chapter 7. The image map CGI script is located on DIGEX's server as:

```
/cgi-bin/imagemap
```

and will appear in your anchor tags as:

```
<a href="/cgi-bin/imagemap/~userid/mapfile.map"><IMG SRC="image.gif" ISMAP></a>
```

where "mapfile.map" is the name of the Web Map file, which corresponds to image.gif in your public_html directory. You may use as many image maps as you like on your pages, but each one must have its own .map file.

WebAccess Counter

DIGEX has installed a flexible counter CGI script that will display the number of times a page has been visited (since the first access) in an easy-to-read odometer format. You can select the width of the counter, increment it by one or more digits, reset it to 0, or keep your access count hidden.

Link to the access counter /cgi-bin/nph-count as you would to a standard image with the <IMG> tag, followed by a question mark (?) and the necessary arguments. Your HTML code will look like this:

```
<img src="/cgi-bin/nph-count?link=/~userid/page.html&width =5">
```

Chapter 11 Population and Maintenance of Your Web Site

where /~userid/page.html is the local URL of any Web page in your public_html directory on which you wish to display an access counter. You may use as many counters as you like. Use multiple counters simply by changing the URL after the link= argument. You can add multiple arguments by separating them with ampersands (&). For example:

```
<img src="/cgi-bin/nph-count?width=5&link=foo.html&arg3= val3">
```

> **width**=number. Specifies the number of digits in the resulting image.
> **link**=URL of the page on which the counter is located. The link argument is used to keep track of a certain counter. It should be unique for each counter.
> **increase**=number (defaults to 1). Specifies the number by which the counter should be increased.
> **show**=NO. You might want to keep track of the number of accesses to a certain page without showing the counter image.

Ongoing Maintenance of Your Site

Remember to check the links on your site once the directories have been populated to make sure that they work, and that the multimedia files to which they take the user download properly and play or display through the appropriate helper application.

Proper site maintenance requires some organization. You'll find that some sites are static: once they are up, they rarely change. In others, the content of the pages will change with some frequency. For those, we recommend that you prepare a maintenance job sheet on which to list the pages in the site, what they are, how they link, and what needs to be updated. And if you have to create multimedia files on an ongoing basis, make a list for yourself as to how you created them.

appendix A

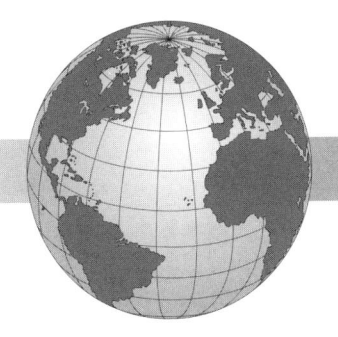

DIGEX Packages

DIGEX Shell Service

E-Mail Shell

News and Mail allows the user to access Internet Electronic Mail and USENET newsgroups (over 10,000 discussion topics and worldwide coverage). This service allows international communications for only $15 a month.

Full Shell builds on the basic package with complete access to all Internet "real-time" functions such as FTP (File Transfer Protocol), Telnet, IRC (Internet Relay Chat), Gopher, WAIS, World Wide Web, and the many other packages available on the network. Full Internet service is $25 per month.

Both services have a one-time set up fee of $20. Each package offers six hours per day of free time and 5 MB of disk storage space. Additional on-line time is billable at $1 an hour; additional disk storage is billable at $1–$2 per megabyte per month.

All DIGEX shell accounts include the capability of making files available via anonymous FTP to others on the Internet, and for making Web pages available via the World Wide Web. DIGEX Shell accounts can be paid for with credit cards or personal checks. Electronic mail invoices are sent, and paper invoicing is provided to corporations or government organizations that require it.

The DIGEX shell service is perfect for the individual or the small corporation just starting to explore the Internet and discover its application to business or personal interests. It allows complete access to all of the resources of the network, but absolutely no requirement that the customer be an expert with the systems and technologies that make it all work. A *User's Guide* is supplied to each user, showing the basic commands, thus enabling the user to begin accessing the Internet immediately. An electronic copy is also available online.

On-line registration is available with a credit card (Visa, MC, Discover, American Express, Diners). Simply use one of the local dial-up numbers to call the system (modem settings 8-N-1) and type **new** at the login prompt. Please allow one to two business days to process the account application.

Personal-IP—Dynamic PPP Dial-Up Connection

PPP (Point-to-Point Protocol) services have become very popular, as they allow individuals to dial up over a phone line and directly connect their workstation to the Internet. Unlike Express Access and Private Domain services, where users are dialing into a system with "dumb" terminal emulation on their PCs, Personal IP service allows a customer's computer to become a fully functional host on the Internet. The advantages include the ability to use all of the latest graphical display technology with Macintosh and Windows front-end applications, such as Mosaic and Cello, and direct FTP from any site on the Net to workstation.

Flexibility comes with a price. PPP requires users to have the expertise to install and manage their own TCP/IP software. DIGEX provides the network link and associated services, such as news feeds, mail routing, and name service, but the system itself is the responsibility of the customers, as is the network software on their end. Some customers may wish to seek the help of a consultant or systems integrator for initial setup.

Suggested configuration:

- PC or Macintosh
- 14.4 Kbps or better modem

- TCP/IP software (TCP Connect II, Chameleon, and many other commercial and shareware packages).

For further information, contact DIGEX as follows.

Digital Express Group, Inc.	301-847-5000 ; 410-898-5000; fax -5215
6800 Virginia Manor Road	201-460-2800; 212-843-8787; 215-349-6100
Beltsville, MD 20705 USA	800-969-9090; info@digex.net
Washington, DC metro	301-847-5000; Help Desk: 847-5050
Baltimore, MD metro	410-898-5000; Help Desk: 898-5050
New York, NY	212-843-8787
Northern NJ (Rutherford)	201- 460-2800
Philadelphia, PA	215-349-6100
All other areas:	800-969-9090
Fax:	301-847-5215; 410-898-5215

Dial-up modem phone numbers for Express Access as of November 28, 1995

Use the following local telephone numbers to connect to the Express Access Service. Set your terminal program to vt100/102 emulation, 8 bits, no parity, and login as **lhtml** at the **login** prompt. Press **Enter** at the **Password** prompt if necessary.

If you are outside the local DIGEX coverage area, call to see if extended coverage is offered.

State/Area code/City	Data Number	Customer Support
Delaware (302)		
Wilmington/Holly Oak	610-558-0707	215-349-6100
Maryland (301/410)		
Annapolis area	410-451-0390	800-969-9090
Baltimore area	410-898-5252	410-898-5050
Easton/Kent Island/Centerville	410-819-8570	800-969-9090
Frederick/Mt. Airy	301-414-0091	800-969-9090
Gaithersburg/Damascus	301-847-5252	301-847-5050

Harford County	410-877-9586	800-969-9090
Waldorf/Indian Head/ Brandywine	301-808-0386	800-969-9090
Washington DC Metro area (14.4)	301-220-0258	301-847-5050
Washington DC Metro area (28.8)	301-847-5252	301-847-5050
Westminster/Sykesville/ Parkton	410-583-5252	800-969-9090
New York (212/516/718/914/917)		
New York City	212-843-2102	212-843-8787
New Jersey (201/908/609)		
Atlantic City	609-348-6203	800-969-9090
Avalon/Cape May/Wildwood	609-390-1496	800-969-9090
Beach Haven/Egg Harbor/ Tuckerton	609-484-9553	800-969-9090
Rutherford/Hackensack	201-460-2804	201-460-2800
Hammonton/Vineland/ Millville	609-476-3894	800-969-9090
Plainfield area	908-753-0050	800-969-9090
New Brunswick area	908-937-9481	800-969-9090
Trenton area	609-278-8909	800-969-9090
Pennsylvania (215/610)		
Philadelphia	215-349-6106	215-349-6100
Doylestown area	215-343-8967	215-349-6100
Lansdale/Collegeville area	610-631-6476	215-349-6100
West Chester/Mendenhall area	610-558-0707	215-349-6100
Pittsburgh	412-565-3104	800-969-9090
Virginia (703)		
Woodbridge/Manassas	703-207-0191	800-969-9090
Tappahannock	804-443-0034	800-969-9090

Special PPP Instructions:

- New Brunswick customers should use a default route/gateway of 199.34.50.63 and call 908-937-5565.
- Plainfield NJ customers should use a default route/gateway of 199.125.190.63 and call 908-753-0336.
- All other customers should use a default route/gateway of 204.91.204.91 and call the appropriate number listed in the table above.

DIGEX Price List and Product Availability as of April 15, 1996

Product	Area Rate	Monthly Rate	Yearly Rate	Start-up Fee
DIGEX Shell (Full)	All	$25	$250	$20
DIGEX Shell (E-mail)	All	$15	$150	$20
Personal-IP	All	$35	$350	$20
Full-time IP	All	$99	$1188*	$295

Some services are not available in all areas.
Frame Relay: Call for pricing
Direct-IP/Leased: Call for pricing
Private Domain: Call for pricing
* Start-up fee is waived if yearly fee is paid in advance
New Jersey customers must add 6% state sales tax.

appendix B

HTML Character Equivalencies

Here's a complete list of the ISO-Latin characters and their metacharacter equivalencies. You might want to make a copy of this table and keep it handy. Or you can tear the page out. If you must. We won't tell!

Description	Char	Character	Entity Name
space, blank		&#032;	&sp;
exclamation mark	!	&#033;	&excl;
double quotation mark	"	&#034;	&quot;
number sign	#	&#035;	&num;
dollar sign	$	&#036;	&dollar;
percent sign	%	&#037;	&percnt;
ampersand	&	&#038;	&amp;
apostrophe/single quote	'	&#039;	apos;
left parenthesis	(	&#040;	&lpar;
right parenthesis	)	&#041;	&rpar;

Description	Char	Character	Entity Name
asterisk	*	&#042;	&ast;
plus sign	+	&#043;	&plus;
comma	,	&#044;	&comma;
minus sign/hyphen/dash	-	&#045;	‐ or − or ‐
period/decimal point	.	&#046;	&period;
slash, solidus	/	&#047;	&sol;
digit 0	0	&#048;	0
digit 1	1	&#049;	1
digit 2	2	&#050;	2
digit 3	3	&#051;	3
digit 4	4	&#052;	4
digit 5	5	&#053;	5
digit 6	6	&#054;	6
digit 7	7	&#055;	7
digit 8	8	&#056;	8
digit 9	9	&#057;	9
colon	:	&#058;	&colon;
semicolon	;	&#059;	&semi;
less-than sign	<	&#060;	&lt;
equal sign	=	&#061;	&equals;
greater-than sign	>	&#062;	&gt;
question mark	?	&#063;	&quest;
Uppercase Letters			
commercial at sign	@	&#064;	&commat;
capital A	A	&#065;	A
capital B	B	&#066;	B
capital C	C	&#067;	C

Appendix B   HTML Character Equivalencies

Description	Char	Character	Entity Name
capital D	D	&#068;	D
capital E	E	&#069;	E
capital F	F	&#070;	F
capital G	G	&#071;	G
capital H	H	&#072;	H
capital I	I	&#073;	I
capital J	J	&#074;	J
capital K	K	&#075;	K
capital L	L	&#076;	L
capital M	M	&#077;	M
capital N	N	&#078;	N
capital O	O	&#079;	O
capital P	P	&#080;	P
capital Q	Q	&#081;	Q
capital R	R	&#082;	R
capital S	S	&#083;	S
capital T	T	&#084;	T
capital U	U	&#085;	U
capital V	V	&#086;	V
capital W	W	&#087;	W
capital X	X	&#088;	X
capital Y	Y	&#089;	Y
capital Z	Z	&#090;	Z
left square bracket	[	&#091;	&lsqb;
backslash/rev solidus	\	&#092;	&bsol;
right square bracket	]	&#093;	&rsqb;
circumflex	^	&#094;	&circ;
underscore	_	&#095;	&lowbar;

Description	Char	Character	Entity Name
Lowercase Letters			
spacing grave accent	`	&#096;	&grave;
small a	a	&#097;	a
small b	b	&#098;	b
small c	c	&#099;	c
small d	d	&#100;	d
small e	e	&#101;	e
small f	f	&#102;	f
small g	g	&#103;	g
small h	h	&#104;	h
small i	i	&#105;	i
small j	j	&#106;	j
small k	k	&#107;	k
small l	l	&#108;	l
small m	m	&#109;	m
small n	n	&#110;	n
small o	o	&#111;	o
small p	p	&#112;	p
small q	q	&#113;	q
small r	r	&#114;	r
small s	s	&#115;	s
small t	t	&#116;	t
small u	u	&#117;	u
small v	v	&#118;	v
small w	w	&#119;	w
small x	x	&#120;	x
small y	y	&#121;	y
small z	z	&#122;	z

Appendix B HTML Character Equivalencies

Description	Char	Character	Entity Name
left brace	{	&#123;	&lcub;
vertical bar	|	&#124;	&verbar;
right brace	}	&#125;	&rcub;
tilde	~	&#126;	&tilde;
Special Characters			
non-breaking space			
inverted exclamation	¡	&#161;	&iexcl;
cent sign	¢	&#162;	&cent;
pound sterling sign	£	&#163;	&pound;
general currency sign	¤	&#164;	&curren;
yen sign	¥	&#165;	&yen;
broken vertical bar	¦	&#166;	&brvbar;
section sign	§	&#167;	&sect;
dieresis or umlaut	¨	&#168;	&uml;
copyright sign	©	&#169;	&copy;
fem ordinal indicator	ª	&#170;	&ordf;
left (double) angle	«	&#171;	&laquo;
logical not sign	¬	&#172;	&not;
soft hyphen		&#173;	&shy;
registered trademark	®	&#174;	&reg;
macron (long) accent	¯	&#175;	&macr;
degree sign	°	&#176;	&deg;
plus-or-minus sign	±	&#177;	&plusmn;
superscript 1	¹	&#185;	&sup1;
superscript 2	²	&#178;	&sup2;
superscript 3	³	&#179;	&sup3;
spacing acute accent	´	&#180;	&acute;
micro sign	µ	&#181;	&micro;
paragraph sign, pilcrow sign	¶	&#182;	&para;

Description	Char	Character	Entity Name
middle dot, centered dot	·	&#183;	&middot;
spacing cedilla	¸	&#184;	&cedil;
masculine ordinal indicator	º	&#186;	&ordm;
right (double) angle quote	»	&#187;	&raquo;
fraction 1/4	¼	&#188;	&frac14;
fraction 1/2	½	&#189;	½ or ½
fraction 3/4	¾	&#190;	&frac34;
inverted question mark	¿	&#191;	&iquest;
Uppercase Latin-1 Letters			
capital A grave	À	&#192;	&Agrave;
capital A acute	Á	&#193;	&Aacute;
capital A circumflex	Â	&#194;	&Acirc;
capital A tilde	Ã	&#195;	&Atilde;
capital A dieresis or umlaut	Ä	&#196;	&Auml;
capital A ring	Å	&#197;	Å or Å
capital AE ligature	Æ	&#198;	&AElig;
capital C cedilla	Ç	&#199;	&Ccedil;
capital E grave	È	&#200;	&Egrave;
capital E acute	É	&#201;	&Eacute;
capital E circumflex	Ê	&#202;	&Ecirc;
capital E dieresis or umlaut	Ë	&#203;	&Euml;
capital I grave	Ì	&#204;	&Igrave;
capital I acute	Í	&#205;	&Iacute;
capital I circumflex	Î	&#206;	&Icirc;
capital I dieresis or umlaut	Ï	&#207;	&Iuml;

Appendix B HTML Character Equivalencies

Description	Char	Character	Entity Name
capital ETH	Ð	&#208;	Ð or Đ
capital N tilde	Ñ	&#209;	&Ntilde;
capital O grave	Ò	&#210;	&Ograve;
capital O acute	Ó	&#211;	&Oacute;
capital O circumflex	Ô	&#212;	&Ocirc;
capital O tilde	Õ	&#213;	&Otilde;
capital O dieresis or umlaut	Ö	&#214;	&Ouml;
multiplication sign	×	&#215;	&times;
capital O slash	Ø	&#216;	&Oslash;
capital U grave	Ù	&#217;	&Ugrave;
capital U acute	Ú	&#218;	&Uacute;
capital U circumflex	Û	&#219;	&Ucirc;
capital U dieresis or umlaut	Ü	&#220;	&Uuml;
capital Y acute	Ý	&#221;	&Yacute;
capital THORN	Þ	&#222;	&THORN;
small sharp s, sz ligature	ß	&#223;	&szlig;
Lowercase Latin-1 Letters			
small a grave	à	&#224;	&agrave;
small a acute	á	&#225;	&aacute;
small a circumflex	â	&#226;	&acirc;
small a tilde	ã	&#227;	&atilde;
small a umlaut	ä	&#228;	&auml;
small a ring	å	&#229;	&aring;
small ae ligature	æ	&#230;	&aelig;
small c cedilla	ç	&#231;	&ccedil;
small e grave	è	&#232;	&egrave;
small e acute	é	&#233;	&eacute;
small e circumflex	ê	&#234;	&ecirc;

Description	Char	Character	Entity Name
small e umlaut	ë	&#235;	&euml;
small i grave	ì	&#236;	&igrave;
small i acute	í	&#237;	&iacute;
small i circumflex	î	&#238;	&icirc;
small i umlaut	ï	&#239;	&iuml;
small eth	›	&#240;	&eth;
small n tilde	ñ	&#241;	&ntilde;
small o grave	ò	&#242;	&ograve;
small o acute	ó	&#243;	&oacute;
small o circumflex	ô	&#244;	&ocirc;
small o tilde	õ	&#245;	&otilde;
small o umlaut	ö	&#246;	&ouml;
division sign	÷	&#247;	&divide;
small o slash	ø	&#248;	&oslash;
small u grave	ù	&#249;	&ugrave;
small u acute	ú	&#250;	&uacute;
small u circumflex	û	&#251;	&ucirc;
small u umlaut	ü	&#252;	&uuml;
small y acute	‡	&#253;	&yacute;
small thorn	fl	&#254;	&thorn;
small y umlaut	ÿ	&#255;	&yuml;

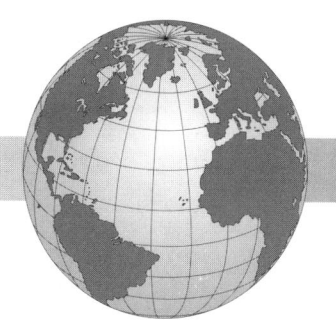

appendix C

Calendar

This table was created for The American Comedy Network (ACN), a site that includes a lot of examples of the typical work that you might be doing for the average Web site. ACN's morning show hosts use the network's Web site to get their daily radio show preparation material; the site is updated daily by ACN's staff of writers. This table was created to enable the radio personalities who visit the ACN site to review prep material throughout the course of the year, in case a topic becomes hot again. They can simply click on a day and see the prep sheet for that day. We created a calendar table (Figure C.1) and you can adapt the interface to suit your application: Feel free to use it, but remember, it needs to be redone every year by hand. To get you started, both 1996.html and 1997.html are in the `Authoring` folder.

The calendar is presented with three months across in each row. The table format requires that each set of three months be grouped together by progressive weeks: since January, February, and March make up the top cells of the 3 × 4 calendar grid, the first week of January, the first week of February, and the first week of March combined comprise the actual data for the first row of the table, followed by the second weeks of January, February, and March in the next row, and so on.

Each month can have dates that fall in up to six different weeks, if the month begins on a Friday or Saturday. So some months have filler blank

Figure C.1
Calendar in table form.

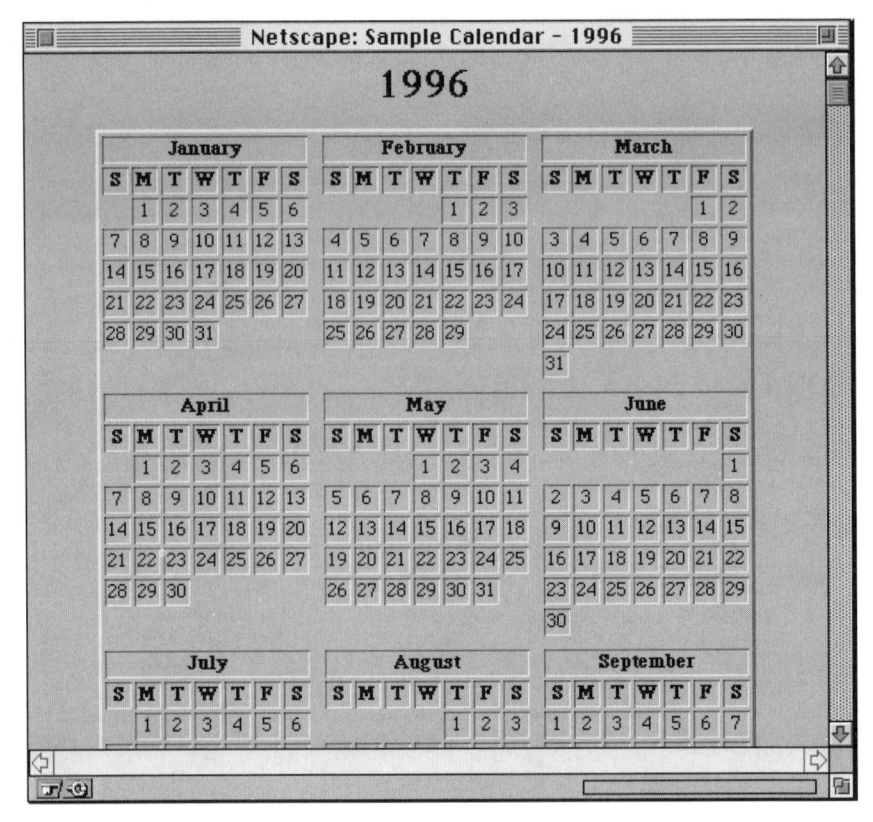

[Figure C.1: Screenshot of Netscape window titled "Sample Calendar - 1996" showing a 1996 calendar in table form with months January through September visible.]

days at the beginning and end of the months, so that each month lines up with the other months in its row. It's a good idea to just go ahead and keep those filler days, since you may need them next year.

Note that the calendar lines up correctly in the figure because it's displayed in centered preformatted text, which you recall is monospaced; in Netscape, it's usually shown in Courier.

Once the table is laid out, it's a simple matter of placing anchor tags around each date. Table data without an anchor looks like this:

```
<!-- Fifth week of March -->
<td align=center>24</td>
```

The same code with an anchor tag linking to the document **stuff.html** in the same directory as the calendar looks like this:

```
<!-- Fifth week of March -->
<td align=center><a href="stuff.html">24</a></td>
```

Finally, if you visit the ACN site it only uses links for the business days of the week, Monday through Friday, but you can obviously use any days you want. You can find it in use at http://american.comedy.com/acn. Here's the entire code:

```
<!doctype html public \"-//W30//DTD W3 HTML 2.0//EN\">

<HTML>

<HEAD>
<TITLE>
Sample Calendar - 1996
</TITLE>
</HEAD>

<BODY>
<center>
<h1>1996</h1>
<table border=2>

<!-- January/February/March -->

<tr><td colspan=7 align=middle><b>January</b></td><td></td><td colspan=7 align=middle><b>February</b></td><td></td><td colspan=7 align=middle><b>March</b></td></tr>

<!-- Days if the week -->

<tr><th>S</th><th>M</th><th>T</th><th>W</th><th>T</th><th>F</th><th>S</th><td></td><th>S</th><th>M</th><th>T</th><th>W</th><th>T</th><th>F</th><th>S</th><td></td><th>S</th><th>M</th><th>T</th><th>W</th><th>T</th><th>F</th><th>S</th></tr>

<tr align=right valign=middle>

<!-- First week of January -->

<td></td>
<td align=center>1</td>
<td align=center>2</td>
<td align=center>3</td>
<td align=center>4</td>
<td align=center>5</td>
<td align=center>6</td>

<td></td>

<!-- First week of February -->

<td></td>
<td></td>
<td></td>
```

```
<td></td>
<td align=center>1</td>
<td align=center>2</td>
<td align=center>3</td>

<td></td>

<!-- First week of March -->

<td></td>
<td></td>
<td></td>
<td></td>
<td></td>
<td align=center>1</td>
<td align=center>2</td>

</tr>

<tr align=right valign=middle>

<!-- Second week of January -->

<td align=center>7</td>
<td align=center>8</td>
<td align=center>9</td>
<td align=center>10</td>
<td align=center>11</td>
<td align=center>12</td>
<td align=center>13</td>

<td></td>

<!-- Second week of February -->

<td align=center>4</td>
<td align=center>5</td>
<td align=center>6</td>
<td align=center>7</td>
<td align=center>8</td>
<td align=center>9</td>
<td align=center>10</td>

<td></td>

<!-- Second week of March -->

<td align=center>3</td>
<td align=center>4</td>
<td align=center>5</td>
<td align=center>6</td>
<td align=center>7</td>
```

```
        <td align=center>8</td>
        <td align=center>9</td>

    </tr>

    <tr align=right valign=middle>

    <!-- Third week of January -->

        <td align=center>14</td>
        <td align=center>15</td>
        <td align=center>16</td>
        <td align=center>17</td>
        <td align=center>18</td>
        <td align=center>19</td>
        <td align=center>20</td>

    <td></td>

    <!-- Third week of February -->

        <td align=center>11</td>
        <td align=center>12</td>
        <td align=center>13</td>
        <td align=center>14</td>
        <td align=center>15</td>
        <td align=center>16</td>
        <td align=center>17</td>

    <td></td>

    <!-- Third week of March -->

        <td align=center>10</td>
        <td align=center>11</td>
        <td align=center>12</td>
        <td align=center>13</td>
        <td align=center>14</td>
        <td align=center>15</td>
        <td align=center>16</td>

    </tr>

    <tr align=right valign=middle>

    <!-- Fourth week of January -->

        <td align=center>21</td>
        <td align=center>22</td>
        <td align=center>23</td>
        <td align=center>24</td>
        <td align=center>25</td>
```

```
<td align=center>26</td>
<td align=center>27</td>

<td></td>

<!-- Fourth week of February-->

<td align=center>18</td>
<td align=center>19</td>
<td align=center>20</td>
<td align=center>21</td>
<td align=center>22</td>
<td align=center>23</td>
<td align=center>24</td>

<td></td>

<!-- Fourth week of March -->

<td align=center>17</td>
<td align=center>18</td>
<td align=center>19</td>
<td align=center>20</td>
<td align=center>21</td>
<td align=center>22</td>
<td align=center>23</td>

</tr>

<tr align=right valign=middle>

<!-- Fifth week of January -->

<td align=center>28</td>
<td align=center>29</td>
<td align=center>30</td>
<td align=center>31</td>
<td></td>
<td></td>
<td></td>

<td></td>

<!-- Fifth week of February (leap year? yes!!)  -->

<td align=center>25</td>
<td align=center>26</td>
<td align=center>27</td>
<td align=center>28</td>
<td align=center>29</td>
<td></td>
<td></td>
```

```
<td></td>

<!-- Fifth week of March -->

<td align=center>24</td>
<td align=center>25</td>
<td align=center>26</td>
<td align=center>27</td>
<td align=center>28</td>
<td align=center>29</td>
<td align=center>30</td>

<tr align=right valign=middle>

<!-- Sixth week of January -->

<td></td>
<td></td>
<td></td>
<td></td>
<td></td>
<td></td>
<td></td>

<td></td>

<!-- Sixth week of February -->

<td></td>
<td></td>
<td></td>
<td></td>
<td></td>
<td></td>
<td></td>

<td></td>

<!-- Sixth week of March -->

<td align=center>31</td>
<td></td>
<td></td>
<td></td>
<td></td>
<td></td>
<td></td>

</tr>

<tr><td></td></tr>
```

```
<!-- April/May/June -->

<tr><td colspan=7 align=middle><b>April</b></td><td></td><td
colspan=7 align=middle><b>May</b></td><td></td><td colspan=7
align=middle><b>June</b></td></tr>

<!-- Days if the week -->

<tr><th>S</th><th>M</th><th>T</th><th>W</th><th>T</th><th>F</th><th
>S</th><td></td><th>S</th><th>M</th><th>T</th><th>W</th><th>T</th><
th>F</th><th>S</th><td></td><th>S</th><th>M</th><th>T</th><th>W</th
><th>T</th><th>F</th><th>S</th></tr>

<tr align=right valign=middle>

<!-- First week of April -->

<td></td>
<td align=center>1</td>
<td align=center>2</td>
<td align=center>3</td>
<td align=center>4</td>
<td align=center>5</td>
<td align=center>6</td>

<td></td>

<!-- First week of May -->

<td></td>
<td></td>
<td></td>
<td align=center>1</td>
<td align=center>2</td>
<td align=center>3</td>
<td align=center>4</td>

<td></td>

<!-- First week of June -->

<td></td>
<td></td>
<td></td>
<td></td>
<td></td>
<td></td>
<td align=center>1</td>

</tr>
```

Appendix C Calendar

```
<tr align=right valign=middle>

<!-- Second week of April -->

<td align=center>7</td>
<td align=center>8</td>
<td align=center>9</td>
<td align=center>10</td>
<td align=center>11</td>
<td align=center>12</td>
<td align=center>13</td>

<td></td>

<!-- Second week of May -->

<td align=center>5</td>
<td align=center>6</td>
<td align=center>7</td>
<td align=center>8</td>
<td align=center>9</td>
<td align=center>10</td>
<td align=center>11</td>

<td></td>

<!-- Second week of June -->

<td align=center>2</td>
<td align=center>3</td>
<td align=center>4</td>
<td align=center>5</td>
<td align=center>6</td>
<td align=center>7</td>
<td align=center>8</td>

</tr>

<tr align=right valign=middle>

<!-- Third week of April -->

<td align=center>14</td>
<td align=center>15</td>
<td align=center>16</td>
<td align=center>17</td>
<td align=center>18</td>
<td align=center>19</td>
<td align=center>20</td>

<td></td>
```

```
<!-- Third week of May -->

<td align=center>12</td>
<td align=center>13</td>
<td align=center>14</td>
<td align=center>15</td>
<td align=center>16</td>
<td align=center>17</td>
<td align=center>18</td>

<td></td>

<!-- Third week of June -->

<td align=center>9</td>
<td align=center>10</td>
<td align=center>11</td>
<td align=center>12</td>
<td align=center>13</td>
<td align=center>14</td>
<td align=center>15</td>

</tr>

<tr align=right valign=middle>

<!-- Fourth week of April -->

<td align=center>21</td>
<td align=center>22</td>
<td align=center>23</td>
<td align=center>24</td>
<td align=center>25</td>
<td align=center>26</td>
<td align=center>27</td>

<td></td>

<!-- Fourth week of May -->

<td align=center>19</td>
<td align=center>20</td>
<td align=center>21</td>
<td align=center>22</td>
<td align=center>23</td>
<td align=center>24</td>
<td align=center>25</td>

<td></td>

<!-- Fourth week of June -->
```

```html
<td align=center>16</td>
<td align=center>17</td>
<td align=center>18</td>
<td align=center>19</td>
<td align=center>20</td>
<td align=center>21</td>
<td align=center>22</td>

</tr>

<tr align=right valign=middle>

<!-- Fifth week of April -->

<td align=center>28</td>
<td align=center>29</td>
<td align=center>30</td>
<td></td>
<td></td>
<td></td>
<td></td>

<td></td>

<!-- Fifth week of May -->

<td align=center>26</td>
<td align=center>27</td>
<td align=center>28</td>
<td align=center>29</td>
<td align=center>30</td>
<td align=center>31</td>
<td></td>

<td></td>

<!-- Fifth week of June -->

<td align=center>23</td>
<td align=center>24</td>
<td align=center>25</td>
<td align=center>26</td>
<td align=center>27</td>
<td align=center>28</td>
<td align=center>29</td>

</tr>

<tr align=right valign=middle>

<!-- Sixth week of April -->
```

```html
<td></td>
<td></td>
<td></td>
<td></td>
<td></td>
<td></td>
<td></td>

<td></td>

<!-- Sixth week of May -->

<td></td>
<td></td>
<td></td>
<td></td>
<td></td>
<td></td>
<td></td>

<td></td>

<!-- Sixth week of June -->

<td align=center>30</td>
<td></td>
<td></td>
<td></td>
<td></td>
<td></td>
<td></td>

<tr><td></td></tr>

<!-- July/August/September -->

<tr><td colspan=7 align=middle><b>July</b></td><td></td><td colspan=7 align=middle><b>August</b></td><td></td><td colspan=7 align=middle><b>September</b></td></tr>

<!-- Days if the week -->

<tr><th>S</th><th>M</th><th>T</th><th>W</th><th>T</th><th>F</th><th>S</th><td></td><th>S</th><th>M</th><th>T</th><th>W</th><th>T</th><th>F</th><th>S</th><td></td><th>S</th><th>M</th><th>T</th><th>W</th><th>T</th><th>F</th><th>S</th></tr>

<tr align=right valign=middle>

<!-- First week of July -->

<td></td>
```

Appendix C Calendar

```
<td align=center>1</td>
<td align=center>2</td>
<td align=center>3</td>
<td align=center>4</td>
<td align=center>5</td>
<td align=center>6</td>

<td></td>

<!-- First week of August -->

<td></td>
<td></td>
<td></td>
<td></td>
<td align=center>1</td>
<td align=center>2</td>
<td align=center>3</td>

<td></td>

<!-- First week of September -->

<td align=center>1</td>
<td align=center>2</td>
<td align=center>3</td>
<td align=center>4</td>
<td align=center>5</td>
<td align=center>6</td>
<td align=center>7</td>

</tr>

<tr align=right valign=middle>

<!-- Second week of July -->

<td align=center>7</td>
<td align=center>8</td>
<td align=center>9</td>
<td align=center>10</td>
<td align=center>11</td>
<td align=center>12</td>
<td align=center>13</td>

<td></td>

<!-- Second week of August -->

<td align=center>4</td>
<td align=center>5</td>
<td align=center>6</td>
```

```html
            <td align=center>7</td>
            <td align=center>8</td>
            <td align=center>9</td>
            <td align=center>10</td>

            <td></td>

            <!-- Second week of September -->

            <td align=center>8</td>
            <td align=center>9</td>
            <td align=center>10</td>
            <td align=center>11</td>
            <td align=center>12</td>
            <td align=center>13</td>
            <td align=center>14</td>

        </tr>

        <tr align=right valign=middle>

            <!-- Third week of July -->

            <td align=center>14</td>
            <td align=center>15</td>
            <td align=center>16</td>
            <td align=center>17</td>
            <td align=center>18</td>
            <td align=center>19</td>
            <td align=center>20</td>

            <td></td>

            <!-- Third week of August -->

            <td align=center>11</td>
            <td align=center>12</td>
            <td align=center>13</td>
            <td align=center>14</td>
            <td align=center>15</td>
            <td align=center>16</td>
            <td align=center>17</td>

            <td></td>

            <!-- Third week of September -->

            <td align=center>15</td>
            <td align=center>16</td>
            <td align=center>17</td>
            <td align=center>18</td>
            <td align=center>19</td>
```

```html
<td align=center>20</td>
<td align=center>21</td>

</tr>

<tr align=right valign=middle>

<!-- Fourth week of July -->

<td align=center>21</td>
<td align=center>22</td>
<td align=center>23</td>
<td align=center>24</td>
<td align=center>25</td>
<td align=center>26</td>
<td align=center>27</td>

<td></td>

<!-- Fourth week of August -->

<td align=center>18</td>
<td align=center>19</td>
<td align=center>20</td>
<td align=center>21</td>
<td align=center>22</td>
<td align=center>23</td>
<td align=center>24</td>

<td></td>

<!-- Fourth week of September -->

<td align=center>22</td>
<td align=center>23</td>
<td align=center>24</td>
<td align=center>25</td>
<td align=center>26</td>
<td align=center>27</td>
<td align=center>28</td>

</tr>

<tr align=right valign=middle>

<!-- Fifth week of July -->

<td align=center>28</td>
<td align=center>29</td>
<td align=center>30</td>
<td align=center>31</td>
<td></td>
```

```
<td></td>
<td></td>

<td></td>

<!-- Fifth week of August -->

<td align=center>25</td>
<td align=center>26</td>
<td align=center>27</td>
<td align=center>28</td>
<td align=center>29</td>
<td align=center>30</td>
<td align=center>31</td>

<td></td>

<!-- Fifth week of September -->

<td align=center>29</td>
<td align=center>30</td>
<td></td>
<td></td>
<td></td>
<td></td>
<td></td>

<tr><td></td></tr>

<!-- October/November/December -->

<tr><td colspan=7 align=middle><b>October</b></td><td></td><td colspan=7 align=middle><b>November</b></td><td></td><td colspan=7 align=middle><b>December</b></td></tr>

<!-- Days if the week -->

<tr><th>S</th><th>M</th><th>T</th><th>W</th><th>T</th><th>F</th><th>S</th><td></td><th>S</th><th>M</th><th>T</th><th>W</th><th>T</th><th>F</th><th>S</th><td></td><th>S</th><th>M</th><th>T</th><th>W</th><th>T</th><th>F</th><th>S</th></tr>

<tr align=right valign=middle>

<!-- First week of October -->

<td></td>
<td></td>
<td align=center>1</td>
<td align=center>2</td>
<td align=center>3</td>
<td align=center>4</td>
```

```
<td align=center>5</td>

<td></td>

<!-- First week of November -->

<td></td>
<td></td>
<td></td>
<td></td>
<td></td>
<td align=center>1</td>
<td align=center>2</td>

<td></td>

<!-- First week of December -->

<td align=center>1</td>
<td align=center>2</td>
<td align=center>3</td>
<td align=center>4</td>
<td align=center>5</td>
<td align=center>6</td>
<td align=center>7</td>

</tr>

<tr align=right valign=middle>

<!-- Second week of October -->

<td align=center>6</td>
<td align=center>7</td>
<td align=center>8</td>
<td align=center>9</td>
<td align=center>10</td>
<td align=center>11</td>
<td align=center>12</td>

<td></td>

<!-- Second week of November -->

<td align=center>3</td>
<td align=center>4</td>
<td align=center>5</td>
<td align=center>6</td>
<td align=center>7</td>
<td align=center>8</td>
<td align=center>9</td>
```

```
<td></td>

<!-- Second week of December -->

<td align=center>8</td>
<td align=center>9</td>
<td align=center>10</td>
<td align=center>11</td>
<td align=center>12</td>
<td align=center>13</td>
<td align=center>14</td>

</tr>

<tr align=right valign=middle>

<!-- Third week of October -->

<td align=center>13</td>
<td align=center>14</td>
<td align=center>15</td>
<td align=center>16</td>
<td align=center>17</td>
<td align=center>18</td>
<td align=center>19</td>

<td></td>

<!-- Third week of November -->

<td align=center>10</td>
<td align=center>11</td>
<td align=center>12</td>
<td align=center>13</td>
<td align=center>14</td>
<td align=center>15</td>
<td align=center>16</td>

<td></td>

<!-- Third week of December -->

<td align=center>15</td>
<td align=center>16</td>
<td align=center>17</td>
<td align=center>18</td>
<td align=center>19</td>
<td align=center>20</td>
<td align=center>21</td>

</tr>
```

```
<tr align=right valign=middle>

<!-- Fourth week of October -->

<td align=center>20</td>
<td align=center>21</td>
<td align=center>22</td>
<td align=center>23</td>
<td align=center>24</td>
<td align=center>25</td>
<td align=center>26</td>

<td></td>

<!-- Fourth week of November -->

<td align=center>17</td>
<td align=center>18</td>
<td align=center>19</td>
<td align=center>20</td>
<td align=center>21</td>
<td align=center>22</td>
<td align=center>23</td>

<td></td>

<!-- Fourth week of December -->

<td align=center>22</td>
<td align=center>23</td>
<td align=center>24</td>
<td align=center>25</td>
<td align=center>26</td>
<td align=center>27</td>
<td align=center>28</td>

</tr>

<tr align=right valign=middle>

<!-- Fifth week of October -->

<td align=center>27</td>
<td align=center>28</td>
<td align=center>29</td>
<td align=center>30</td>
<td align=center>31</td>
<td></td>
<td></td>

<td></td>
```

```
<!-- Fifth week of November -->

<td align=center>24</td>
<td align=center>25</td>
<td align=center>26</td>
<td align=center>27</td>
<td align=center>28</td>
<td align=center>29</td>
<td align=center>30</td>

<td></td>

<!-- Fifth week of December -->

<td align=center>29</td>
<td align=center>30</td>
<td align=center>31</td>
<td></td>
<td></td>
<td></td>
<td></td>

<tr><td></td></tr>

</table>
</center>
<hr>
</BODY>

</HTML>
```

Index

A

<a>...</a> (anchor tag), 50, 59, 125–29
   in-document, 127–28
   linked documents and, 50, 59, 124–25
   name of, 129
   sound integration and, 198, 204
   uses of, 124
<abbrev>...</abbrev> (abbreviation tag), 112
Absolute URLs, 48, 122, 163
acn.gif file, 151
ACN home page
   client-side image maps and, 157–58
   server-side image maps and, 149–56
      creating, 151–55
      preparing graphic, 150–51
      testing, 155
   tables for, 253–72
<acronym>...</acronym> (acronym tag), 112
action= attribute, 163
Adaptive command, 140
<address>...</address> (physical address information tag), 82–83
address.txt file, 83
.aif or .aiff files, 194, 199
align= attribute, 31, 60, 69–70, 79–81, 181
all value, 69
alt= attribute, 135
American Comedy Network. *See* ACN home page
America Online (AOL), 35, 119
Ampersand, 33, 237
anchor list.txt file, 125
Anchor tag. *See* <a>...</a> (anchor tag)
Angle brackets, 18, 29
Apple Event, 209
Apple Extras folder, 209
<area>...</area> (area tag), 156–57
Asterisks, 101, 174, 216, 218
Attributes, 29–30. *See also specific types*
   of body element tags, 59–60
<au>...</au> (author tag), 110–11
Audio Interchange File Format, 199
AudioShop (Opcode Systems), 199
.au files, 194, 199, 202
Auto-Load Images preference, 135

B

... (bold tag), 106
Back button (Netscape), 14
Background colors, 62
<base> (URL address tag), 47–49, 75–76
BBEdit Lite, 12
   fonts and, 17
   short version of, 42–43
   in Web page design, 4
<big>...</big> (large text tag), 107–8
Binary mode, 232–33
Bit depth, 138–39
Bit rate, 195–97
_blank reserved name, 222
block-quote.txt file, 84
Body element tags, 23, 47, 59–113. *See also* <a>...</a> (anchor tag)
   attributes of, 59–60
   block elements, 78–88
      <address> (physical address information), 82–83
      <blockquote> (block quotations), 84–85
      <h*n*> (headings), 24–27, 85–88
      <p> (paragraph boundaries), 24, 33–34, 78–81
      <pre> (preformatted text), 24, 26, 81–82, 166–67, 221
   <body> (displayed content of HTML), 23, 61–67

 (line break), 67–69, 76
   <hr> (horizontal rules/lines), 69–71, 168
   <img> (inline images), 30–31, 72–77, 129
   list elements, 88–97
      <dl> (definition list), 95–96
      <li> (itemized list), 88, 93–94

273

Index

Body element tags *(continued)*
   nested lists, 96–97
   <ol> (ordered list), 88–90
   <ul> (unordered list), 91–93
 location of, 41
 physical format elements,
     105–13
   <abbrev> (abbreviations),
       112
   <acronym> (acronyms), 112
   <au> (author), 110–11
   <b> (boldface), 106
   <big> (large text), 107–8
   <del> (delete), 112–13
   <i> (italic), 83, 106
   <ins> (insert), 112–13
   <lang> (language), 110
   <person> (name delimiter),
       111
   <q> (quote), 110
   semantic tags vs., 105–6
   <small> (small text), 108
   <sub> (subscript), 108–9
   <sup> (superscript), 108
   <tt> (teletype), 107
   use of, 97, 105
   <u> (underline), 107
 semantic format elements,
     97–105
   <cite> (citations), 98–99
   <code> (programming
       code), 99–100
   <em> (emphasis), 100–101,
       103–4
   <kbd> (keyboard), 101–2
   physical tags vs., 105–6
   <samp> (sample text), 102–3
   <strong> (bold, emphasized
       text), 103–4
   use of, 97
   <var> (variable name),
       104–5
Body section, 22, 23
Boldface type, 103, 106
Bookmarks, 41–42, 52, 231–32
border= attribute, 147, 187, 189
Borders in tables, 187–92
Brackets, angle, 18, 29

 (line break tag), 67–69, 76
Browsers, 16, 52. *See also specific
   names*
Bullet characters, 91–92, 174
Button bar navigation, 147–48

C

Calendar for ACN Web site,
   253–72
<caption>...</caption> (figure
   or table legend tag),
   182–83
cd command (UNIX), 229
CD-ROM drive, 200
Cell enhancement in tables,
   187–92
cellpadding= attribute, 187, 189
cellspacing= attribute, 187,
   188–89
<center>...</center> tag, 35
CERN format, 154
CGI, 50
Cgi-bin directory, 50, 151,
   155–56, 163
Cgi script. *See also* Mailto CGI
   script
 forms and, 159–60
 image maps and, 151, 156
 URLs and, 155, 163
Channels, number of, 195–97
Character equivalencies, 33,
   245–52
Character sets, 33–34
Checkboxes, 173–74
chmod command (UNIX), 230,
   234
Choose file button, 130
<cite> (citations tag), 98–99
class= attribute, 55, 60
clear attribute, 60, 69
Client pull feature (Netscape),
   54
Client-side image maps, 149,
   156–58
<code>...</code> (programming code tag), 99–100
Color Picker (Apple), 63

Colors, 61–67
 background, 62
 GIF files and, 62–63, 139
 hexadecimal triplets and,
     62–63
 HTML ColorPicker and,
     63–65
 of link states, 61
 in Netscape Navigator, 61
 transparent, 140–41
cols= attribute, 215, 218
colspan= attribute, 185
Comment command (BBEdit
   Lite), 76
Comment tags, 32–33
Common Gateway Interface
   (CGI), 50
Compressed document, 26–27
Config button (FreePPP), 228
Config PPP control panel
   (FreePPP), 227
Constructionalists, 38
Convert To command
   (SoundApp), 201
coords= attribute, 157
Copyright, 52
Courier type, 81, 99, 101
Create New Directory command
   (Fetch), 233
Custom command (Photoshop),
   140
Customize menu (Fetch), 233
Custom sample rate (Sound-
   Machine), 202

D

definition.html file, 95
Definition lists, 95–96
<del>...</del> (delete tag),
   112–13
Diffusion command (Photo-
   shop), 140
DIGEX (Digital Express Group)
 advantages of, 226
 connecting to, 227–28
 E-mail and, 235–36, 239–40
 free use of, 9, 226

DIGEX *(continued)*
   information about, 226
   packages, 239–43
   Personal IP plan of, 226
   price list, 243
   product availability, 243
dingbat= attribute, 87, 174
directions.html file, 129, 131
Directories menu (Fetch), 233, 234
Directory, 122
   cgi-bin, 50, 151, 155–56, 163
Directory path, 229
<dl>...</dl> (definition list tag), 95–96
DOCTYPE declaration, 37, 43
<>Document command, 42–43, 46
<>Document dialog box, 43
Documents
   compressed, 26–27
   help, 52
   linked, 50–52, 59, 124–25
   parent, 52
Document Source command (Netscape), 17
Domain name, 116–17, 120–22
Duplicate command (BBEdit Lite), 124

E

Editors, text, 4, 5, 12, 15. *See also* BBEdit Lite
8 bits/pixel command, 140
Element tags, 20–21. *See also* Body element tags; Head element tags
11.025 kHz, 8-bit, mono command (SoundApp), 200–201
... (emphasis tag), 100–101, 103–4
E-mail
   addresses on business cards, 2
   DIGEX and, 235–36, 239–40
   mailto CGI script and, 161, 166, 176, 235–36

   monospaced font for, 81
Empty tags, 20, 21, 49, 89
End tag, 21, 86
Executable program, 5
Extensions menu (BBEdit), 24, 42, 46, 76, 93, 127, 130

F

Fetch (program), 230–34, 235
File names, 22, 117
File service protocol, 117–18
File Transfer Protocol (FTP), 118, 230–34
Find command (Netscape), 74
Finder menu (BBEdit Lite), 123, 134, 193
FlattenMooV application, 212
Fonts, 17–18, 56–57, 81. *See also* Physical format elements
   monospaced, 17, 81
Fonts and Colors item (Netscape), 66
Fonts & Tabs command (BBEdit), 17
<font> tag, 222
Foreign language tag, 110
form.html file, 161
Forms, 159–77
   building, 161–68
   checkboxes in, 173–74
   element tags
      <form>, 161–63
      <input> (input field), 163–68, 172–74
      <option> (menu options), 168, 169–72
      <select> (list selection), 168–69, 170–72
      <textarea> (multiline text box), 174–77
   forms-processing CGI script and, 159–60
   location of, 161
   password and, 174
   radio buttons in, 172–73
   server queries and, 160
   types of, 161

   use of, 10, 159, 160
Forms-processing CGI script, 159–60
Frames, 213–24
   advantages of, 213–14
   concept of, 214
   describing, 215–19
   disadvantages of, 213
   names for, 219–22
   reserved names for, 222
   tags
      <frame> (frame reference), 218–19
      <frameset> (frame container), 214–15, 218
      <noframes> (non-Netscape 2.0 client container), 223
   Web pages and, 214
Frames per second figure, 211
Free-form text forms, 161
Freeware, 9
from= attribute, 55
FTP, 118, 230–34
Full Shell, 239
FusionRecorder, 209

G

General Preferences command (Netscape), 198
Get info window (Netscape), 200
Get method of server queries, 160
Getstats package, 236
GIF files
   color and, 62–63, 139
   defined, 73–74
   graphic displays and, 150
   location of, 75
   maneuvers with, 140–42
   Photoshop and, 137–42
Glossary, 52
Gopher service protocol, 119
Gothic typeface, 18
Graphics, 150–51. *See also specific graphic file formats*
   inline, 72–77

Index

Graphics *(continued)*
  navigational tools for. *See*
    Photoshop (Adobe)
  raw, 138
  shapes of, 151–52
  with URLs, 129–32
  in Web page design, 4–5
Graphics Interchange Format.
  See GIF files
Guided tour button (WebMap),
  153

H

Head element tags, 39–57
  <base> (URL address), 47–49,
    75–76
  <head>, 22, 41
  <html> (main container), 21,
    23, 40–41
  <isindex> (searchable index),
    49–50
  <link> (document linkage),
    50–52
  location of, 41
  <meta> (user-defined informa-
    tion), 52–55
  <range> (document range),
    55–56
  <spot> (user-defined identifi-
    ers), 56
  <style> (style characteristics),
    56–57
  <title> (HTML document
    title), 22–23, 41–42
Headers, table, 180–81, 187
headings.html file, 25–27
Headings tag, 24–27, 85–88
height= attribute, 30–31
Help documents, 52
Helper applications, 8, 198–99
Helpers tab (Netscape), 198
Helping folder, 12
Hexadecimal triplet, 62–63
<h*n*>...</h*n*> (headings tag),
  24–27, 85–88
Home directory, 229
Home page, 52

Host names, 121
Hotspots, 18
href= attribute, 49, 51, 52, 124,
  127, 157, 198
<hr> (horizontal rules/lines tag),
  69–71, 168
<html>...</html> (main con-
  tainer tag), 21, 23, 40–41
HTML Format command
  (BBEdit), 93
HTML (HyperText Markup
  Language), 15–27
  browser variations of, 16
  character equivalencies, 33,
    245–52
  character sets, 33–34
  comments, 32–33
  computer skills needed for
    using, 7–8
  defined, 3
  Extensions, 42–43
  file names, 22
  hardware needed for using,
    8
  history of, 18–19
  package offered with, 9
  sample pages of, 19–26
  source, 17–18, 25–26
  technical information on, 19
  text file extensions and, 15
  tools, 12–14, 42
  versions of, 16, 19, 34–38,
    86–87, 163
HTML Link command, 127,
  130
.html or .htm files, 15
http-equiv= attribute, 54
HTTP (HyperText Transfer
  Protocol)
  address, 48
  defined, 44, 115
  RealAudio and, 207
  server, 44, 117
  URLs and, 115
HyperText Markup Language.
  See HTML (HyperText
    Markup Language)
Hypertext Reference, 49

Hypertext system, 1

I

... (italic tag), 83, 106
Icons, 144–46
  sizing, 134
id= attribute, 55, 59
Image mapping tag, 156–57
Image map reference file, 151
Image maps, 149–58
  cgi script and, 151, 156
  clickable, 236
  client-side, 149, 156–58
  example of, 30
  server-side, 149–56
  URLs and, 152–53
  use of, 6–7
Images, inline, 72–77, 123,
  129–32
<img> (inline images tag), 72–77
  attributes of, 30–31
  uses of, 30, 129
Import to QuickTime command
  (SoundApp), 200
increase= argument, 237
Index, 52
  searchable, 49–50
index.html file, 129, 204
  creating, 46
  described, 45
  headings in, 86
  images in, 123, 129–32
  in-document anchor in, 127–28
  line break tag in, 67–68, 76
  reloading, 75–76
  toc.html file linked to, 124,
    125–27
Indexed Color command
  (Photoshop), 139
In-document anchors, 127–28
<input> (input field tag), 163–68,
  172–74
<ins>...</ins> (insert tag),
  112–13
Interface guidelines, human,
  134–36
Interlacing, 141–42

Index 277

International Standards Organization (ISO), 18
Internet Electronics Mail, 239
Internet Explorer, 13
Internet Information Clearinghouse, 121
InterNIC, 121
<isindex> (searchable index tag), 49–50
ismap attribute, 30
ISPs (Internet Service Providers), 225–37. *See also* DIGEX (Digital Express Group)
   connection type for, 226–28
   cost of space on, 225
   faster work on, 235
   host names and, 121
   maintenance of site and, 237
   server preparation for, 228–35
      directory path and, 229
      loading files, 233–35
      permissions and, 229–30
      populating directories and, 230–33
   staff on, 225, 235
   Unix and, 4
   use of, 8
   variations in, 225
   Web design options with, 235–37
Italic type, 83, 100, 104, 106
Itemized lists, 88, 89, 93–94

J

Jacks, 209
JPEG files, 73–74, 137–38
justification.html file, 79

K

<kbd>…</kbd> (keyboard entry tag), 101–2

L

<lang>…</lang> (language tag), 110

lang= attribute, 59, 110
Large icon view (BBEdit), 134
Large text display, 107–8
Learn HTML on the Macintosh CD document, 13
left value, 69
<li>…</li> (itemized list tag), 88, 89, 93–94
Line breaks, 67–69, 76
link= argument, 237
<link> (document linkage tag), 50–52
Linked documents, 50–52, 59, 124–25
Link states, color of, 61
List button (WebMap), 153
List element tags, 88–97
   <dl> (definition), 95–96
   <li> (itemized list), 88, 89, 93–94
   nested lists, 96–97
   <ol> (ordered list), 88–90
   <ul> (unordered list), 91–93
   use of, 88
location.gif file, 129
ls command (UNIX), 229
Lynx, 35

M

MacTCP, 8, 227
Mailto CGI script
   e-mail generated by, 161, 166, 176, 235–36
   forms and, 160–61, 166
   loading of, 159–60
   mailto service protocol vs., 160, 163
Mailto service protocol, 118–19, 160, 163
<map>…</map> (image mapping tag), 156–57
marginheight= attribute, 222
marginwidth= attribute, 222
md= attribute, 60, 87
<meta> (user-defined information tag), 52–55
method= or methods= attribute, 51, 163

MicroTek ScanMaker IIsp scanner, 138
minimum.html file, 20–25
Mode menu (Photoshop), 139
Monaco 9, 18
Monospaced font, 17, 81
Mosaic, 13
MoviePlayer, 209
Movies, 5, 7, 209–12
   QuickTime, 204, 209, 211
.mp2 files, 194
MPEG audio, 194, 209
μ-law sound file extension, 194
Multiline text boxes, 174–77
Multimedia. *See* Movies; Sound
Multimedia file link, 204
Multiple attribute, 171
Multiple-option choices forms, 161

N

name= attribute, 51, 54, 124, 127, 166, 219
Name command (Netscape), 74
names.html file, 221
Navigational tools, 133–58
   button bar, 147–48
   icons, 134, 144–46
   image maps, 149–58
      cgi script and, 151, 156
      client-side, 149, 156–58
      server-side, 149–56
      URLs and, 152–53
   interface guidelines, 134–36
   text, 135, 148–49
   using Photoshop, 136–44
NCSA format, 154, 160
NCSA Telnet, 119, 226, 229
Nested lists, 96–97
Netscape Navigator
   alignment in, 79–81
   block of quoted material in, 84–85
   <body> tag and, 61
   bookmarks in, 41–42
   browsing with, 1–2, 12
   cassette2.html file in, 147, 148
   cellspacing in, 188–89

Netscape Navigator *(continued)*
　checkboxes in, 173
　citations in, 99
　client pull feature of, 54
　colors in, 61
　Courier type in, 99
　default screen, 42
　default temporary folder, 200
　definition list in, 95–96
　Get info window and, 200
　headings.html document and, 26
　headings in, 86–87
　height= attribute and, 30–31
　HTML and, 16, 34–35
　italic type in, 100
　nested list in, 97–98
　ordered list in, 89–90
　radio boxes in, 173
　RAM necessary for, 8
　sound and, 198, 200
　SoundApp and, 198
　subscripts in, 109
　table headers in, 185
　tags of, 19, 33–35, 37
　　emphasis, 100, 104
　　meta-information, 54
　　paragraph, 78
　titles in, 22, 41–42
　type= attribute and, 92
　underlined text and, 107
　unordered list in, 92
　URLs and, 22, 47
　value= attribute and, 167
　variable names in, 105
　versions of, 12
　width= attribute and, 30–31
NetShark (Intercon), 16
New Connection command (Fetch), 231
News groups (USENET), 118, 239
News service protocol, 118
NeXT option (SoundApp), 201
Next/Previous document, 52
<noframes>…</noframes> (non-Netscape 2.0 client container tag), 223
Noref attribute, 157
Noresize attribute, 222
nowrap attribute, 60, 86
Now Software, 111

O

<ol>…</ol> (ordered list tag), 88–90
OmniWeb, 70
One-option forms, 161
Open button (Netscape), 13
Open File (Netscape), 13
Open Transport, 8, 227
<option> (menu option tag), 168, 169–72
Options menu (Netsape), 66, 198
ordered.html file, 89
Ordered lists, 88–90

P

<p>…</p> (paragraph tag), 24, 33–34, 78–81
Parent document, 52
_parent reserved name, 222
Password, 174
Path, 117, 122
Pause command (Sound-Machine), 203
Permissions, 229–30, 234
<person>…</person> (name delimiter tag), 111
Personal IP (DIGEX), 226
Personal-IP-Dynamic PPP Dial-Up connection, 240–43
phonebook.html file, 214, 219–20
PhotoGIF shareware, 143–44
Photoshop (Adobe), 136–44
　advantages of, 137
　cost of, 137–38
　GIF files and, 137–42
　graphics created with, 138–40
　shareware plug-in to, 143–44
　use of, 9–10
Physical format elements, 105–13
<abbrev> (abbreviations), 112
<acronym> (acronyms), 112
<au> (author), 110–11
<b> (boldface), 106
<big> (large text), 107–8
<del> (delete), 112–13
<i> (italic), 83, 106
<ins> (insert), 112–13
<lang> (language), 110
<person> (name delimiter), 111
<q> (quote), 110
semantic tags vs., 105–6
<small> (small text), 108
<sub> (subscript), 108–9
<sup> (superscript), 108
<tt> (teletype), 107
use of, 97, 105
<u> (underline), 107
PICT files, 137–38
Pixels
　frame description and, 216, 217–18
　of icons, 134
　image height and width in, 30
　movie size in, 210
Playback software, 209
pnm service prefix or protocol, 207
Point-to-Point Protocol (PPP), 226–27, 229, 240–43
Ports, 117, 209
Post method of server queries, 160
Pound sign, 156
<pre>…</pre> (preformatted text tag), 81–82, 99, 166–67, 221
Preferences command (Fetch), 233
Preferences dialog box (Real-Audio), 206
Preferences menu (Netscape), 66, 198
Premier (Adobe), 209
Presentationists, 38
Preview command (BBEdit), 24, 26, 81–82, 166–67, 221

Index

Process button (RealAudio), 206
Prodigy, 52
Programming code tag, 99–100
Progressive Network Metafile (pnm), 207
Progressive Network web site, 208
PSI, 9
public_html directory, 230, 232, 234–35, 236

Q

<q>...</q> (quote tag), 110
Quality slide bar (Fusion-Recorder), 211
Quarter Size, 210
Question mark, 236
QuickCam (Connectix), 211–12
QuickTime (Apple), 7
  movies and, 204, 209, 211
  sound and, 200–202
Quotation marks, 31
Quoted material, 84–85, 110

R

Radio buttons, 172–73
.ra files, 205–6
.ram files, 206–8
<range> (document range tag), 55–56
Raw Data command (Fetch), 233
Raw Image mode, 232–33
RealAudio Encoder, 205
RealAudio (Progressive Networks), 7, 204–8
RealAudio server, 235
Record command (Sound-Machine), 203
Record dialog box (Sound-Machine), 203
Recorder Preferences dialog box (FusionRecorder), 210
Recording menu (Sound-Machine), 202
Record menu (FusionRecorder), 210

Record WindowSize command (FusionRecorder), 210
Refresh File List command (Fetch), 234
Relative remainders, 216, 218–19
Relative URLs, 48, 122–23, 150
rel= attribute, 52
Reload button, 131
Reserved names, 222
Reset button, 175
resources folder, 74–75, 123, 212, 234
rev= attribute, 51
right value, 69
rows= attribute, 215, 218
Rows in tables, 181, 184

S

<samp>...</samp> (sample text tag), 102–3
Sampling frequency, 195–97
Save As command (Netscape), 17
Save Bookmark command (Fetch), 232
Scanners, 138
Searchable indexes, 49–50
Search engines, 53
Security, in UNIX, 234
<select>...</select> (select from list tag), 168–69, 170–72
_self reserved name, 222
Semantic format elements, 97–105
  <cite> (citations), 98–99
  <code> (programming code), 99–100
  <em> (emphasis), 100–101, 103–4
  <kbd> (keyboard), 101–2
  physical tags vs., 105–6
  <samp> (sample text), 102–3
  <strong> (bold, emphasized text), 103–4
  use of, 97
  <var> (variable name), 104–5
Semi-colon, 33

seqnum= attribute, 86–87
Serial Line Interface Protocol (SLIP), 226–27, 229
Server queries, 160
Servers, 44
  HTTP, 44, 117
  preparation of, 228–35
    directory path and, 229
    loading files, 233–35
    permissions and, 229–30
    populating directories and, 230–33
  RealAudio, 235
Server-side image maps, 149–56
  creating, 151–55
  inaccessibility to cgi-bin directory and, 155–56
  preparing graphic and, 150–51
  testing, 155
Service protocols, 116, 117–19
Set Format (µ-law) command (SoundMachine), 202
SGML, 18, 37
Shareware, 9, 143–44
show= argument, 237
SimplePlayer, 209
SimpleText (Apple), 4
size= attribute, 69–70, 167
Sizing icons, 134
Slashes, 75, 122
SLIP connection, 226–27, 229
<small>...</small> (small text tag), 108
smushed.html file, 26–27
.snd files, 194
software.net (computer company), 2–3
Sound, 193–208
  bandwidth of users and, 194–95
  converting, 200–202, 204–8
  file format of, 193–94, 199
  hearing, 199–200
  helper application for, 198–99
  lengthy files of, 204–8
  multimedia file link and, 204
  Netscape Navigator and, 198, 200

Sound *(continued)*
   properties in files of, 195–97
   recording, 202–4
   streaming and, 204–8
   in Web site, 5, 7
SoundApp, 198–99, 202, 211
Sound Control Panel (SoundMachine), 203
SoundMachine software, 202–4
Sound Settings dialog box (FusionRecorder), 211
Source, 5, 17–18, 25–26, 37
spiderworks.com, 39, 120
spiderworks.gif file, 75
spiderworks web site, 45, 75, 86
<spot> (user-defined identifiers tag), 56
src= attribute, 30, 60, 75, 87, 218–19
staff.html file, 124
Standard General Markup Language (SGML), 18, 37
start= attribute, 89–90
Start tag, 21, 86
Statistics on web page, 236
Streaming, 204–8
StreamWorks (Xing Technologies), 7, 204–5
… (bold, emphasized tag), 103–4
Stuffit, 199–200
<style> (style characteristics tag), 56–57
_… (subscript tag), 108–9
Submit button, 175
Suffixes for domain name, 120–21
[…] (superscript tag), 108
System 7.0 or 7.5, 8

T

Table of contents, 52
Tables, 177–92
   for ACN Web site, 253–72
   borders and cell enhancement in, 187–92
   building, 183–87
   tags
      <caption> (legend for table or figure), 182–83
      <table> (create table), 178–80
      <td> (table data), 181–82
      <th> (table header), 180–81, 187
      <tr> (table rows), 181, 184
   use of, 177
<tag>…</tag> convention, 21, 36
Tags, 3, 15, 20, 34. *See also* Body element tags; Forms; Frames; Head element tags; Tables
   defined, 3, 15
   element, 20–21
   empty, 20, 21, 49, 89
   end, 21, 86
   format of, 18, 29
   names of, 22
   of Netscape Navigator, 19, 33–35, 37, 54, 78, 100, 104
   recognizing, 18
   start, 21, 86
   structure of, 29–31
   uses of, 16, 18, 21
   white space and, 31–32
Tag tables
   defined, 11
   sample, 36–37
   use of, 36
target= attribute, 219, 222
TCP/IP packets, 8
<td>…</td> (table data tag), 181–82
TeachText (Apple), 4
Tech blocks, 11
Telnet, 119, 226, 229
<textarea>…</textarea> (multiline text box tag), 174–77

Text boxes, multiline, 174–77
Text editor, 4, 5, 12, 15. *See also* BBEdit Lite
Text file extensions, 15
Text menu (BBEdit), 17
Text navigation, 135, 148–49
<th>…</th> (table header tag), 180–81, 187
Tilde, 229
<title>…</title> (HTML document title tag), 22–23, 41–42
toc.html file, 124, 125–27
ToC (table of contents), 52
Tognazzini, Bruce, 135
Toolbars, 52
Tools palette (WebMap), 151, 153
_top reserved name, 222
<tr>…</tr> (table rows tag), 181, 184
Transfer mode, 232–33
Transparency, color, 140–41
<tt>…</tt> (teletype tag), 107
Tufte, Edward, 135
type= attribute, 89, 92, 166, 174, 175
type instruction tag, 101–2

U

<u>…</u> (underline tag), 107
<ul>…</ul> (unordered list tag), 91–93
Universal Resource Locators. *See* URLs
Universal Resource Name (URN), 40, 51
UNIX
   commands, 229–30
   security on, 234
   users, 229
   web and language of, 3–4
Unordered List command (BBEdit), 93
Unordered lists, 91–93

Index

until= attribute, 55
Upload command (Fetch), 233
Up value, 52
URLs, 115–32
  absolute, 48, 122, 163
  area associated with, 156–57
  CGI script and, 155, 163
  construction of
    domain name, 116–17, 120–22
    file name, 117
    path, 117, 122
    port, 117
    service protocol, 116, 117–19
  creating links and, 123–29
  defined, 7
  graphics with, 129–32
  image maps and, 152–53
  inline images and, 129–32
  metaphor of, 116
  Netscape Navigator and, 22, 47
  relative, 48, 122–23, 150
  tag containing, 47–49, 75–76
  use of, 45
  web page and, 45
URN, 40, 51
usemap= attribute, 156
USENET, 118, 239

V

Validator, 37
value= attribute, 167
<var>…</var> (variable name tag), 104–5
Version attribute, 40

Video, 209–12
Video Settings dialog box (FusionRecorder), 211
VideoShop (Avid), 209
View menu (Netscape), 17, 74

W

WAIS, 119
.wav files, 194, 199
Web
  beginning of, 1
  browsing, 1–2, 6–8
  publishing on, 2–3
  server, 44
  UNIX language and, 3–4
  versatility of, 2, 159
WebAccess Counter, 236–37
WebCrawler, 53
Web forms, 235–36
WebMap folder, 151
WebMap tool, 151
Web page(s)
  accessing, 13
  browsing, 12
  clickable images on, 236
  colors of, 61–67
  counting visits to, 236–37
  designing
    BBEdit Lite in, 4
    camps in, 38
    CD-ROM package for, 9–10
    computer skills needed for, 7–8
    graphics, 4–5
    hardware needed for, 8
    learning about, 5–7

    tools for creating, 4–5
  links to, 48, 204
  sample, 19–25
  source for, 17–18, 25–26
  statistics, 236
  URLs and, 45
Web site(s)
  ACN, 149–56
  building tools, 11–14
  construction of average, 44–45
  files in, 44, 45
  movies in, 5, 7
  navigational tools, 133–58
    button bar, 147–48
    icons, 134, 144–46
    image maps, 149–58
    interface guidelines, 134–36
    text, 135, 148–49
    using Photoshop, 136–44
  planning, 43–47
  Progressive Network, 208
  reaching other users with, 5–6
  sample, 39, 45–47
  sound in, 5, 7
Website Mirror folder, 13, 19
WebSTAR (StarNine), 44
White space, 31–32, 221
Wide Area Information Server (WAIS), 119
width= argument, 237
width= attribute, 30–31, 69–70
Windows 95, 15, 193
Window width or height, percentage of, 215
Word processors, 17
World Wide Web. *See* Web

Addison-Wesley Developers Press publishes high-quality, practical books and software for programmers, developers, and system administrators.

Here are additional titles from A-W Developers Press that might be of interest to you. If you'd like to order any of these books, please visit your local bookstore or:

FAX us at: 800-367-7198

Call us at: 800-822-6339
(8:30 A.M. to 6:00 P.M. eastern time, Monday through Friday)

Write to us at:
Addison-Wesley Developers Press
One Jacob Way
Reading, MA 01867

Reach us online at:
http://www.aw.com/devpress/

International orders, contact one of the following Addison-Wesley subsidiaries:

Australia/New Zealand
Addison-Wesley Publishing Co.
6 Byfield Street
North Ryde, N.S.W. 2113
Australia
Tel: 61 2 878 5411
Fax: 61 2 878 5830

Southeast Asia
Addison-Wesley
Singapore Pte. Ltd.
15 Beach Road
#05-09/10 Beach Centre
Singapore 189677
Tel: 65 339 7503
Fax: 65 338 6290

Latin America
Addison-Wesley Iberoamericana S.A.
Blvd. de las Cataratas #3
Col. Jardines del Pedregal
01900 Mexico D.F., Mexico
Tel: (52 5) 568-36-18
Fax: (52 5) 568-53-32
e-mail: ordenes@ibero.aw.com
 or: informaciona@ibero.aw.com

Europe and the Middle East
Addison-Wesley Publishers B.V.
Concertgebouwplein 25
1071 LM Amsterdam
The Netherlands
Tel: 31 20 671 7296
Fax: 31 20 675 2141

United Kingdom and Africa
Addison-Wesley Longman Group Limited
P.O. Box 77
Harlow, Essex CM 19 5BQ
United Kingdom
Tel: 44 1279 623 923
Fax: 44 1279 453 450

All other countries:
Addison-Wesley Publishing Co.
Attn: International Order Dept.
One Jacob Way
Reading, MA 01867 U.S.A.
Tel: (617) 944-3700 x5190
Fax: (617) 942-2829

If you'd like a free copy of our Developers Press catalog, contact us at: devpressinfo@aw.com

Planning and Managing Web Sites on the Macintosh®: The Complete Guide to WebSTAR and MacHTTP

Jon Wiederspan and Chuck Shotton
ISBN 0-201-47957-5, $39.95 w/CD-ROM

This book, written by two acknowledged experts in the field, teaches you everything you need to know about using WebSTAR, the best known Mac HTTP server software and its shareware predecessor MacHTTP, as well as about writing CGI applications for your server. A special version of WebSTAR, plus tons of useful software are on the CD-ROM.

Web Weaving: Designing and Managing an Effective Web Site

Eric Tilton, Carl Steadman, and Tyler Jones
ISBN 0-201-48959-7, $24.95

Covering UNIX®, Windows®, and the Macintosh®, *Web Weaving* shows you how to install and configure Web servers, use authoring tools, implement security, and build structured, well-organized Web sites. The authors, experienced Webmasters, include tips for planning for growth, building in maintenance schemes, catering to your users' needs, and creating a logical, underlying infostructure.

Hooked on Java™: Creating Hot Web Sites with Java Applets

Arthur van Hoff, Sami Shaio, and Orca Starbuck,
Sun Microsystems, Inc.
ISBN 0-201-48837-X, $29.95 w/CD-ROM

Written by members of Sun's Java development team, *Hooked on Java* is a concise and practical introduction to using applets to add interactive capabilities to World-Wide Web sites. The CD-ROM contains a wealth of cool Java applets ready to plug into your home pages, examples of HTML pages that are already Java-enabled, Java source code, the Java Developer's Kit for Windows® 95, Windows NT, Solaris 2.x, and more.

The Internet Publishing Handbook For World-Wide Web, Gopher, and WAIS

Mike Franks
ISBN 0-201-48317-3, $22.95

The Internet Publishing Handbook takes you through the process of Internet publishing from beginning to end, using examples and advice gathered from Internet publishers around the world. You'll learn how to assess hardware and software server needs for your site; choose server setup options and features for World-Wide Web, Gopher, and WAIS; design HTML documents; implement digital cash, digital checks, charging, and more.

Growing and Maintaining a Successful BBS: The Sysop's Handbook

Alan D. Bryant
ISBN 0-201-48380-7, $39.95 w/CD-ROM

This book contains advice, tools, and tips from an industry expert on how to go from "up and running" to front runner BBS status. Alan Bryant's first book, *Creating Successful Bulletin Board Systems* covered the basics—this book takes you to the next level, covering topics such as discussions of why, when, and how you might choose to connect your BBS to the Internet; information on legal issues relevant to board content and sysop responsibility; online databases, and more.

Online Law: The SPA's Legal Guide to Doing Business on the Internet

Thomas J. Smedinghoff, Editor
ISBN 0-201-48980-5, $34.95

Written for the layperson, but extensively annotated for the experienced lawyer, *Online Law* provides clear guidance through the rapidly developing law of electronic commerce. Based on sound legal principles, this comprehensive handbook draws on the extensive knowledge of experienced attorneys at the forefront of today's emerging online legal issues.

BBEdit
Your Weapon of Choice

BBEdit 4.0 is the weapon of choice for designing Web pages on the Macintosh. BBEdit 4.0 includes an entire suite of features in addition to those found in BBEdit Lite:

Syntax Coloring for Easier Reading

Users can have BBEdit automatically color keywords and tags to make HTML documents easier to read. BBEdit offers syntax coloring for other languages, as well, such as Java. There's also a popup menu for easy navigation of headings and named anchors within a file.

Spell Checking

The full version of BBEdit gives users the ability to check the spelling in their text documents with an integrated spelling checker. The spelling checker provides a 100,000+ word US English dictionary, as well as dictionaries for UK English, French, Dutch, Spanish, and several specialized dictionaries. The built-in spelling checker is HTML-aware, so authors creating content for Web pages can easily ensure correct spelling in their HTML files.

HTML Tools

BBEdit includes an expanded version of Lindsay Davies' popular "BBEdit HTML Tools", which adds support for tables, enhanced HTML checking, and automatic insertion of images or anchor markups when image files or HTML files are dragged into an HTML editing window. The new HTML tools also provide a tool palette within BBEdit, from which HTML tags may be dropped into their desired locations, for quicker and easier markup than ever before.

Java Support

BBEdit 4.0 includes support for Java, making it the ideal companion for the Java development environments by Symantec, Metrowerks, Sun Microsystems, and Natural Intelligence.

It's Fast, Fast, Fast

BBEdit 4.0 is fully native for the Power Macintosh, making it a powerful step up from the already speedy BBEdit Lite.

Full Integration with Frontier 4.0, for Even More Powerful Web Tools

BBEdit includes full integration with Frontier 4.0, the advanced scripting system. This combination provides "Web Site Scripting", a powerful system for HTML authoring and web site management. Web Site Scripting includes an extensible Glossary; any keyword typed in "double quotes" is expanded to its glossary definition automatically. It also features automatic substitution of HTML escape sequences; instead of writing complicated HTML escape sequences to display special characters, simply type the characters as you would normally, and the appropriate escape sequences are inserted automatically. With URL and e-mail link generation, simply type a URL or e-mail address, and the macro processor will construct the correct HTML anchor tags for you. Web Site Scripting also offers one-key processing and previewing of pages.

About BBEdit

BBEdit was the first HTML editor to be included with the Apple Internet Server Solution, and has become the weapon of choice for HTML authors and webmasters all over the world, due in large measure to its power and ease of use.

BBEdit and the Bare Bones Software logo are trademarks of Bare Bones Software, Inc. Other product names mentioned are trademarks or registered trademarks of their respective holders.

BBEdit Special Offer

We are pleased to extend you, as a reader of "Learn HTML on the Mac," a special offer on BBEdit — the popular and critically acclaimed text editor for use by HTML authors, programmers, and anyone else who needs plain text editing with maximum performance and usability. Its integrated HTML editing tools have made it the weapon of choice for Web authors and designers all over the world, and its power and ease of use make it suitable for anyone from novice to professional.

For more information about BBEdit, visit us at:
http://www.barebones.com/

Customer Information:

Name: _____

Company: _____

Address: _____

Phone: _____ Fax: _____

E-Mail: _____

Payment Information:

VISA / MC / AMEX #: _____ Exp. Date: _____

Cardholder Signature: _____

Order Information:

BBEdit CD-ROM Special Offer:	$79.00
Sales Tax (MA residents only):	$ 3.95
Shipping (US Priority or Airmail):	$ 5.00
Total:	$

Bare Bones Software, Inc.
Post Office Box 1048
Bedford, MA 01730 USA

voice: 617.676.0650
fax: 617.676.0651
bbsw@barebones.com

Bare Bones Software, Inc.

Warranty

Addison-Wesley warrants the enclosed disc to be free of defects in materials and faulty workmanship under normal use for a period of ninety days after purchase. If a defect is discovered in the disc during this warranty period, a replacement disc can be obtained at no charge by sending the defective disc, postage prepaid, with proof of purchase to:

Addison-Wesley Publishing Company
Editorial Department
Developers Press
One Jacob Way
Reading, MA 01867

After the 90-day period, a replacement will be sent upon receipt of the defective disc and a check or money order for $10.00, payable to Addison-Wesley Publishing Company.

Addison-Wesley makes no warranty or representation, either express or implied, with respect to this software, its quality, performance, merchantability, or fitness for a particular purpose. In no event will Addison-Wesley, its distributors, or dealers be liable for direct, indirect, special, incidental, or consequential damages arising out of the use or inability to use the software. The exclusion of implied warranties is not permitted in some states. Therefore, the above exclusion may not apply to you. This warranty provides you with specific legal rights. There may be other rights that you may have that vary from state to state.